Unlocking the Customer Value Chain

Unlocking the Customer Value Chain

*

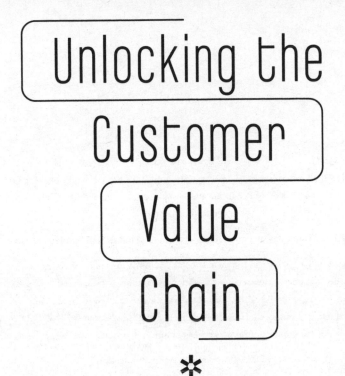

How Decoupling Drives Consumer Disruption

THALES S. TEIXEIRA

with Greg Piechota

CURRENCY
New York

Published in the United States by Currency, an imprint of the Crown Publishing Group,
a division of Penguin Random House LLC, New York.
currencybooks.com

CURRENCY and its colophon are trademarks of Penguin Random House LLC.

Currency books are available at special discounts for bulk purchases for
sales promotions or corporate use. Special editions, including personalized covers, excerpts
of existing books, or books with corporate logos, can be created in large quantities for
special needs. For more information, contact Premium Sales at (212) 572–2232
or e-mail specialmarkets@penguinrandomhouse.com.

Library of Congress Cataloging-in-Publication Data
Names: Teixeira, Thales S., author. | Piechota, Greg.
Title: Unlocking the customer value chain : how decoupling drives consumer
disruption / Thales S. Teixeira, Greg Piechota.
Description: 1 Edition. | New York : Currency, 2019. | Includes
bibliographical references and index.
Identifiers: LCCN 2018027655 | ISBN 9781524763084 (hardback) |
ISBN 9781524763091 (eISBN)
Subjects: LCSH: Customer relations. | Consumer satisfaction. | Marketing. |
BISAC: BUSINESS & ECONOMICS / Management. | BUSINESS & ECONOMICS /
Entrepreneurship. | BUSINESS & ECONOMICS / Leadership.
Classification: LCC HF5415.5 .T459 2019 | DDC 658.8/12—dc23
LC record available at https://lccn.loc.gov/2018027655

ISBN 978-1-5247-6308-4
Ebook ISBN 978-1-5247-6309-1

Printed in the United States of America

Book design by Chris Welch
Illustrations by Mekanism
Jacket design by Josh Smith

10 9 8 7 6 5 4 3 2 1

First Edition

Origins matter. To my parents,
Joao Batista and Assunta Teixeira. And to Iva, my wife,
Kalina, my daughter, and Marley, my son:
you are the three great waves of disruption
in my life. I love you all!

CONTENTS

Unlocking the Customer Value Chain

INTRODUCTION

Borders was once one of the largest bookstores in the United States. But in 2011, following the disruption of its business model by Amazon, the company went bankrupt. According to CEO Mike Edwards, the experience of closing Borders was "humbling." Principles that Edwards had learned over an entire career suddenly didn't work due to what he described as a "digital tsunami."[1]

Nokia, once the global leader in mobile phones, had to sell itself in 2013 to avoid bankruptcy, also a victim of digital disruption. Its CEO, Stephen Elop, was brutally honest in acknowledging that he didn't know what he didn't know. In a tearful interview that has since become famous, Elop claimed, "We didn't do anything wrong, but somehow we lost."[2]

More recently, in 2017, J. Crew, once one of the world's most fashionable clothing companies, had to close many stores after multiple quarters of declining same-store sales. Its founder and ousted CEO, Mickey Drexler, acknowledged that he hadn't known how to deal with the pace of digital change. "If I could go back 10 years," he said, "I might have done some things earlier."[3]

But what, exactly? Edwards, Elop, and Drexler never offered any alternatives to their failed strategies. Nor have many other executives who have seen their businesses implode.

Today, digital disruption affects every industry, geography, and market, and it isn't going away. Rather than a single, pivotal event, disruption has become a permanent condition of modern markets. New entrants. New technologies. New investors. New business models. How should large, established companies respond?

Innovation Alone Is Not the Answer

Innovation, many leaders say. If new and more innovative companies are disrupting their businesses, then leaders of incumbents need to out-innovate these competitors. The argument seems sound, and it enjoys strong support. In 1997, Clayton Christensen published *The Innovator's Dilemma: When New Technologies Cause Great Firms to Fail*, which roughly equated disruption with innovation. When a specific type of innovation existed (what in this book Christenson calls "disruptive technology" and what in his subsequent books he calls "disruptive companies, strategies, and products"), so, too, did the risk of market disruption exist. Where this innovation didn't exist, neither did disruption. Inspired by Christensen, and influenced by an avalanche of other books on innovation, business leaders have dedicated massive amounts of time and resources to helping their companies become more innovative. If certain "new technologies" adopted by competitors "cause great firms to fail," as Christensen's subtitle suggests, then it makes sense for incumbents to respond by investing in new disruptive innovations themselves.[4] But what if innovation and disruption are not so tightly connected?

Technology Is Not What's Disrupting Most Markets

In particular, I argue in *Unlocking the Customer Value Chain* that new technology isn't driving most disruption today. Consumers are. And that in turn means incumbents require a different kind of innovation in order to thrive—not technological innovation, but a transformation in *business models.* A business model describes how a company works—how it creates value and to whom; how it captures value and from whom. Innovating your business model requires a deep knowledge of customers. You must understand what your customers want, and in particular, the main steps or activities they undertake in order to satisfy their desires. You need to understand *their* value chain.

Once you learn to look at markets from the customer's perspective, a whole new wave of digital disruption opens up for you, one spanning industries such as retailing, telecom, entertainment, consumer goods, industrials, services, transportation, and more. Traditional companies in these industries have enabled customers to conduct most if not all consumption activities in partnership with them as customers go about acquiring goods and services. These companies bind together as a single "chain" all the steps that consumers undertake in order to acquire products and services. In today's new wave of disruption, upstart firms are breaking apart these chains, offering customers the chance to fulfill just one or a few activities with them, and leaving incumbents to fulfill the rest. I call this process of breaking apart the chain of consumption "decoupling." Startups decouple to gain a foothold in the market, and they grow by offering to fill a specific activity for customers—what I call "coupling." Both the initial decoupling and the subsequent coupling allow startups to quickly steal a substantial amount of market share at incumbents' expense. In short, the startups become disruptors.*

* For a precise definition of key terms in this book, please refer to "Note on Terminology" at the end of the book.

(De)couplers Are Changing the Game

Unlocking the Customer Value Chain will examine many specific examples of decoupling. Amazon, for instance, initially broke apart the series of activities customers typically fulfill in order to shop for durable goods. Customers could purchase goods from Amazon, while turning to traditional retailers as showcases for discovering products and educating themselves about them. Netflix broke apart the chain of activities by which customers consumed video entertainment, offering only the delivery of content, while leaving it to telecom operators to provide investment-intensive infrastructure for customers to connect their households to the internet. Facebook targets and distributes news. But it doesn't produce the news itself—traditional news organizations and users do. These disruptive companies, and many lesser-known firms that we'll analyze, all deploy innovative technologies, but they use technology to enable their business models. The business models themselves represent the true innovations.

The present wave of customer-driven innovation in business models is fundamentally new. It follows that incumbents seeking to master it should embrace a new strategic framework. While frameworks such as SWOT analysis,* game theory, and even Michael Porter's Five Forces proved extremely useful for companies in the 1980s, 1990s, and early 2000s, the nature of competition has changed. Most industries used to have only two or at most a few major global players. Today industries contain many competitors, mostly small ones acting globally. Game theory loses much of its value when one larger, more predictable player has to play a strategic "chess match" with not one, not two, but hundreds and in some cases thousands of small, unpredictable players. Other traditional approaches to strategy are similarly ill-equipped

* SWOT stands for "strengths, weaknesses, opportunities, and threats."

to handle present-day realities. This book aims to complement these established frameworks.

Customers Are Disrupting Markets

As a rule, these traditional strategy frameworks tend to be firm-centric, oriented toward what's best for the company relative to its competitors. But since the new wave of digital disruption is driven by customers, a company needs new frameworks and tools that focus primarily on *them*. In *Unlocking the Customer Value Chain*, I outline powerful, customer-centric responses to digital disruption, as opposed to firm-centric responses. Instead of reacting to each new, potentially threatening startup, I advise that incumbents devise a system for responding to the *overall pattern* of disruption produced by changing customer needs. Incumbents should take a general approach to what is essentially a generalized problem.

I've written *Unlocking the Customer Value Chain* for managers and executives of established businesses, but I believe it will also prove valuable for entrepreneurs who wish to learn how to disrupt markets in a more disciplined, orderly fashion, with less risk. The book should also help general readers who wish to understand how digital businesses really work. Customers truly are changing the business landscape. *We* are changing. Small, frequent, and spontaneous actions in our daily lives—staying in a rented home versus a hotel, hailing a private car versus a taxi, comparing prices on an app versus going from store to store—can eventually take down entire industries. These actions seem innocuous at first, yet they accumulate momentum as more consumers adopt the behavior, new companies jump in to exploit it, and consumers flock to these startups. That is how big, century-old firms fall. And it's how new billion-dollar companies are born.

I've divided *Unlocking the Customer Value Chain* into three sections. Part I explains the new reality of markets, what has changed, and *why* it has changed. I conclude with a chapter detailing a step-by-step process for engineering disruption. In Part II, written primarily for incumbents, or established companies, I provide a generalized framework for responding to disruption, as well as analytical tools to help you determine the best response to this new class of disruption. I intend the framework to help you decide *what* to do, as well as give you tools to help you understand *how* to do it. In Part III, I apply the theory of decoupling to the life cycle of companies, deriving new insights into how to start, grow, and avoid the decline of a customer-centric disruptive business.

Decoupling Is Occurring Everywhere

I formed my theory of decoupling in the course of performing extensive research into digital disruption. During an eight-year period, I visited large tech companies such as Airbnb, Google, Facebook, Netflix, and Wayfair, among others, as well as smaller startups including Houzz, Enjoy, zulily, Tower, Rebag, and Birchbox. I also visited incumbents such as Coca-Cola, Disney, Warner, Walmart, Paramount Pictures, Electronic Arts, and Sephora, and non-U.S.-based firms such as Globo, Nissan, Siemens, and Zalora. In every case, I talked to company founders or top executives, and I conducted in-depth research on the company's customers—those that incumbents lost, those that disruptors gained, and those that incumbents and disruptors had in common.

The more I looked, the more I discerned the same, common pattern of disruption. It was everywhere, affecting many kinds of businesses in different industries. A case-based, cross-industry vantage point allowed me to spot the commonalities of this disruption and to frame generally applicable concepts, lessons, and frameworks. As you read the following chapters, I encourage that you set aside your industry-specific focus and consider with an open mind how the disruption occurring in other industries might relate to recent developments in your own. Case-based research helps decision makers formulate guiding principles, which is precisely why we use it at Harvard Business School. But such research doesn't test strict casual assertions (if X happens, then you should always do Y). If you're seeking equations that can unambiguously describe something as complex as digital disruption, this book won't help you. But if you're looking for common patterns that can help you interpret this new phenomenon, and if you'd like to learn from others' successes and failures, *Unlocking the Customer Value Chain* will prove a valuable starting point.

Mindful of executives' busy schedules and their need for novel, actionable ideas, I have avoided the highly technical language found in many academic books. Still, a brief word on terminology is in order. When I use the term "disruption," I am referring to an abrupt and sizable change of market shares among participants in an industry. As I've suggested, I employ "decoupling" to refer to the breaking of the links between adjacent customer-related activities. Unlike other forms of business model innovation, decoupling occurs at the level of the customer's value chain, not at the product level. I define "customer value chain" (CVC) as the series of activities that customers perform in order to fulfill their needs and wants. These activities include searching for, evaluating, purchasing, using, and disposing of products. The customer value chain is analogous to Michael Porter's value chain (the series of activities such as operations, logistics, and marketing that companies execute in order to create value for themselves), but it reflects the customer's vantage point, rather than the company's. For more on these terms, please see "Note on Terminology" at the end of the book.

Understand Customers, and You'll Understand Disruption

As an academic, I am duty-bound to be transparent about my intellectual bias toward the discipline of marketing. For the past eight years, I've taught courses at Harvard on traditional and digital marketing strategy, marketing analytics, and e-commerce. These courses focus on consumer behavior, teaching students how to apply a marketing perspective to solve common business problems. By analyzing digital disruption from a customer vantage point, this book indirectly argues for the usefulness of the marketing discipline for understanding business model innovation. To my knowledge, few marketing executives bear direct responsibility for innovation in large companies. That reality needs to change. As I hope you'll see, executives who are versed in consumer behavior are the ones who are best equipped to carry out customer-driven innovation.

Unlocking the Customer Value Chain aims to provide not merely an exciting new perspective on digital disruption but also concepts and tools you can use to take meaningful action. Don't become another cautionary tale like Borders, Nokia, and J. Crew. The leaders at these firms tried relentlessly to respond to digital disruption. Borders tried to be "an innovative company," launching its own e-commerce website, e-reader, and e-book store.[5] Nokia for years invested heavily in smartphones, touch screens, and other technologies, earning multiple innovation awards. J. Crew engaged in digital marketing, invested in a digital platform, and employed various innovative fabrics. Yet technological innovation alone didn't save them. It likely won't save your business, either. Your fate lies in the hands of customers. So let's understand the logic of their needs and wants. By doing so, we can devise reliable strategies and tools for directly managing disruption to their advantage, and indirectly to yours as well.

PART I
The New Reality of Markets

1

THE DISCOVERY JOURNEY

If you're a big-box retailer, you want your stores jammed with customers. The busier your stores are, the more sales you'll log. Pretty obvious, right? Well, not always, as it turns out. At the height of the 2012 holiday shopping season, Best Buy, the world's largest electronics retailer with almost fifteen hundred U.S. locations, saw its stores packed with people. The customers marveled at the glowing displays of forty-two-inch Sharp flat-screen TV sets. They crowded around to test new Samsung laptops with Intel Pentium processors. They browsed through Blu-ray sets of *Mad Men* seasons. Yet there was one thing that customers weren't doing as much of as in the past: pulling out their wallets. Best Buy's sales *fell* that quarter by almost 4 percent.[1]

Instead of buying, many visitors played with their smartphones as they shopped. Tapping at their screens, they scanned barcodes from TV sets and laptops, or snapped pictures of DVD covers. Within seconds, price comparison apps on their phones searched the inventory of Amazon.com and other online competitors, often locating prices that were 5 to 10 percent lower. With a few clicks, users made purchases online and arranged to have items delivered directly to their doorsteps.[2] Again and again, Best Buy employees watched as would-be customers left the store empty-handed.

These customers were engaging in a practice called "showrooming." And in 2012, Best Buy was hardly the only victim. Apps such as Price Check by Amazon turned the brick-and-mortar stores of Walmart, Bed Bath & Beyond, and Toys "R" Us into showrooms for many shoppers. As Google reported, more than six in ten smartphone owners used their phones in-store to help in shopping.[3] In surveys, shoppers reported that their top three reasons for "showrooming" were better online prices, their desire to see products in person before ordering online, and the unavailability of items at retail stores (e.g., due to stocking shortages).[4] For the first time, technology presented what former Best Buy chief marketing officer Barry Judge called "an opportunity [for a competitor] to steal a sale right when someone is in the throes of making a decision."[5]

Showrooming, while seemingly a physical retailer problem on the surface, is a prime example of the digital disruption that has unsettled so many industries, from media to telecommunication, finance to transportation. In Best Buy's case, disruption exacted a steep toll. After the 2012 holiday shopping season, the company reported a $1.7 billion quarterly loss. Sales continued to decline for the next year and a half, and Best Buy's stock price plunged to a twelve-year low. "Are We Witnessing the Death of the Big-Box Store?" one newspaper headline wondered.[6] Inside the company, management floundered. The company's veteran CEO resigned,[7] and his successors differed on how to respond. Although the interim chief executive wanted to tackle showrooming head-on and put an end to the practice, the board's final appointee initially doubted whether the practice even posed a problem.[8] Academics, analysts, and journalists also articulated conflicting views. Some argued that Best Buy should follow Amazon's lead, expanding its differentiated offer and selling cheaper online.[9] Others believed Best Buy should model itself after Apple, stocking fewer products and focusing on high-end stores.[10] The outlook for Best Buy seemed so dire that the company's founder came out of retirement with a bid to buy out the company.[11]

Best Buy wound up deploying an array of tactics to prevent customers from showrooming and to entice them to buy at the store. It tailored its in-store barcodes to prevent customers from attempting to showroom using mobile apps. It refrained from placing barcodes on some products inside stores and used in-store exclusive barcodes to prevent shoppers from finding lower prices through price-comparison apps on their phones.[12] It renovated stores, retrained staff, relaunched its online store, and offered exclusive products only available at Best Buy, such as special editions of Blu-ray movies.[13] The company also went on the attack, creating its own shopping app. None of these tactics seemed to deter consumers from showrooming.

In the spring of 2013, after another lost holiday shopping season, Best Buy finally made a bold move: it promised to match prices with Amazon and other online retailers. The decline in sales flattened, and by the end of the year, CEO Hubert Joly announced: "Best Buy has killed showrooming."[14] But had it? Was the strategy sustainable in the long term? Unlike its online competitors, Best Buy still employed retail staff, maintained stores, and carried inventory across numerous locations. As a result, its costs were fundamentally higher than those of online retailers with centralized warehouses and no retail staff. Price matching stopped the leak of customers, but it ate into profit margins without addressing the root cause of the industry's disruption.[15]

You might think Best Buy had little choice but to experiment wildly with one-off tactics. After all, the threat it faced—showrooming—was unprecedented. As a result, Best Buy executives had little science to call upon, and no general frameworks or theories to deploy. They also had no cases in other industries to study for guidance, inspiration, or best practices. What did disruptive phenomena in other industries have to do with what they were facing? Feeling besieged by a threat that seemed to come out of nowhere, all they could do was retreat into their industries and take tentative stabs in the dark. Of course, the executives at Best Buy were hardly alone in their powerlessness: their peers at other large companies, including Comcast (facing disruption from Netflix) or AT&T (under threat from Skype), also hunkered down, focused on what they knew, and waged a series of indiscriminate campaigns against their digital challengers.

Today, executives at incumbents fare little better. They remain stymied by disruption, uncertain of what to do. But what if disruption is actually the *same* across industries? What if the threat posed by Amazon to Best Buy bears a *structural similarity* to disruptive threats in a range of other industries? What if just a *single* dynamic has unsettled markets in recent years, a hidden pattern of attack by upstart competitors? That would change everything for leaders of incumbent firms. If you could understand this hidden pattern, then you wouldn't be blindly feeling your way any longer. Even if disruption is rearing its head in your industry for the first time, you'd be able to respond in a methodical way by deploying a generalized framework. Threats that seemed uniquely yours and existential in nature would become more comprehensible, predictable, and thus manageable. Disruptors would no longer be so, well, disruptive after all.

Puzzled by Disruption

It turns out that individual instances of disruption aren't nearly as unique as most executives assume. A pattern *does* exist—one that I uncovered almost by accident. In 2010, a year after I began teaching at Harvard Business School, I sat down to write my first case study. I had chosen to focus on how online streaming services such as Netflix had challenged Globo, Brazil's biggest media company. As a conglomerate of television and radio stations, newspapers, websites, and other media properties, Globo captured 70 percent of all TV advertising revenue at the time. But their most successful product—

telenovelas (soap operas), popular in Latin America since the 1960s—wasn't doing so well.

I visited Globo's headquarters and interviewed about a dozen of its executives, including the chairman of the board. Writing up the case study, I recounted how younger audiences weren't watching much TV anymore, especially *novelas,* which were traditionally shown during prime time, 6:00 to 10:00 p.m. Instead, younger consumers were going online to watch their favorite shows on YouTube or Netflix. Proud of my work, I sent the finished case study to Globo for approval (standard practice for our case studies). To my great shock, my request for approval was declined. And not just declined: the corporate communications people with whom I interfaced essentially told me that I could never publish the case.

I couldn't believe it. It was my first case, and I had spent quite some time researching and writing it. But I thought I understood the company's decision. Globo was frightened about the threats its *telenovelas* faced, and executives didn't want to "wash their dirty laundry" publicly. So I let it go.

I went on to write a series of cases on other topics in digital marketing, studying companies such as PepsiCo, Groupon, Dropbox, Trip Advisor, and YouTube. In 2013, I again tried to publish a case study about a firm in the throes of being disrupted. This time the company was Telefonica, Spain's largest telecom company. For decades, Telefonica had made a killing on international calls. Then, in 2003, Skype came along, and in less than a decade, Telefonica's and other European operators' revenues from international calls plummeted by more than two-thirds.[16] What consumer would pay 40 cents a minute to call New York City from Madrid when you could Skype another person anywhere in the world for free? Telecom executives lost billions of euros under their watch. Again, after I interviewed almost a dozen of Telefonica's executives and wrote up the case, someone at the top refused to sign off on its publication. I later discovered that the then CEO had refused permission, likely for a similar reason to that of the executives at Globo. The pain was real, and a cure was not yet available or well understood.*

These two setbacks got me thinking: Why were executives struggling so much with disruption? Did they know how to respond but just needed more time? Or were they genuinely baffled, regarding disruption as utterly novel and unknown? I decided to approach a number of large companies facing disruption and talk to them off the record. My goal wasn't to publish cases but simply to understand what they were facing and how they were responding. Between 2013 and 2017, I spoke with executives at Sephora, a beauty retailer that at the time was fending off a challenge by upstart Birchbox; at Best Buy, which was grappling with Amazon; and at Electronic Arts, a videogame publisher that faced threats from developers including Zynga, Rovio, and Supercell. At each company, I found that executives were acutely aware of the threats that upstarts posed, yet unsure how to best respond. Mind you, they did react, but mostly with pointwise tactics akin to Best Buy's initial attempts at discouraging shoppers from practicing showrooming.

In the course of these conversations, I began to notice a recurring theme. As dangerous as disruptors were to incumbents, they weren't replacing or unsettling *everything* about an incumbent's business, just a small part of it. Amazon, as we've seen, wasn't dissuading customers from browsing the aisles at Best Buy to discover products, test them out, and compare features. Amazon's app came into play only once a customer had finished comparison shopping and was looking to make a purchase. In a sense, Amazon and Best Buy were sharing customers. This was a different type of competition, one that big-company executives were not used to seeing and responding to.

Or take Sephora and Birchbox. Consumers had been visiting

* Unlike TV Globo's case, at Telefonica, top executives did have a couple of options to combat the new disruptor.

Sephora's physical stores to test and evaluate Yves Saint Laurent lipsticks or Chanel perfumes and make purchases on the spot. Customers could later repurchase items from Sephora either on the company's website or in the store. In 2010, when Birchbox came along, it disrupted Sephora using a "subscription box" model. For a fee, Birchbox sent customers monthly boxes of beauty products to sample. Yet customers didn't get to decide what went into their boxes—Birchbox did that for them. In this way, Birchbox made it unnecessary for customers to visit Sephora to test makeup, lipstick, perfume, and skincare products—they could now do this in the convenience of their own homes. Consumers were delighted. As one Birchbox subscriber related, "I live in a small town and have very little access to high-end brands."[17] For a customer like this, Birchbox was a godsend.

At first, Birchbox was solely in the business of facilitating sampling, offering sample-sized products in its subscription boxes. If customers liked a particular sample of a product, they could then purchase the full-sized version of the product at Sephora or elsewhere.[18] Over time, as more people subscribed to these boxes to trial and learn about new products, fewer people casually entered Sephora stores to learn about new products on the shelf. Birchbox had come to pose a major threat because it interfered with just one part of the consumer's activities: testing. As one industry executive stated, "You're going to have more and more young clients who . . . will buy their product without being in a store."[19]

Likewise, in the videogame industry, developers such as Zynga, Rovio, and Supercell didn't focus on replicating the entire business of traditional videogame developers. What they did in taking on incumbent Electronic Arts was simply change how consumers paid for them. Prior to internet-enabled gaming consoles, consumers had to pay a one-time up-front price of $40 to $80 to purchase a physical videogame before they could play it. Then new channels including social media and app stores came along, and upstart developers began making their games available for free. They made money by selling customers inexpensive add-ons (some cheaper than $1) that allowed gamers to better compete and advance. Around 98 percent of mobile gamers, the casual players, played for free. The other 2 percent, the loyal players, were more than willing to pay.[20] This strategy worked so well that by 2019, most mobile game developers had abandoned the pay-to-play model in favor of "freemium" pricing models.

The Concept of Decoupling

Wondering precisely how disruptors were unsettling small parts of incumbents' businesses, I turned to a basic framework that my colleagues and I teach our students: the customer's value chain, or CVC.* A CVC is composed of the discrete steps a typical customer follows in order to select, buy, and consume a product or service. CVCs vary according to the specifics of a business, industry, or product. For example, the key stages in a CVC for purchasing a flat-screen TV involve going to a retailer, evaluating the options available, choosing one, purchasing it, and then using the TV at home. For a beauty product such as skin cream or for a videogame, the value chain is basically the same. In the case of videogames, players evaluate the available game titles, choose one or more, purchase it, and then play it.

FIGURE 1.1 **A TYPICAL CONSUMER'S VALUE CHAIN (CVC)**

Traditionally, consumers completed all these activities with the same company in a joint or coupled manner. To buy a TV, consumers

* Also referred to as the decision-making process.

found it most convenient to go to physical stores such as those operated by Best Buy, choose one of the available options after evaluating them all, and buy the TV right then and there. While people could browse in one store and buy at another, Best Buy knew that most of the time, consumers who had arrived in the store to buy a TV would purchase it there if the price seemed reasonable. Similarly, a shopper for beauty products would go to a Sephora store, evaluate perfume options, choose one, buy it, and consume it. And a gamer would do the same for games produced and sold by Electronic Arts.

What I realized, as I thought about these examples, was that disruptors had posed a threat by *breaking the links between some of the stages of the CVC* and then "stealing" one or a few stages for themselves to fulfill. To facilitate comparison shopping, Amazon created a mobile application (app) that allowed shoppers in brick-and-mortar stores to search, scan the barcode, or snap a picture of any product to easily discover Amazon's price. This enabled Amazon's customers to easily break the connection between *choosing* a product and *purchasing* it. Best Buy did the former, Amazon the latter. Similarly, Birchbox enabled its customers to easily separate the *testing* of beauty products (fulfilled by Birchbox) from the *choosing* and *purchasing* stages (fulfilled by other retailers). Upstart game developers allowed customers to separate out the *purchasing* of games from the act of *playing* them.

In effect, upstarts were culling just a portion of the CVC that had traditionally been provided by an incumbent, and they were building entire businesses around it. Disruptors were *decoupling* discrete activities that customers performed. Upstarts weren't trying to replace incumbents entirely, as traditional competition was based upon. Why do that if they could steal a customer just by offering a narrow slice of the value pie? Plus, the cost of completely replacing an incumbent could prove prohibitive for a startup—billions of dollars of investment in stores, salespeople, production facilities, and other assets. Upstarts let Best Buy, Sephora, and Electronic Arts still offer some parts of the CVC, often those that are expensive to replicate. Of course, to incumbents, this was no consolation. Even the loss of one core stage in the CVC wreaked havoc in an incumbent's business, particularly if that portion was where the incumbent made most of its money.

Decoupling, Decoupling, Everywhere

As the concept of decoupling came into focus, I found myself taken aback by it. Best Buy, Sephora, and Electronic Arts were in different consumer retail industries, and the upstarts that challenged them seemed to be doing so using different weapons (Amazon used an app, Birchbox a subscription box, and game developers such as Supercell a different pricing strategy). I could see why executives at these incumbent companies were considering disruptors only in their own industry when crafting their responses. Yet disruption in each of these industries ultimately amounted to the same process: decoupling. Upstarts were peeling away a portion of the customer's value chain that used to be the sole province of incumbent companies. And on this count, they were dangerous. Disruptions thus weren't all unique events, disconnected from one another. Rather, they were, possibly, a general phenomenon.

By 2014, I was eager to tell others about the common approach I was seeing. Was I genuinely on to something? I was invited to present some of my early work on decoupling at the National Retail Federation Week in New York City. Executives in the audience were as intrigued as I was about the possibility of commonalities between disruptors across retail industries. Later that year, I presented decoupling at a prominent San Francisco venture capital firm. This firm invested in disruptive companies in a number of industries, not just retail. As investors there suggested, the decoupling pattern might extend into sectors such as business software, media, and e-commerce, comprising a truly general phenomenon. They advised that I study a range of companies to verify whether this was true.

Over the past few years, I have taken that advice, investigating disruption in industries such as food, apparel, beauty, healthcare, hospitality, transportation, education, media, and entertainment. Everywhere, I spotted evidence of decoupling. Take television. Traditionally, broadcasters required that viewers watch advertisements in order to enjoy their favorite programs. People could of course change channels, but there was no guarantee they would avoid other commercials. And they also risked missing some of the original program by skipping around. During the early 2000s, TiVo disrupted the market by introducing digital video recorders (DVRs) that allowed viewers to record programs and then fast-forward through commercials. In effect, TiVo decoupled viewing TV programs from watching ads. Fifteen years later, a startup named Aereo promised the same benefit of decoupling ads from shows without any need to buy a DVR. Subscribe to their service, and you could stream shows devoid of ads on demand from anywhere.[21]

Decoupling has also riven the automobile industry. Traditionally, people visited dealers and bought cars from automakers such as General Motors. Car-sharing companies such as Zipcar ushered in the first generation of decoupling in this industry, providing drivers with access to cars without having to purchase and maintain the vehicle, or sign frequent rental agreements. Zipcar is a membership service that provides access to company-owned cars placed at multiple locations around a city. Its members pay a fee based on how long they use the vehicle. They bear no responsibility for fuel, maintenance, or insurance. Zipcar breaks the links between purchasing and driving a car, as well as between driving and maintaining a car. For those who prefer to be driven, on-demand ride-hailing services such as Uber, Lyft, and Didi Chuxing in China allow passengers to decouple the act of owning and driving a car from traveling in one. Whether you prefer to drive or be driven, a decoupler exists that caters to your desire to avoid buying and maintaining an automobile.

Most people who use these ride-hailing services to decouple car usage from car ownership tend to be younger residents of densely populated urban centers. A larger population of consumers has been using these services to disrupt the taxi industry, decoupling the act of hailing a taxi from riding in one. In many cities around the world, hailing a taxicab on the street or calling a dispatch service hardly guarantees that a car will actually appear where and when you need it. With their online apps, Uber and its look-alikes eliminate this element of uncertainty. They make transportation easier, less stressful, and more reliable by enabling customers to ride in private cars.

In financial services, I found—you guessed it—more decoupling. The act of investing in the stock market is actually a four-stage process. First you arrive at an investment strategy (e.g., you believe in the rising trend of online sales). Then you find individual stocks compatible with the strategy (e.g., e-commerce companies). Next you pass this information on to a stockbroker, who buys and sells shares of companies such as Amazon, eBay, and Wayfair. Finally, you pay these agents a management fee.

Motif, a financial technology startup, has decoupled the first two stages of this process. It allows investors to devise investment strategies themselves, called "motifs," without an advisor. Investors then hire Motif to match their strategies with a portfolio of stocks. An investor might anticipate that biotechnology will grow, or that in a few decades the world will experience a tremendous water shortage. Using a matching algorithm, Motif allows investors to place bets on their visions, identifying the companies that would stand to benefit the most should the investor's prediction come to fruition. Motif makes money by charging a subscription fee for the building and management of an investor's motifs. Since it doesn't create the strategy, it doesn't take a performance fee on the gain in value of the stocks—a standard practice among traditional brokerage firms.[22]

We can also observe decoupling in foreign exchange. In recent years, a wave of online peer-to-peer platforms has inundated the financial markets. Disruptors such as TransferWise have made it cheaper to transfer money across different currencies. Traditionally, banks offering international money transfers have needed to execute three operations. Suppose you want to send money to your cousin in England. The bank accepts your deposit in dollars, performs a currency conversion, and deposits British pounds in your cousin's account. For the deposits, the bank charges a service fee, and for the currency conversion, it charges a sales commission (the rate spread). TransferWise, on the other hand, decouples these operations and never actually does the latter. When you deposit American dollars, it holds the funds until another transaction occurs in the opposite direction (for example, when a person transfers British pounds to someone in the United States). TransferWise pays the recipient of that second transaction with your money, using the originator's British pounds to pay your cousin. Since TransferWise never (to be precise, rarely) needs to convert currency, it doesn't charge a sales commission on currency trading to anyone. That is how it can offer a cheaper service to its customers. The only problem with this approach is TransferWise's eventual risk of having too much of one currency deposited and not enough of another to pay out. The company's solution is to play with the service fee. If TransferWise possesses a surplus of American dollars, the service fee from depositing in this currency rises to dissuade more people from depositing dollars. Conversely, if the company has a deficit of British pounds, it lowers the service fee to deposit with it, potentially even forgoing the fee entirely. TransferWise has figured out a clever, or should I say wise, way of decoupling the receiving of currency X and the depositing of currency Y in a foreign exchange transfer.

Let's move on to an entirely different industry, home meals, where we also see decoupling at work. During the 1950s, middle-class American families ate most meals at home, with women—wives, mothers, domestic servants—usually doing the cooking. Since the 1960s, many women have pursued careers outside of the home, leaving them with less time to cook. Most men, meanwhile, have proven decidedly unwilling to perform domestic chores. By 2015, 43 percent of men engaged in home chores such as food preparation or cleaning up, compared with 70 percent of women.[23] With restaurants providing meals that were cheap, convenient, and of reasonably high quality, more people began to eat out. Today, Americans eat out more than they eat in: in 2015, sales at U.S. restaurants and bars surpassed those of grocery stores for the first time in history.[24] In fact, households with families have given up preparing meals to such an extent that they now have started to miss it. The challenge is that many people no longer know how to prepare more elaborate dishes because their parents did not teach them. They also don't have time to spend an entire morning making lunch or an afternoon making dinner.

Enter the meal delivery kit startups—companies such as Blue Apron, Chef'd, HelloFresh, and hundreds of copycat businesses. Suppose you like Chinese cuisine and have spotted a recipe for kung pao chicken in a magazine. You'd like to prepare it yourself for a family dinner this Saturday, and maybe invite some friends over. Traditionally, you would find the recipe, drive to an Asian grocery, and spend an hour shopping for ingredients. Then you would go home and wash and cut the ingredients yourself before starting to cook. Companies such as Chef'd allow amateur chefs to decouple the acts of finding a recipe and shopping for ingredients from the cooking itself. Sign up for their subscription service, and they'll send you boxes with a simple recipe to follow, along with all the ingredients, pre-cut, pre-washed, pre-measured, and ready for cooking. With prices as low as $60 for three two-person meals per week, becoming a kitchen hero becomes simpler, and health-conscious consumers know exactly what ingredients they're eating.

What if you don't care about cooking and you just want to eat a home-cooked meal? There's a decoupler for that, too. Companies such as Hire-A-Chef allow people to book chefs to cook at their homes, on demand, and at the reasonable price of $48 for a four-person meal. Wealthy individuals have been hiring chefs to cook in their homes for ages. Hire-A-Chef allows middle-class customers to do this cheaply and on demand. Further, customers can select from among a long list of chefs available at a particular date and time. One San Francisco–based chef has worked his way through several Michelin-starred restaurants in Europe and suggests dishes like an Indonesian-spiced bison steak with caramelized endive, pickled lemon, and Jerusalem artichoke freekeh.[25] Hire-A-Chef and other copycats decouple three key stages of the customer's value chain—recipe creation, ingredient shopping, and cooking—from a fourth stage, the actual consumption of a meal cooked at home. Last but not least, the chefs clean up the kitchen!

Decoupling is not strictly a consumer-facing phenomenon. Business-to-business incumbents can also be decoupled. Consider Salesforce.com, the leading software company for sales and customer relationship management (CRM). Its main product is a sales automation tool that provides salespeople in medium and large companies with data, analytics, and productivity tools for them to contact potential customers and close deals. The software is run over the cloud and is sold as a software-as-a-service (SaaS). This means it runs remotely in Salesforce.com's servers, in what is called the back-end solution. And what Salesforce.com's customers see is the client interface, or the front end. RocketVisor is a startup founded by one of my former students to allow users to link together information in their Salesforce.com dashboards with other information on potential clients available on sites such as LinkedIn, Google, and the prospective client's website. RocketVisor does this via a browser plugin that connects all this information in an easy-to-use interface and overlays it on top of Salesforce.com's dashboard. In effect, what RocketVisor has cleverly done is to allow their clients to decouple the front-end user interface—what you see—from the back-end software that processes everything shown on the user's screen. According to RocketVisor's founder, Michael Yaroshefsky, major software vendors aren't necessarily great at both engineering great software and designing the user experience. When they are lacking in the latter, a better company (his) can come in and offer to do just the front-end portion for the user. Business-to-business software can be decoupled, too.

In all of these examples, you might wonder *why* decoupling has taken place. Why does it make sense? Why does it work? The answer ties back to value, which all consumers want. Traditionally, incumbents provide value *across* the multiple stages of the customer's value chain. However, value is never equally distributed throughout the stages of the CVC. No matter how great the TV commercial is, it is never as good as the show I chose to watch. And in some cases, people value different stages of the process differently. When eating home-cooked meals, some value the opportunity to choose the recipe, while others do not. Some value the chance to choose the ingredients or to prepare the food, while others only value eating it. Customers flock to upstarts to decouple because they see an opportunity to "consume" the value-creating portion of activities such as watching television, playing videogames, testing electronics, talking on their phones, or using cars to get somewhere. But here's the crucial part: with decoupling, they gain the ability to claim value *without* the parts of the chain that *don't* create value, such as peeling the onions, watching ads, buying a game, or maintaining the car. Given the choice, customers will happily separate out the value-creating portions from the non-value-creating portions. What do they have to lose?

FIGURE 1.2 **EXAMPLES OF DECOUPLED ACTIVITIES AND THEIR DISRUPTORS**

		VALUE-CREATING PORTION		NON-VALUE-CREATING PORTION	DISRUPTORS
Watching TV	=	watch show	+	watch ads	TIVO
Playing videogames	=	play game	+	purchase game	zynga
Eating home-cooked meal	=	cook meal	+	procure ingredients	CHEF'D
Shopping	=	test/try	+	buy	amazon
Communicating	=	talk/text	+	connect	Skype
Driving	=	use	+	maintain	zipcar

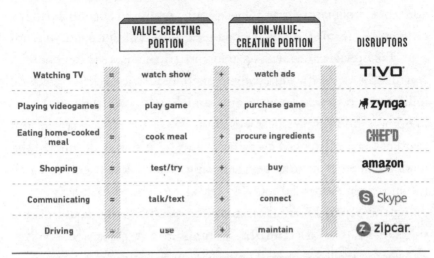

Source: Adapted from Thales S. Teixeira and Peter Jamieson, "The Decoupling Effect of Digital Disruptors," *European Business Review*, July–August 2016, 17–24.

In the End, It Really Is All Decoupling

As I began to uncover decoupling as a general phenomenon across industries, I received invitations from companies including BMW, Nike, Google, Microsoft, and Unilever to explain decoupling to them. Focused mostly on their industries, they were eager for a broader approach that would allow them to better understand the competitive challenges afflicting them. I found myself in a curious position: I wanted to advise these companies to deemphasize other concepts that people were using in relation to disruption (for instance, the "sharing economy," "webrooming," and "freemium") and to see everything in terms of just one phenomenon: decoupling. I believed that focusing solely on decoupling would simplify the conversation, allowing busy executives to home in on the essence of the disruptive threat they faced and forge strategies to counter it. Why does an executive need ten terms to describe disruption when one will do? But was "decoupling" the one?

The more I investigated decoupling, the more I appreciated the concept's explanatory power. Decoupling really did encompass many of the other terms that people had used to talk about digital disruption. Take review sites such as Yelp and TripAdvisor. These onetime startups have drastically changed their industries. They aggregate millions of reviews of restaurants and hotels worldwide, influencing diners' and travelers' choices about where to eat and stay. From another perspective, however, these sites have simply decoupled the links between evaluating and choosing. They allow users to search for and evaluate restaurants and travel services, respectively, while doing the actual booking on another website.* Why would people suffer the hassle of comparing options in one place and booking elsewhere? Well, because they regard review aggregators as more trustworthy and unbiased. Aggregators often don't receive commissions from the businesses they showcase, and they tend to treat all businesses identically, affording them the same content format and space. What distinguishes individual restaurants or hotels on aggregator sites are the objective features of these establishments, as well as the reviews that other like-minded consumers post on these sites.

Decoupling also accounted for another form of disruption, showrooming. As I've suggested, showrooming separates out the act of choosing a product from the act of purchasing it. Decoupling also helps us understand a reverse phenomenon, whereby consumers search online and then buy in a physical store—what some have called webrooming. Pop-up stores used by retailers such as Warby Parker (eyewear) and Bonobos (clothing) have decoupled the link between purchasing and receiving by allowing customers to see and buy items in a small store but not take them home immediately, since these stores carry little if any on-site inventory. Now, why would consumers ever do that? The answer is that it is more conve-

* In a later stage of their lives, some of these decouplers eventually rejoined these two activities to generate a new source of revenues (e.g., TripAdvisor).

nient for a shopper to receive at home the exact item that she wants, particularly when it is a bulky item such as furniture or mattresses, or when fit is critical, as in the case of eyewear. For online retailers, not having to stock all items in all colors, shapes, and sizes in multiple stores is a great benefit, one that allows for lower inventory costs and potentially lower prices offered to consumers.

We also hear a lot these days about the "sharing economy"—services such as Airbnb and Turo that allow consumers access to special experiences, such as living in a nineteenth-century granite lighthouse on a rock just off Long Island ($350 per night on Airbnb) or riding in a 2017 gold chrome Maserati Ghibli ($699 per day on Turo).[26] Here, too, we see decoupling in action, this time in the form of ruptured links between purchasing and consuming. Likewise, Rent the Runway has been disrupting the haute couture industry by allowing women to use expensive jewelry and dresses for special occasions without having to buy them: for just $139 a month you get access to $40,000 worth of designer clothing per year. This is yet another example of decoupling, a separation of the activities of using (the value-creating portion) from owning (the non-value-creating portion). People are opting to rent products they never would have rented in the past, particularly products with high price points, such as cars (Turo) and bicycles (Hubway), or products with a high cost of ownership, such as bulky sports equipment (Comoodle), and even dogs (Borrow My Doggy). Business models based on the renting and sharing economies represent huge new opportunities for consumers to reduce their ownership burden—thanks to decoupling.

We can also spot decoupling in two other business models that have been gaining prominence online, software-as-a-service (SaaS) models and freemium. Under the SaaS model, companies offer software such as Microsoft Office 365 by subscription rather than as a perpetual license with a large up-front cost. Home PC users do not need to pay the $149.99 up-front cost to use the product. Instead, they might pay just $6.99 per month. We can regard SaaS as a special case of decoupling usage from ownership. Freemium models used by Dropbox, an online storage service, go even further, decoupling usage from (pre)payment. Users of a basic software or service online do not need to pay anything up front. Only heavy users interested in a premium version pay. Decoupling is a flexible and multifaceted concept indeed.

In the years ahead, more new decoupling-style businesses may disrupt established players. Decoupling of the consumption and disposal stages remains a potentially significant, untapped opportunity. For example, Spoiler Alert is an app targeting food businesses in the United States, which throw away $165 billion a year of soon-to-expire or spoiled products. The startup connects shops, restaurants, and food producers to nearby nonprofits taking donations or to companies that make fertilizer and animal feed.[27] Using this service, restaurants can consume food without worrying about the disposal of unused ingredients or leftovers.

FIGURE 1.3 **GENERALIZING DECOUPLING TO OTHER FORMS OF DISRUPTION**

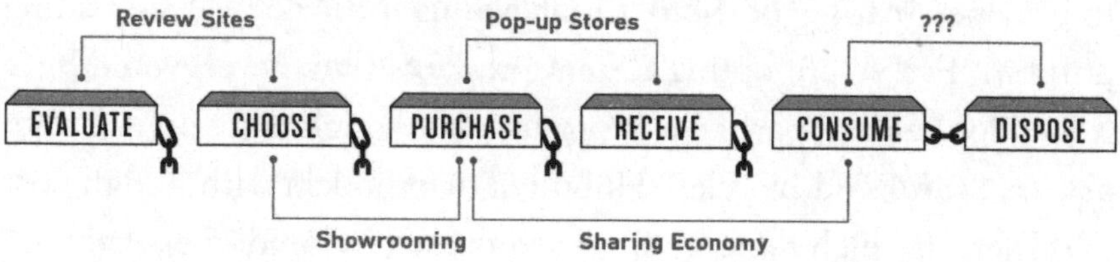

Common Problems Suggest a Common Solution

As I've suggested, disruptions across industries aren't nearly as idiosyncratic as they might seem to be at first glance. An underlying pattern is at work, one that permeates many of the most notable disruptions in the business world today. That pattern is one of customers decoupling entire CVCs traditionally fulfilled by established businesses. If we look closely, we can discern this phenomenon in industries such as automobiles, banking, consumer goods, and many more. We can also spot it in sharing-economy startups, among software-as-a-service providers, and among review sites. Decoupling has been cropping up all along, without many executives realizing it.

I was fortunate: as a business school professor who advised many companies large and small, my vantage point was broader than most. It's very hard to see generalizable patterns when you operate in only one industry and dedicate 99 percent of your time and mental energy to it. Our natural tendency is to think that the problems we face are unique to us. In our highly specialized professional worlds, we tend to think in terms of silos—particular fields, disciplines, functions, or specialties. Such extreme focus has its benefits, but it can also prevent us from spotting general patterns that can help us develop more appropriate responses.

The executives I interviewed were focused primarily on *their* businesses and the challenges they faced. At best, they were exposing themselves in depth to one or two structurally distinct forms of disruption: those affecting their businesses and their competitors'. They might have been aware of disruptions in other industries, but they weren't looking closely enough to see the underlying pattern of decoupling. It takes time to realize that others have similar problems, and that we can learn by analyzing them. But it's worth spending that time and making a discipline of looking broadly. If you're being disrupted, look at companies in completely different industries that find themselves in similar positions. And before seeking out solutions, try looking for common problems. What are companies going through? What can you learn?

If you don't attempt to take a broader view, you'll doom yourself, in effect, to reinventing the wheel—looking for a solution that others might have already invented for you. Consider Best Buy. As we've seen, the company's senior executives, led by newly appointed CEO Hubert Joly, tried many different approaches to fending off Amazon. First, executives tried to block consumers from showrooming.

Best Buy tried to offer exclusive products that online retailers did not carry. It tried to tamper with barcodes, and it even considered using radio-frequency jamming inside stores to prevent shoppers from using their mobile devices to price-compare with Amazon. That alone hints at the level of desperation the executives were likely experiencing.

Eventually, Joly resolved to offer low prices that rivaled Amazon's. According to Joly, "price is table stakes"; it would help Best Buy to avoid losing the customer to Amazon. Of course, price matching would not help Best Buy gain incremental revenues, let alone profits. Ultimately, Joly and his U.S. retail executives realized that the company couldn't win either by fighting customers' increasing desire to practice showrooming or by competing head-to-head against Amazon. The only solution was somehow to find a way to *coexist* with both showrooming shoppers and Amazon. Best Buy needed to "relearn" how to make money. And relearn it did.

During a meeting with Samsung, Best Buy proposed that the manufacturer locate Samsung-branded kiosks inside its stores. There was a catch: Samsung would have to pay a fee.[28] Yes, the *retailer* would charge the *manufacturer* for the opportunity—the privilege—of having its products showcased prominently. As Best Buy saw it, if its showrooming of new products was proving to be a valuable service for Samsung, Best Buy should be compensated. Whether a consumer who walked into a Best Buy store and tested Samsung's electronics eventually bought it at Best Buy, Amazon, or elsewhere, Samsung was benefiting. Samsung initially was unwilling to pay. But in light of compelling data supporting Best Buy's claim, it eventually agreed. And in the wake of this deal in 2013, Best Buy struck similar arrangements with other manufacturers, including LG, Sony, Microsoft, and AT&T.[29] This was the first time, to my knowledge, that a retailer in the electronics category charged a manufacturer a substantial sum for space (not sales) in the store. As we will see in the next chapters, some precedents for this approach exist in other industries.

After securing the Samsung deal, Best Buy began to drastically change its business model, transforming itself from a standard retailer to a business that essentially served as a showroom for major manufacturers. Requiring minimal investment from Best Buy and no need for fancy new technologies, this new model dramatically increased Best Buy's profitability. As of 2019, a sizable portion of Best Buy's profits came from so-called slotting fees paid by manufacturers for the opportunity to showcase products in the best areas of the store, away from competitors, and with well-marked brand signage. According to an article in *Fortune* magazine, the solution was devised by Joly, a veteran hotelier, and three other executives, two of whom had built careers in other industries.[30]

Although Best Buy eventually solved its decoupling problem, it took years of trial and error. As we'll see later in this book, the model of decoupling lends itself to a powerful framework for systematically understanding and, more important, responding to this type of disruption. Armed with a broader view of disruption that transcends your industry, you'll be able to arrive at effective responses to disruptors more quickly, avoiding trial and error and much of the stress, chaos, and uncertainty that come with it. A key principle of my framework is to do exactly what Best Buy eventually did: find ways to coexist peacefully with decouplers and decoupling, rather than trying to destroy or buy them out. You can kill a startup, but it's only a matter of time before another disruptive business pops up. Likewise, you can tie customers' hands so that they can't move their business to the startups, but it's only a matter of time before customers figure out how to free themselves from the bonds. To fend off disruption, coexistence is key! Later in this book, I will show you how to accomplish coexistence and position yourself for a more prosperous future.

Before we can understand *how* to forge a more stable relationship with decoupling and decouplers, we must first broaden our understanding of the underlying phenomenon. Executives have so much trouble responding to disruption in part because they get lost in the noise. There are so many threats on the horizon, so many challenges, and, of course, so many consultants and media experts talking about technological trends that can, they claim, spell the death of large companies. Surprisingly, though, the decoupling phenomenon isn't just or even primarily about technology. Business executives focus so much on technology that they often miss the essence of what most decouplers do: innovate on top of the dominant business model in an industry. As we'll see in Chapter 2, business model innovation is all around us. We neglect it to our peril. And if, like Best Buy, we can learn to harness it, well, watch out!

2

WHAT'S *REALLY* DISRUPTING YOUR BUSINESS?

It's October 26, 1958, and a sparkling new Pan American World Airways Boeing 707 has left the gate on its inaugural flight from New York to Paris. To the passengers on board, the 707 is a technological wonder. As the world's first commercial jetliner, it can fly much higher, faster, and farther than existing propeller-driven planes. Inside the cabin, the atmosphere is jubilant. The gentlemen have donned coats and ties, the ladies pearls and heels. The actress Greer Garson is on hand, having been driven to the plane in a silver Rolls-Royce.[1] Stewardesses stroll the aisles, attending to passengers' every need. No peanuts and ginger ale for these folks. They savor "gourmet meals of *foie gras* and lobster thermidor and Mouton Rothschild catered by Maxim's of Paris." It is, in the words of one historian, quite the "sky party."[2]

Most passengers today are hard-pressed to imagine a time when flying was a luxurious "sky party." During the second half of the twentieth century, jet travel became a fixture in the lives of middle-class Americans, fueled in part by technologies such as the wide-body jumbo jet. Initially, the airlines managed to retain some of the glamour of those first commercial jet flights, at considerable cost to their bottom lines. The food was fresh, cocktails were made to order, and some airlines even offered bunk beds for longer flights.[3] By the 1980s, however, many airlines were suffering financially, and not just because of customer perks. Airlines had long been terrible businesses—heavily subsidized national monopolies that were hobbled by government regulations and that emphasized adoption of new technology and broader geographical footprints over profits. The deregulation of U.S. and European airlines during the 1970s, 1980s, and early 1990s expanded competition and set off pricing wars. Free booze and fancy meals were the first features to go.[4]

In this tumultuous landscape, one airline would soon find a path to profit. In 1988, an accountant named Michael O'Leary joined the struggling Irish carrier Ryanair to help turn it around. Inspired by Southwest Airlines, a low-cost carrier in the United States focused on short-haul and point-to-point flights, O'Leary proposed a new strategy. He would offer no-frills flights around Europe, dispensing once and for all with the glamour of midcentury air travel. In his view, "air transport is just a glorified bus operation. You get on, you want to get there quickly, with the least amount of delays, and cheaply."[5] To keep airfares low and on par with bus or train tickets, Ryanair would slash all nonessential costs and charge extra fees for many services that traditional airlines bundled together in the price of a ticket.

During the 1990s and 2000s, Ryanair gained notoriety among consumers for its low prices and bare-bones service. Like Southwest, Ryanair usually flew to smaller and cheaper airports, many of which were located far from main destinations. The airport serving Ryanair's "Paris-Disney" destination was actually in the city of Reims, up to two hours from Paris by bus. Ryanair's planes had no curtains, reclining seats, seat pockets, or even airsickness bags. Passengers who experienced motion sickness en route had to manage on their own, like a bus passenger would. Nor did the airline offer assigned seating. The first passengers to the gate claimed the aisle and window seats, and everyone else had to scrunch into those uncomfortable middle seats. No more free drinks or courtesy meals. If you wanted mediocre airline food, you had to pay for it.[6] On the other hand, ticket prices were shockingly low—in many cases, only a few euros for an international flight.

If the company charged so little, how did it make money? That's where Ryanair's story gets interesting. Instead of profiting by selling airline seats and keeping expenses low, Ryanair earned money by charging for incidentals. From the minute passengers booked their tickets, the company offered them additional services, levying fees they often found hard to avoid or resist. Ryanair charged debit and credit card fees for buying tickets, airport fees for checking in, fees for checked bags, and, obviously, fees for "luxuries" like priority boarding.[7] Ryanair also acted as a travel agent, selling access to airport parking, airport lounges, bus and train transfers, car rental, hotel bookings, theme park tickets, tours, and activities. It sold financial services, exchanged foreign currencies for its passengers, and sold travel, home, and even life insurance. On board, it offered streaming movies and TV shows, access to online bingo, and tickets for theater, concerts, and sports events. Passengers could also buy watches, Bluetooth headsets, pocket lights, and so on.

These incidental revenue streams might seem trivial, but they added up. In 2016, Ryanair lost money on its transportation operations, as many airlines still do. Yet it reported a US$1.56 billion operating profit thanks to its high-margin cross-selling business.[8] After decades in which dozens of airlines in the United States and hundreds in Europe either went bankrupt or were bought out by others, Ryanair has defied the odds, big-time. As with most other airlines, customers complain about their experience on Ryanair, but they flock to the airline anyway in search of a bargain. Their loyalty has made Ryanair Europe's most popular and profitable carrier.[9]

Ryanair's extraordinary success alerts us to an important and counterintuitive truth about consumer markets. Many businesspeople assume that innovative products and services and the advanced technology behind them determine market share outcomes. If you want to disrupt a market in the digital age, they think, get your hands on the latest technology that nobody else has and use it to develop innovative offerings. On the strength of these beliefs, companies invest billions in research and development to secure patents for proprietary technologies.

And yet technologies may not be the grand solution that executives in the digital age often suppose. I conducted a statistical analysis of patents and revenues of digital technology companies that were startups on or after 1995. These companies included Google, Amazon, Facebook, Yahoo, Salesforce.com, eBay, LinkedIn, Zynga, PayPal, and eleven others. I wanted to discover whether the accumulation of patents led these startups to grow revenues, as commonly assumed, or whether it worked the other way around: accumulated cash from revenues allowed tech companies to invest in patents to protect their earnings. On average, I found, the number of patents granted was a consequence of revenues, not their cause.[10] This finding held true in eighteen of the twenty companies I analyzed.

Although my quantitative analysis didn't include Ryanair, it's worth noting that the airline became a disruptive powerhouse without possessing unique technologies or product innovations. Its planes and booking systems were comparable to those of other airlines, and its product, the customer experience, was arguably much worse. So how could Ryanair win in a highly competitive market with an inferior product? The company possessed something else that competitors lacked: an innovative business model. Although Ryanair initially made money much like other airlines did, it abandoned the standard approach of selling high-priced tickets to transport passengers and then earning a return after subtracting out costs. Its new business model—virtually unmatched at the time—entailed filling up planes and then acting as a monopoly retailer in the skies.[11]

For much of the twentieth century, business model innovation developed slowly in many industries, reshaping them over multiple decades. In the digital economy, however, this type of innovation has occurred much more quickly, becoming a profoundly disruptive force that separates winners from losers, survivors from the deceased, often in just a few years. Further, three distinct waves of business model innovation have appeared over the past few decades—a phenomenon with enormous implications for companies. Upstarts typically catch incumbents by surprise; the latter don't see business model innovation as part of a pattern. But if you can spot a wave of digital business model innovation early enough, you can get ahead of it. You can anticipate how likely startups will be to join the wave, and you can craft an appropriate response in advance. "Wave-spotting" is an essential skill for executives seeking to understand and master digital disruption in their industry.

The Incredible Changing Business Model

Before examining the role that business model innovation has played in disrupting digital markets, let's first define our terms. Although choosing a business model is one of the most important decisions any businessperson makes, executives don't always reflect much on what a business model actually is or does. Academics like myself have made the task of reflection harder, offering multiple and often conflicting definitions.[12] For our purposes, here's a simple definition, one that applies both to large businesses with established models and to small startups that are experimenting with and evolving their models:

> **A business model** specifies how the firm creates value (and for whom), and how it captures value (and from whom).*

* The definition I offer is not my own. It conforms well with those proposed by most authors writing on the subject. In particular, Allan Afuah's book *Business Model Innovation* opts for this definition. For details on the various definitions put forth by academics, as well as explanation of why I chose this particular definition, please see the endnotes.

A business model, as defined above, describes how a business is supposed to function *in theory*. Although businesses will differ from one another in their particulars (name, location, number of employees, financials, and so on), a model allows us to look beyond the particulars to identify conceptual similarities and differences between businesses, whether or not they happen to operate in the same industry.* Likewise, a model allows us to chart how business concepts evolve over time.[13] Take supermarkets. Traditionally, these businesses have *created value* for shoppers (and differentiated themselves from smaller food markets and shops) by enabling one-stop shopping, allowing customers to buy many products in one place rather than visiting multiple retailers. Supermarkets, meanwhile, have *captured value* by purchasing produce and packaged goods from growers and food manufacturers and selling these items to shoppers at a markup. On an individual-item basis, supermarkets tend to have lower markups than small shops selling similar goods in the same region. However, since most people visiting the store purchase multiple items, these markups yield meaningful profits for supermarket owners.

By 2019, retailers ranging from Walmart to most mom-and-pop supermarkets around the world still made money according to this model. But not all large retailers did. Some supermarkets—mostly national chains in the United States and other countries—had hatched a strategy of reducing their markups and competing more vigorously on price. To make up for their lower profits, they developed a new revenue source: they charged suppliers for space on their shelves. If you were Nestlé and you wanted eye-catching space at the corners of aisles for that new brand of cookies you were launch-

* According to scholars of business strategy, business models enable their managers to accomplish three tasks: classify businesses based on their similarities, experiment by changing inputs and observing outcomes, and replicate successful models. In this chapter, we address the first two goals. We leave the last goal for Chapter 4.

ing, you had to pay these supermarkets more for the added shelf space. And manufacturers such as Nestlé did agree to pay more, since doing so allowed them to feature new products without sacrificing space they already claimed for their existing items. This practice of selling shelf space to manufacturers represented a whole new class of business models. Innovative supermarkets *created value* in two distinct ways. Like traditional supermarket chains, they created value for customers by allowing for one-stop shopping and low prices. But they also created value for manufacturers by allowing them to launch new products without compromising the performance of their traditional top sellers. Unlike their predecessors, the new supermarkets *captured value* from suppliers as well as from shoppers. As we saw in Chapter 1, Best Buy made a similar move to help solve its showrooming problem. As of this writing, slotting fees were the top source of income for the average national U.S. supermarket chain, Walmart excluded. Margins on goods sold constituted only the fourth-largest income source.* So the next time you walk into a supermarket, take time to marvel at what you're seeing. A supermarket is no longer an establishment that just buys groceries, adds a markup, and sells the food to you. To the extent that it attracts and sells attention to brands, it resembles a media company more than a retailer.

New supermarkets were hardly the only retailers to have diverged from the traditional business model. Decades ago, discount clubs such as Costco, Sam's Club, and Makro in Europe began to make money by offering even lower prices on bulk quantities of consumer packaged goods. With shoppers clamoring to enter their stores, discount clubs could charge a yearly membership fee to shop there,

* In second place among top sources of income is float on cash. And in third place is real estate speculation, both in and around the store. For more, see *Inside the Mind of the Shopper: The Science of Retailing*, by Herb Sorensen (Upper Saddle River, NJ: FT Press, 2009).

and shoppers would willingly pay it. As an example of this new business model, Costco *created value* by offering one-stop shopping and extremely low prices. It *captured value* through its membership fees (upward of $60 per year), as well as by selling products at a markup.[14] Initially, most of Costco's profits accrued from markups, but that has gradually shifted. Guess what percentage of Costco's total 2016 profits of $2.35 billion owed to the fees it charged its members. Fifty percent? Eighty percent? One hundred percent? Try 112 percent.[15] Costco *lost* money in its traditional supermarket retail business model and more than made up for it with membership fees. Costco stands as an incredible example of business model innovation in the groceries retail sector.

These two variations of business model innovation illustrate how even relatively minor changes to a business model's value creation and value capture components can dramatically change the face of a firm. And they suggest how our simple business model definition can help us spot conceptual differences between businesses as they innovate and evolve. Yet we've described business model innovation in only one industry. What happens when we consider the evolution of business models over time across many different industries? And in particular, what happens when we look at business models in the online space?

TABLE 2.1 **COMPONENTS OF BUSINESS MODELS**

BUSINESS MODEL	VALUE CREATION	TO WHOM?	VALUE CAPTURE	FROM WHOM?
Old supermarkets	One-stop-shopping	Shopper	Margins on goods sold	Shopper
New supermarkets	One-stop-shopping + attention	Shoppers + suppliers	Margins + slotting fees	Shopper + suppliers
Discount clubs	One-stop-shopping + very low prices	Shoppers	Margins + club fees	Club members

Business Model Innovation on Fire

As I've indicated, the creation of new business models tended to happen slowly prior to the internet. In the supermarket industry, it took half a century or longer for slotting fees and club membership fees to make their debut as a means of capturing value. Even after they appeared, it took decades for other companies within the industry to embrace them. In the airline industry, Southwest appeared about thirty years after U.S. airlines first began offering coach service, and it took Ryanair another twenty years to perfect the model.[16] A similar story holds for other industries.

This slow pace of change made life comparatively easy for executives. No matter what market or sector you were entering, the choice of a business model was pretty simple. By default, you were handed a standard model or method for creating value and making money. At best, a second option of business model was available to you as well. In media, for instance, a single model for making money dominated for much of the twentieth century. Companies created value for customers by offering free content such as broadcast television shows, news articles, or radio songs to consumer audiences. They captured value by selling viewers' attention to advertisers, in what was termed an "ad-supported" model. Over time, premium cable television channels such as HBO and satellite radio SiriusXM embraced a different model for making money. They created value for customers in the same way—by providing content. But they captured value by charging for subscriptions, what was called a "paid media" model. For decades, these two models were basically it. If you wanted to compete, you chose one of the two and gave it your best shot. Switching was rare.

This situation changed dramatically with the advent of the commercial internet in the mid-1990s. Previously, the internet had been used mainly by academics and the military. As millions of ordinary people became interested in accessing the World Wide Web, companies rushed to exploit the online space as a business tool. At first, businesses used the web to advertise products and present their brands. They viewed the web as just another communication channel akin to television, print, and radio. Then businesses began to sell retail goods online, retaining the same basic business models that had long existed in their industries. By the late 2000s, e-commerce evolved to include not just retail products but increasingly complex services with innovative business models such as on-demand taxis or subscription-based grocery offerings. What started as a communication channel had transformed into a full-fledged sales channel.

Renowned innovation expert David Teece has observed, "The internet era has fueled the need to understand and design innovative business models. It has caused many companies to rethink their business models."[17] And rethink they have. A 2015 study of eighty U.K. companies from creative industries found that digital technologies enabled "pervasive changes" in business models.[18] But many business executives have not kept up with the times. In a 2016 KPMG global study of thirteen hundred CEOs, 65 percent of respondents felt concerned that new entrants were disrupting their business models, and more than half admitted that their own companies were not disrupting their industry's business models enough.[19] In Chapter 9, I'll suggest some reasons why incumbents typically lag in disrupting their own business models.

Many factors have spurred business model innovation in the digital age, but three deserve further elaboration. First, the global tech community is tightly knit or *co-located*, with companies clustered in a few geographical areas, such as San Francisco, New York, Boston, Tel Aviv, Bangalore, London, and Berlin. This clustering effect allows startups to share services, talent, ideas, and other valuable resources. Second, ample *capital* exists to fund startups as they experiment with new business models. Third, a great *fluidity* exists in the appropriation of business models. When a new business model seems promising, it's hard to prevent people from replicating it not only within one industry or sector but across industries. People talk, and employees are constantly switching jobs, transferring their knowledge to new employers. As a contributing factor, business model innovations are hard to protect legally via patents or other measures.[20]

Co-location, capital, and fluidity of people and ideas create ideal conditions for business model innovations to spread. And in many instances, the speed of the spread can be breathtaking. Take the private car transportation industry. When Uber appeared, it generated attention by offering on-demand private car service that customers could request by mobile app. As this model showed early signs of success, copycats emerged. In addition to direct competitors like Lyft in the United States, Didi Chuxing in China, and Ola in India, other startups arose to offer apps for a variety of on-demand services. There was Uber for fast-food delivery (Valk Fleet), Uber for laundry (Lavanda), Uber for alcohol (Drizly), Uber for massage (Soothe), and my favorite nonsensical example, Uber for gasoline (WeFuel). As the *Wall Street Journal* announced, "There's an Uber for everything now."[21]

The appearance of business model innovation in and across industries happens so suddenly that executives and entrepreneurs often struggle to understand it. Disruptors tend to use a surfing metaphor, perceiving promising business models as powerful ocean waves. Seeking to catch and ride these waves, they anticipate them by directing their gazes in a direction where waves will likely appear. When they sense that a wave is imminent, they position themselves by paddling directly in front of the wave. Of course, spotting the right wave to ride requires focus and some luck, and staying atop of the wave once it appears requires learning and patience. For incumbents, the spread of business model innovations feels far less fun, and far more threatening. Incumbents tend to think of them, consciously or not, as wildfires that pop up unpredictably, propagate quickly, and wreak devastation in their paths. Their instinctive response is to suppress the wildfire by attacking or buying the startup. If a business model innovation flares up in your industry, turn on the siren, quick!

Which of these metaphors is most accurate? The answer is both—and neither. In his theory of special relativity, Albert Einstein observed that light behaves both as a particle and as a wave. "It seems as though we must use sometimes the one theory and sometimes the other," Einstein said, "while at times we may use either. . . . We have two contradictory pictures of reality; separately neither of them fully explains the phenomena of light, but together they do."[22] Similarly, we might think of digital disruption as behaving like both a random forest fire *and* a predictable tidal wave. The analogy depends on one's vantage point—incumbent or disruptor. In the next section, I emphasize disruption's predictability over time by adopting the perspective of the disruptor.

Unbundling, Disintermediation, Decoupling

Although many promising specialized digital business models have appeared in one or a few adjacent industries, a few others have spread further into most industries, giving rise to a broader, recognizable wave of digital disruption.* To date, the internet has seen three great waves.† The first—called unbundling—began in the mid-1990s and has been amply discussed by scholars.[23] Since the internet is a digital medium, the first commercial enterprises to join it were those that sold easily digitized content such as text, images, music, ads, and media content in general. Traditionally, media companies had com-

* For example, crowdsourcing, reverse auctions, user communities, and fractional ownership.

† Like ocean waves, these waves of digital disruption have arrived sequentially, one after the other. Unlike ocean waves, once a new wave of disruption hits, the previous one doesn't disappear.

bined content, creating value for customers by charging less for the content bundle than if customers had acquired each element separately. These media companies captured value through bundling because in the aggregate, bundling prompted buyers to purchase more content, even if they didn't wind up consuming the entire bundle. Physical newspapers such as the *New York Times* used to be a bundle of content, including news articles, classified advertisements, and restaurant reviews. The internet enabled businesses such as Google, Craigslist, and Yelp to specialize in each of these types of content, respectively, thereby *unbundling* the newspaper.[24] Cable television likewise amounted to a bundle of channels. In this first wave, Hulu, Sony, and HBO unbundled cable channel packages into single television channels and series, and iTunes unbundled TV series into single episodes that people could purchase and consume one at a time.

The unbundling unleashed by the internet was hardly limited to newspapers and cable TV. In music, companies such as EMI had long controlled access to content by selling bundled songs on compact discs (CDs).[25] Digital services such as Apple's iTunes unbundled the CD by allowing consumers to purchase songs individually.[26] In book publishing, firms such as McGraw-Hill sold entire textbooks even when students only wanted to read individual chapters. Amazon unbundled the textbook by allowing users to purchase a single chapter using their Kindle e-readers.

In each of these examples, digital disruptors grabbed an opportunity to distribute content online and deliver only what people wanted to consume, even if it represented just a small portion of the full content. In the aggregate, consumers purchased less content, not because they consumed less but because finally, for the first time, they could buy only what they wanted. This development delighted consumers, but it disrupted bundled-content firms, slashing the revenues of established players including the *New York Times*, EMI, and McGraw-Hill's textbook publishing division.[27] Some incumbent companies recovered from this wave of innovation, but others didn't. At the *Times*, advertising revenue fell by 50 percent between 1999 and 2016, although the newspaper managed to recover some of the losses by building a successful digital subscription business.[28] EMI Records' revenue fell by a third in the decade and a half beginning in 1996. The company was subsequently acquired by a bank, broken into pieces, and sold off.[29] McGraw-Hill's educational arm lost two-thirds of its revenue between 2005 and 2016. In 2013, the division was spun off from the company's financial information and media businesses.[30]

By the late 1990s, most online content that could be unbundled profitably had been. This first wave of business model innovation began to give way to a new wave: the disintermediation of goods and services. Because it enabled more personalization, unbundling had made it advantageous for content creators and distributors to sell directly to the end consumer. Service providers in a broader array of industries, not just content, took note of the internet's potential as a low-cost, high-reach sales channel and further removed the middleman from their transactions.[31] Prior to the internet, for instance, many consumers used travel agents to book vacation airfare, accommodations, and activities. These businesses didn't produce the services they sold. They only act as intermediaries, acquiring customers for other service providers (e.g., hotels, airlines, rental car companies). Customers regarded local agents as the only way to access a range of travel options that they wanted.

With the internet's emergence, agents no longer enjoyed a local monopoly on these travel options. Customers could communicate easily with service providers and book travel themselves, bypassing the travel agent. They could book flights online directly with United Airlines, their hotels with Hilton, and their tours by accessing the website of a local tour guide.[32] The financial services industry saw similar disintermediation, for example in the appearance of websites allowing investors to purchase and sell stocks without a broker or advisor.[33] Unlike unbundling, disintermediation affected both digital and physical service providers. Therefore, its impact was arguably larger, as it afflicted many more industries, from home video (disrupted by Netflix) and home improvement (disrupted by BuildDirect) to dating services (disrupted by eHarmony).

This tidal wave flooded markets during the 2000s, beginning to ebb by 2010. As an incumbent that was disintermediated, there was little you could do except hang on and try to adjust as best you could. But more disruption was on its way. By 2012, I began to discern a third wave of business model innovation on the horizon. The most innovative companies were no longer responding to shifting consumer behavior by unbundling products or disintermediating services. Rather, they were stealing customers by "decoupling" specific activities that customers normally performed in the course of shopping. As we saw in Chapter 1, Birchbox decoupled the sampling of products from their purchase. Amazon decoupled the purchase of products from browsing. Turo decoupled the usage of cars from their purchase. Because this latest wave was afflicting companies that sold physical products such as beauty supplies, electronics, and cars in addition to companies that sold content and services, the wave's devastating power was potentially even larger.

This third digital wave also differed from the other two in that now disruption was taking place across the customer's value chain. The first wave, unbundling, largely took place at the product level and in the consumption stage: some consumers read only newspaper articles, others only the classified ads. The second wave, disintermediation, occurred within the supply chain (e.g., cellulose companies selling pulp directly to the newspapers, bypassing paper manufacturers). Decoupling also broke down important linkages, but this time between customer activities, not products or supply chain stages (*see Figure 2.1*).

FIGURE 2.1 **HOW DECOUPLING DIFFERS FROM THE OTHER TWO WAVES OF DIGITAL DISRUPTION**

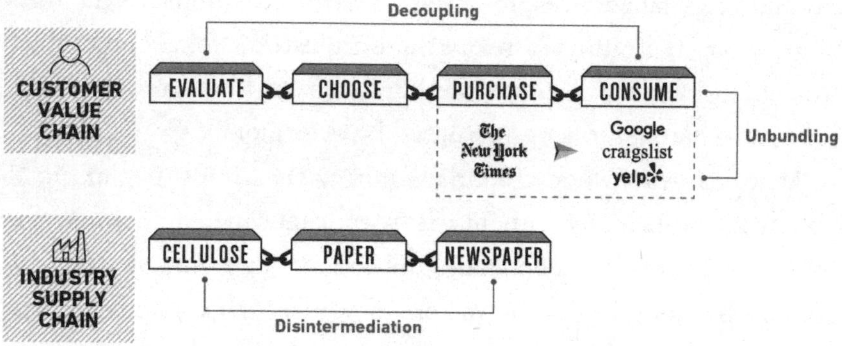

Continuing to research innovative businesses, I realized that decoupling perpetrated by startups was afflicting multiple incumbents across a variety of industries. It was no isolated phenomenon. As I related in Chapter 1, the entrepreneurs I spoke with didn't know they were "decoupling."[34] They had detected an unmet consumer need and were simply—and intuitively—doing their best to satisfy it. In the process, they were quickly stealing customers from established companies. Likewise, executives I interviewed at large, established companies such as Four Seasons Hotels, mall developer Westfield, Disney, Paramount Pictures, and Microsoft didn't understand "decoupling" as a general approach. They saw disruption rising up all around them, and they were concerned that their established businesses were or soon would be besieged. Not knowing the root cause, they scrambled to respond, often futilely.

DECOUPLING'S RIPPLING EFFECTS

In some sectors where decoupling was gaining prominence, the size of potential markets was so huge that many startups sought to decouple the same activities for customers. As markets grew crowded, these startups decoupled in slightly different ways so as to differentiate themselves from one another. This created what we might term a "rippling" effect within an industry or sector. Take the auto industry. Historically, people consumed private automobile transportation by buying cars from local dealers who represented the major automakers. In addition to paying to acquire the car, drivers assumed the costs of maintenance, fuel, and insurance. Car dealers, meanwhile, earned large profits by selling shiny new vehicles at a markup. In 1999, the average U.S. car dealer earned 40 percent of its profits through the sales of new vehicles.[35]

Those days are over. Car dealers now make hardly any money on car sales themselves—less than 10 percent of total net profits. Rather, their profits arise from the sale of financing, insurance, extra warranties, and maintenance, which now represent 67 percent of their net income.[36] Car dealers have evolved and today resemble banks selling financial services much more than they do auto retailers. No wonder the famed investor Warren Buffett surprised the investor world when, starting in 2014, he decided to acquire large, privately owned U.S. auto dealers.[37] These were not highly profitable businesses, but to Buffett, that wasn't the point. Holding investments in multiple local and national auto financing banks (e.g., Berkshire Hathaway Automotive), insurance companies (e.g., Geico), and car warranty providers (e.g., Applied Underwriters), Buffet spotted an opportunity to secure another sales channel for his other companies. Conversely, he was shrewd enough to anticipate what car dealer innovations could mean for his investments if he did *not* control them directly.

The impact of all this business model innovation on consumers has been huge, leaving car buyers to bear a large and increasing financial burden. In addition to the price of a car, they now have to pay more to own and operate a 1.5-ton machine. Fortunately for these customers, other companies have jumped in with a number of different solutions, all based around variations of decoupling. Zipcar, as discussed before, and other on-demand car-renting companies such as Enterprise's CarShare and Gig provide drivers with access to a car without the need for contracts and reservations. Zipcar's prices are reasonable for short periods of time, say a few hours. But what if you want a car for longer than that? You're in luck: car-sharing companies such as Turo (formerly RelayRides) allow non-car-owners to rent directly from individual car owners via a peer-to-peer model.[38] Turo's prices tend to be more reasonable than Zipcar's for longer periods of time such as a weekend, although customers must forgo convenience in order to benefit from the lower cost. This group of car-sharing disruptors has broken the links between purchasing and driving a car, as well as those between driving and maintaining the car.

A subsequent generation of auto disruptors—ride-hailing businesses including Uber, Lyft, and Curb (Boston Taxi's response to ride-hailing)—took decoupling further, severing the links between driving a car and traveling in one. They provided platforms through which individual car owners could pick up passengers and drive them to their destinations in exchange for a modest fee. Previously, customers could obtain service like this only through a limited number of licensed taxi and limousine services. The decoupled solutions of firms such as Uber and Lyft made economic sense for consumers looking to make short trips. For longer trips, French startup BlaBlaCar adapted the ride-hailing model by providing a platform for passengers to prearrange cost-effective long-distance trips with car owners.[39] As on a bus, customers purchased seats with set itineraries. Since passengers and drivers had to coordinate times and dates among themselves, customers were again in the position of trading off convenience for cost. Given the size of the U.S. passenger automobile market, with $570 billion worth of new cars sold in 2015, we can expect the segmentation of decoupling models to continue in the years to come, with rippling effects in other markets (*see Figure* 2.2).[40]

FIGURE 2.2 **SEGMENTATION OF DECOUPLING IN THE AUTO INDUSTRY**

	DRIVE	BE DRIVEN
SHORT	zipcar	UBER lyft curb
LONG	TURO	BlaBlaCar

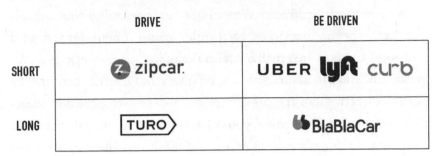

Business Model Innovation, Not Technology

In many cases, the innovative companies I studied as examples of decoupling seemed to be disrupting their industries thanks to the use of innovative technologies. After all, Uber, Amazon, and Birchbox are all regarded as technology companies, right? I decided to talk to these firms and learn about the new technologies they developed and were leveraging. It soon became clear to me that the initial success of these companies didn't hinge on new and innovative technologies, but rather on the power of their business model innovations. Similarly, others have argued that even well-regarded "tech" companies such as Google, in their early days, didn't invent completely new technologies, but rather invented or perfected new business models.[41] These innovations represented the *real* engine of disruption. To illustrate the point, let's look at a couple of lesser-known examples.

Founded in 2012, Trov has been trying to disrupt the insurance industry with its mobile app that allows users to insure single products for a specific amount of time.* No longer do users need to sign a

* Trov is a unique example in that it decouples as well as unbundles insurance, the latter by selling product-specific insurance.

yearly contract covering all of their possessions, as traditional insurance companies required.[42] Why might customers find this appealing? Let's say you plan to go to Rio de Janeiro, Brazil, for ten days and would like to insure the Canon camera you recently bought. With Trov, you can insure only your camera and for only the ten-day period, directly from the app. Further, once you've provided information for every possession you'd like to insure, you can turn the insurance on and off with the touch of a button. The app instantly provides prices based on a series of risk factors. And if your camera is broken, stolen, or misplaced, you can file a claim using the app with no human intervention.

In the traditional process, a typical insurance customer undertakes a seven-step value chain. You purchase a valuable item, feel the need to insure it, learn about various insurance companies, request a quote from one or more insurers, wait for the company to write and send the policy, purchase the policy on an annual basis, and eventually cancel the policy. Trov allows customers to decouple the requesting of a quote (i.e., turning the insurance on) from the writing of the policy. It also allows customers to decouple the purchasing of an annual policy from the canceling of the policy (i.e., turning it off).

Consumers have found this decoupling extremely attractive—so much so that Trov has attracted five investment rounds totaling $46.3 million as of this writing.[43] Millennials are looking for easier and more convenient solutions, and Trov's model is one way to create value for them. Trov captures back some of this value not from customers but from insurance companies, who hand Trov a portion of the premiums that customers pay to the underwriters of the insurance policies they sell. Trov, in essence, is the insurance agent of the future, offering insurance without a year-long commitment and serving you twenty-four hours a day, instantly.

Trov seems like a technology company through and through. But while technology plays a role in Trov's success, it doesn't play the lead role. Trov relies on a mobile app, but many incumbents and startups have access to that technology. In fact, all of the technology Trov uses, including commercial or custom software and basic algorithms, was fairly standard and available off the shelf when Trov hit the market. In addition to an actuarial model that allows the startup to assess risk on a single-product basis, Trov's real advantage comes from its highly innovative business model. Standard technology *enables* Trov to deliver services to customers. The new business model built around decoupling is what really allows Trov to stand out in a saturated market.

Trov isn't an isolated case. Consider the online payments industry. Shopping online might seem easy, but in some respects it isn't. A typical online shopping value chain actually includes at least nine steps: accessing an e-retailer's site, browsing products, choosing products, placing products in a virtual shopping basket, signing into the website or signing up for an account, inputting credit card information, choosing a shipping address and other shipping options, and confirming the purchase. Although the first several steps are convenient enough, the need to fill out payment information tends to deter many people from finishing an online shopping session. By some accounts, on average 69 to 80 percent of online shoppers abandon their basket before completing a purchase.[44]

Enter Klarna, a Swedish online payments startup founded in 2005.[45] The company facilitates online payments for e-commerce retailers, eliminating the need for individuals to have a credit card on hand and to input payment information for every online transaction. If an e-commerce website has allowed its shoppers to pay with Klarna, shoppers need only enter their email and zip code—Klarna does the rest. It pays the retailer immediately and then charges the shopper either within two weeks or after the person received the item and has decided to keep it. In effect, Klarna provides the shopper very short-term financing, capturing value not from customers but by charging a fee from merchants (Klarna justifies this fee by arguing that it reduces risk and friction in the online shopping process, increasing sales for merchants by preventing people from giving up at the last stage of the purchase process). Klarna thus decouples the act of buying from the act of paying, particularly when it comes to inputting credit card information.

In Sweden, Klarna has disrupted a payments industry that had been dominated by big banks, global credit card companies, and entrenched telecom operators. As of 2016, Klarna was responsible for nearly 40 percent of all e-commerce sales in the country, had received $332 million in venture capital investments, and was valued at $2.3 billion.[46] Like Trov, however, Klarna didn't achieve its success because of breakthrough technology. It didn't have some unmatched new algorithm or a high-tech customer interface—all of its technology was off the shelf. Klarna's decisive advantage owed to its business model, one that nobody in its industry had thought of before, and one that at its core involved decoupling.

Most of the other digital disruptors described in this and the previous chapter did not rely on breakthrough technologies, either. Yes, startups like Uber and BlaBlaCar needed mobile apps for their customers, access to GPS linked to maps, and online scheduling tools. Yes, Birchbox and Trov developed their own apps. Yes, Klarna needed a credit scoring algorithm to decide which shoppers to give credit. But by the time these companies were founded, the digital technologies that they used had already spread widely and had been accessible to incumbents and other startups alike. Most were even regarded as standard technologies.

Among businesses in which digital technology plays a significant role in value creation and capture, many are actually *not* technology companies, in the sense that they did not develop new and innovative technologies core to their business model (think of Disney, a company that I have visited to present my research). In general, I refer to digital businesses as for-profit organizations that use the internet (web, mobile apps, etc.) as a channel to acquire customers and/or deliver products and services. These firms are essentially "users" of technology innovations rather than "builders"—a key distinction. Companies such as Apple, Tesla, and some divisions of Amazon and Alphabet are technology innovators, but these represent the exception in the digital economy, not the rule. Overall, if digital businesses are a subset of all businesses, we can regard tech firms as a subset in turn of digital businesses (*see Figure 2.3*).*

FIGURE 2.3 **SCHEMA OF TYPES OF COMPANIES**

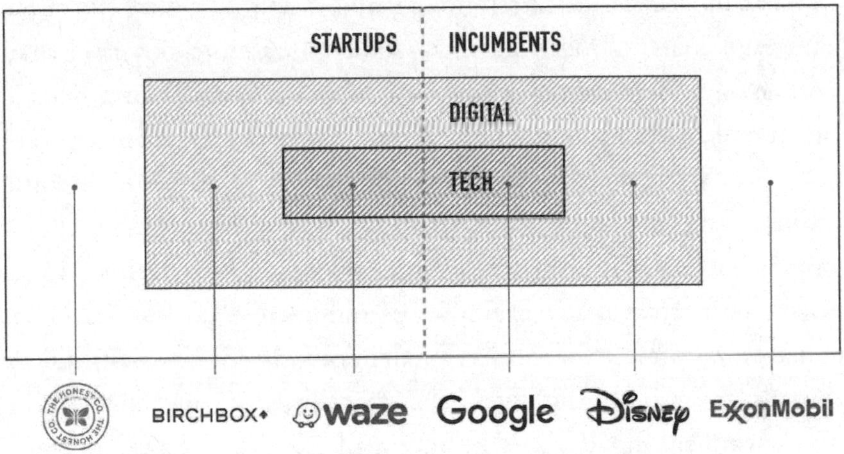

Clearly, some technology innovators are not doing business in the digital space. However, these companies are not the focus of this book.

In distinguishing between digital and "pure" technology companies, I am by no means suggesting that the former are any less valuable or less innovative than the latter. Rather, their source of

* I admit that, in reality, the lines separating these classes of businesses are somewhat fuzzier than I have portrayed them in Figure 2.3. Still, this working definition helps us convey the concepts here in a relatively simple manner.

innovation is simply *different*. For Trov, Klarna, and most of the other examples of decoupling that I have presented thus far, the source of their disruptive power lies in business model innovation. A novel way of creating and capturing value comprises the essence of the competitive advantage for these startups, enabling them to access capital and acquire customers.

Similarly, and setting aside decoupling for a moment, we likewise find that technological innovation was not the primary driver that enabled players such as Ryanair, Costco, or car dealers to disrupt their markets. Rather, all of these firms built their success on the back of important changes to the business models that had prevailed in their industries. Business model innovation is a powerful force of abrupt market-level change, in some cases more powerful than technology. Technology, as Jim Collins put it more than a decade and a half ago in his bestselling book *Good to Great*, "is an accelerator, never a creator of momentum and growth."[47] After researching twenty-eight very successful companies, he concluded that technology "is not by itself the primary source of greatness or decline." Likewise, Teece gives many examples of remarkable technologies that failed to deliver market success for their original inventors, including Xerox's invention of the personal computer, EMI's invention of the CAT scanner, and Kodak's invention of the digital camera. These failures owed in part to the lack of an appropriate business model that would drive these incumbents' businesses forward. As Teece notes, "Technology alone does not disrupt markets, it rarely does."[48]

Stop Blaming Your Lemonade

As we've seen in this chapter, business models have grown more diverse and complex over time. This appears to be a general phenomenon: as markets develop and grow, the number of unique business models evident among competing companies increases, and the models themselves become increasingly refined, specific, and differentiated from one another. As an analogy, consider the humble lemonade stand that kids set up on their front lawn. The model is simple and age-old: obtain ingredients at subsidized prices (i.e., free from Mom and Dad), make lemonade, and sell it at a huge markup. Kids in neighborhoods across America have competed in this way. Today, in many industries, you no longer see the equivalent of simple lemonade stands winning out. Rather, you see lemonade entrepreneurs who give away lemonade for below-cost prices so they can get long lines of captive customers lingering around their yards, like Costco does. Then these entrepreneurs might entertain customers while they wait and, like Ryanair, sell them "add-ons" like snacks or bathroom privileges. That's where the *real* profit now resides. Or lemonade entrepreneurs might engage a band to entertain their customers and require the band to *pay them* for the chance to promote themselves to their captive audience, like new media companies do. Or entrepreneurs might make money selling their captive customers insurance and warranty contracts that provide for "thirst quenching guaranteed," like car dealers do. It all sounds outlandish, yet a glance around your industry will show that this is precisely what's happening.

Although such rapid and extreme business model innovation might seem daunting to incumbents, it doesn't have to be. Understanding how business model innovation drives markets can *empower* incumbents like never before. If you think technology drives innovation, then you'll feel beholden to a few Silicon Valley illuminati who purport to understand sophisticated technologies better than anyone, and who end up selling you on the tech flavor of the month. You'll assume that you must somehow tap into these tech visionaries and their wisdom, and you'll focus your efforts on that task. By contrast, disruption through business model innovation—including that specific form of business model innovation known as decoupling—is readily accessible to any businessperson anywhere. As an executive, you *know* business models already. You've learned to dissect them in business school or in your career. To compete in the digital age, it turns out that you don't have to gain significantly more in-depth technical expertise than you already have. Rather, you must go back to the basics and reflect on how businesses make money—and on how *your* business *might* make new money.

Forget for a moment about wearables, drones, chat bots, the internet of things, machine learning, and augmented or virtual reality. They all might have a place in your future business, but your role, as a senior business executive, is to figure out the *business* side. As Erik Zingmark, senior executive at Nordea, the largest bank in the Nordic countries, put it, "You should never forget about why you are in the bank[ing business], and that is to serve the customer. . . . [T]here is a risk that we focus too much on technology and how to be in the forefront. We could forget about what is the customer value in what we're doing."[49] Erik should know. His employer is the incumbent being disrupted by Klarna in Sweden.

Likewise, don't let an excessive focus on your products prevent you from paying attention to your business. Many executives at incumbent businesses, wedded to their business models, react to disruption by blaming their products. As they see it, all the newfangled lemonade stands out there are stealing customers because they have created better-tasting lemonade. Stop blaming your lemonade![50] The truth is that the upstart's lemonade tastes the same as yours, or maybe even worse. It's the new business model that is stealing your customers, not the product. Of course, in a few cases, small, inexperienced, cash-strapped, unproven, or unknown startups do produce a far superior product than the pool of large established businesses in a market. But that's the rare exception. As University of Michigan researcher Allan Afuah argues, most profitable business model innovations have little to do with the underlying product. Profiting from a technology or product innovation still requires an innovative business model.[51]

After many years spent obsessing over technology, it seems that we are collectively starting to take note of what really matters. Between 2004 and 2016, Google searches for websites about "technology innovation" declined globally (indexed to 2004 = 100). Conversely, searches for "business model innovation" increased over the same period. Still, we have a long way to go. In 2016, people searched for "technology innovation" ten times more often than they did for "business model innovation" (*see Figure 2.4*).

FIGURE 2.4 **INTEREST IN TWO TYPES OF INNOVATION, GOOGLE SEARCHES 2004 TO 2016**

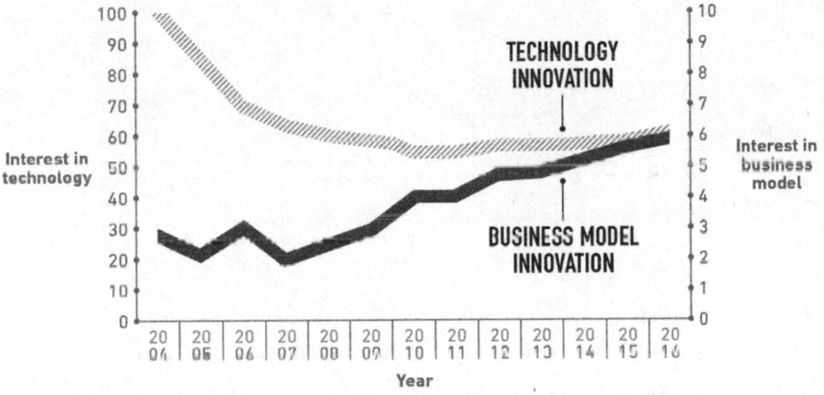

Source: Google Trends.

If you're still keen on constantly identifying new technology innovations for your company, then it's time to make a change. You should spend as much time or more evaluating and evolving your firm's business model(s) as you do worrying about new technologies. After all, if you don't focus on new waves of business model innovation, and decoupling in particular, others will. Your first task should be to understand the component(s) of your business model that is (are) not working. As it turns out, incumbents rarely have to replace their entire model. In Chapter 3 we'll see precisely how to assess your business model and identify possible changes. We'll also examine decoupling's inner logic and underlying drivers. As I argue, you shouldn't just analyze specific startups that are enabling your customers to decouple you. In assessing your business model, it's vital that you get to the core of the phenomenon: the customer's changing needs and wants.

3

BROKEN BY THE CUSTOMER

Airbnb, one of the best-known players in the so-called sharing economy, is a remarkable success story. By 2018, three million people in 190 countries were using the platform to "share" or rent out real estate they owned or even just individual rooms on a per-day basis.[1] Almost three times as many rooms were listed on Airbnb than the world's largest hotel chain Marriott managed in its six thousand properties across 120 countries.[2] At the heart of Airbnb's allure was decoupling. From the customer's perspective, Airbnb broke apart the act of *using* real estate from *owning* it. Travelers didn't have to buy a condo in Barcelona to enjoy the experience of living in one for a few days or a week. They could enjoy a condo that someone else owned, in exchange for a fee. It was often cheaper to rent rooms on Airbnb than to stay at a local hotel of comparable quality, and in most local markets Airbnb offered a wealth of lodging options. In Barcelona, for instance, you could rent a bunk bed in a shared room near La Sagrada Familia for $11 per night, a sunny studio by La Rambla near the Gothic Quarter for $100 a night, or a modernist mansion with sweeping views over the city and the Mediterranean for $10,000 a night. With a few clicks of a mouse, users could arrange not merely to stay in a given city or town but to experience it as the locals did. No wonder the market valued Airbnb at a whopping $31 billion scarcely a decade into the platform's existence.[3]

I wondered how incumbents in the hotel industry were responding to Airbnb's meteoric rise, so I sat down with Susan Helstab, at the time senior vice president of marketing of Four Seasons Hotels. As Susan related, Airbnb's rise built on a consumer trend that she and her colleagues had been seeing for at least fifteen years before Airbnb's founding. It all started, she said, in Paris in the early 2000s. Although first-time visitors to the city often preferred to stay in hotels, some visited Paris multiple times a year either for business or for a mix of business and pleasure. Discovering the unique character of Paris's dozens of neighborhoods, these travelers began asking travel agents to find private residences in desirable neighborhoods where they might stay. Large families, too, sought residences when traveling together, since these often had adjacent living and dining rooms where families could spend time together, a setup more difficult to obtain in a conventional hotel.

Four Seasons Hotels wasn't alone in spotting this trend—other established hotel chains had, too. Worried about losing their most valuable customers (wealthy globetrotters traveling with their entire families), hotel chains started to address customers' desire for multiple rooms clustered together in a single place. And their first big innovation was . . . to guarantee bookings for adjoining rooms. Some hotel chains added more adjoining rooms by installing connecting doors between standard rooms. That way, parents could stay in one room and park their kids or the grandparents in another.

During the late 2000s, hotels began to open new properties in neighborhoods with a more residential feel—places like Knightsbridge or Hyde Park in London, or Shanghai's Pudong district neighborhood.[4] For high-end customers, Four Seasons created two-, three-, and four-bedroom penthouse suites that mimicked condos. The Empire Suite at the Four Seasons George V in Paris featured a master bedroom, two bathrooms, open living and dining rooms, a study, a kitchen, and a terrace with a view over the Eiffel Tower.

Yet Four Seasons and other big chains didn't necessarily identify the *real* reason customers wanted multi-room suites in residential areas of cities like Paris. It wasn't just because customers wanted to feel comfortable when traveling with their families. It was because they didn't want to feel like regular tourists during their tenth trip to the City of Light. This desire turned up in customer surveys and was confirmed by travel agents. As the president of the U.S. Tour Operators Association once noted, "Travelers want to forge deeper connections to the people, traditions and customs of the places they are visiting, and these experiences add a meaningful and memorable component to a vacation."[5]

Airbnb understood this insight. As its founders realized, hotels, airlines, restaurants, and attractions all purported to offer travelers an immersion in local life. But that's not what travelers staying in hotels received. Once they arrived in a locale, they encountered standardized meals and hotel rooms, as well as tours that in no way enabled contact with the authentic local lifestyle. Airbnb would be different. The platform got its name (originally Air Bed and Breakfast) by providing its first customers—college students with no money—a chance to crash on an air mattress in someone's apartment, as well as a hot breakfast. Over time, the company allowed people to rent private rooms, and then entire apartments and houses. Today you can rent an eighty-eight-foot-long houseboat in Barcelona docked near Gran Casino, a barn in Iceland with views over the lava coastline, even a medieval castle next to Galway, Ireland. Yes, some locals do live in these types of homes. As Airbnb realized, travelers wanted to adapt to the living conditions of the place, not the other way around. In Paris, they wanted to stroll around a typical market and buy the perfect piece of *fromage* for dinner. In Rome, they wanted to take their morning espresso in an out-of-the-way neighborhood café. Such authenticity and proximity to local life were precisely what hotels were failing to deliver.

As Helstab of Four Seasons Hotels confided, even she occasionally stayed in private residences while on vacation. She loved the experience of seeing her rental for the first time—spotting an old, ivy-covered gate, taking a long metal key and inserting it into the lock, swinging the gate open, and then traversing a picturesque courtyard to the rental's front door. It was equally thrilling to open that door and see the unique decor inside. For a few days, this comfortable home was all hers. In the travel industry, the decoupling of owning from using enables an experience of make-believe, a chance to fantasize about an alternative lifestyle.

Most executives of established companies credit startups with disrupting their markets. They regard individual entrepreneurs as abrasive disruptors who single-handedly forced a change in the status quo. And in their assessments, they focus primarily on competitors big and small who threaten to unsettle their businesses. Such thinking is at best incomplete, and at worst inaccurate. Airbnb didn't disrupt Four Seasons Hotels. *Customers* did—by changing their behaviors to satisfy their evolving desires. Travelers wanted family spaces beyond bedrooms. They wanted authentic travel experiences. Airbnb and its many clones simply managed to deliver more completely and quickly on those requests than the dozens of global hotel chains around the world.* If you examine other instances of decoupling, you will find that they, too, originate with customers, not with startups or their founders. To get ahead of disruption, we need to pay far more attention to customers than we ordinarily do, and commensurately less attention to competitors. We need to discipline ourselves to look at markets from the customer's perspective, not just the company's, and to understand customers' evolving desires and behaviors.

* Home-sharing services similar to Airbnb include VRBO, Home Away, House Swap, Guest to Guest, and many others. In the luxury property segment, Airbnb competes with specialized services such as One Fine Stay and Luxury Retreats.

Acquiring Customers, Not "Winning"

At first glance, executives might resist shifting their strategic focus from competitors to customers. In my experience, most executives care about customers, but they are *obsessed* with competitors—and understandably so. Modern business strategy has focused squarely on the firm, on assessing the competitive landscape, and on responding to competitors. Using phrases like "business as a competition" or "business as war," academics, consultants, and established CEOs have turned to game theory and to ancient military handbooks such as Sun Tzu's *The Art of War*, written in the fifth century BC, for advice on how to kill the competition. Meanwhile, traditional competitive strategy frameworks have downplayed the critical role of customers. In the case of Michael Porter's Five Forces, for instance, only one of the forces relates to customers, in the form of the customer's bargaining power. Three of the other forces—industry rivalry, threat of new entrants, and threat of substitutes—arguably focus on different types of competitors.* Game theory models, meanwhile, conceptualize games as played with a competitor. Customers are secondary, conceived as the "prize" for which competitors are vying. One reason for this traditional emphasis on competitor over customers no doubt has to do with the accessibility and interpretability of data. It's relatively easy to spot what the competition is doing in a given market, whereas it is considerably harder to discern customers' motivations and actions. As a consequence, competitors allow for clean, unambiguous input into the strategic framework at hand.

Focusing on competitors has worked well in the past, and it might still work in some situations, but it has become less applicable for companies competing in markets threatened with disruption. Traditional corporate strategy assumed a situation in which

* The last force is supplier bargaining power.

companies faced only one or a few competitors, and in which opponents' actions were somewhat predictable. Under such conditions, competition really did bear more similarity to a chess match or to warfare. In today's markets, incumbents across many industries often square off against not one or two large and predictable opponents, but dozens more of small, nimble, and less predictable challengers. These entrants are unpredictable, as they often employ innovative business models and drastically pivot in order to adapt to changing circumstances. In the hotel space, as of late 2016, at least sixty-two U.S. venture-backed startups have attacked the Marriotts and Four Seasons of the world by decoupling activities traditionally served by them, such as booking, concierge, event and meetings facilitation, or wedding planning.[6] Meanwhile, more than ninety venture-backed startups operated in the travel industry. In the restaurant business, that number was 100; in brick-and-mortar retail, over 130; in banking, over 400, and so on. Planning for war or deliberately thinking many steps ahead as a chess player does is a requirement of game theory, and it just isn't practical in such industries anymore—a big reason why executives frequently feel so overwhelmed and baffled.

For these reasons alone, executives would do better to return to the basics of business—not "winning," "beating," or "defeating" competitors, but acquiring and retaining customers. Entrepreneurs at disruptive startups see the world in precisely this way, paying heed to Peter Drucker's famous dictum "The purpose of a business is to create a customer."[7] Indeed, entrepreneurs perceive the focus on customers as a defining quality of startups as opposed to incumbents. As Amazon CEO Jeff Bezos has remarked, "When [executives of other companies] are in the shower in the morning, they're thinking about how they're going to get ahead of one of their top competitors. Here in the shower, we're thinking about how we are going to invent something on behalf of a customer."[8]

Rethinking Business Models and the Customer's Value Chain

Taking customers more seriously than we have doesn't just mean asking the marketing department to run a few more focus groups or surveys. It means modifying some of our most basic definitions, starting with how we think about business models. In Chapter 2, I observed that businesses exist to create value. Once they achieve this, it might be possible for them to also capture some of this value as revenue by charging for their products and services. In shifting our focus toward customers, we should revisit this definition. When a traveler chooses between two hotel chains, she is selecting *within* the same basic business model. But when she considers Airbnb as an alternative to a hotel, she implicitly selects *between* different business models. If customers must choose between renting a suite on Airbnb or at a Four Seasons property, they're actually comparing the value that respective offerings create *for them* and the value that *they must pay* for each of these offerings. In addition, the businesses under comparison also often create inefficiencies or waste for their customers while attempting to deliver and charge for value. In this way, businesses sometimes *erode* customer value. To refocus on the customer, we therefore modify our definition of a business model as follows:

A business model from the customer's point of view:
"A business model consists of the value a business creates for me, what it charges me in exchange for that value, and what value it erodes for me."

For any business in any industry, we can take our updated definition of a business model and layer it on top of the customer's value chain. Doing so allows us to clearly determine whether each activity creates, charges for, or erodes value. Every customer engages in these three types of activities in the course of dealing with companies. Here are a few examples:

TYPE OF ACTIVITY	VALUE CREATING	VALUE CHARGING	VALUE ERODING
DEFINITION	An activity that creates value for the customer.	An activity that is solely added to charge for the value created.	An activity that neither creates value for the customer nor charges for the value created.
EXAMPLES	A cooked meal.	Paying $20 for a cooked meal.	Going to a restaurant to get a cooked meal to eat at home.
	Selling a used car.	Paying 2% commission on the sale price of a car.	Taking pictures and describing the used car in a classifieds listing.
	Staying in a hotel room.	Paying $200 per night.	Providing personal and payment information every time to book a hotel.

Consider, for instance, the process of consuming radio programming. You might choose to listen to a given station because it plays Tears for Fears as well as your other favorite 1980s rhythm and blues artists (i.e., it creates value). But every hour or so, the station also plays that damn Justin Bieber song you hate. To stay on the air, your local radio station has to make money. And one way it makes money, besides airing advertisements, is by promoting new songs and charging record labels for playing them.* You could turn down the volume or change stations when an ad or a Justin Bieber song comes on and turn it back up a minute or two later, but doing so requires effort. From a listener's standpoint, the station delivers value, charges for the value it has created, and erodes value to some extent, too.

* In the United States this is legal as long as the radio station discloses it as being "sponsored airtime." In certain countries, it is more common.

iHeartMedia owned and operated 855 U.S. radio stations by the end of 2016, attracting some 245 million listeners each month.[9] The company provided four distinct activities to its radio listeners in a coupled manner. Here's the type of value the consumer received and relinquished across those four activities:

FIGURE 3.1 **VALUE CLASSIFICATION IN A RADIO LISTENER'S CVC**

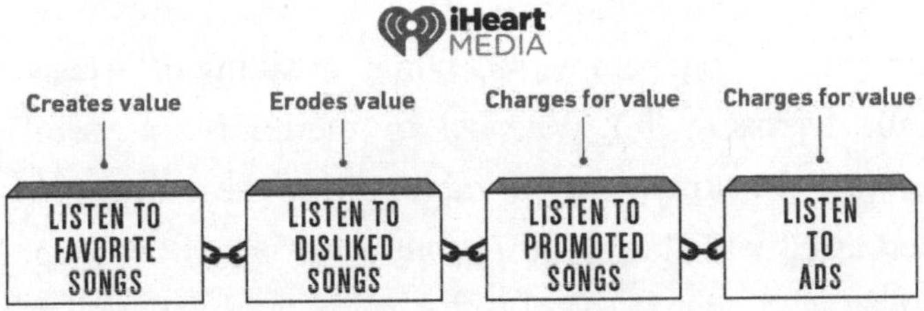

Now, how might a disruptor decouple this particular assemblage of activities that create, erode, and charge for value? We don't need to speculate. Founded in 2000, Pandora Radio disrupted the traditional radio model by decoupling all four stages of what I call the customer value chain.[10] Through an innovation called the Music Genome Project, Pandora mapped out and measured the (dis)similarity between a wide range of songs. Pandora used this algorithm, together with users' input about their musical preferences, to ensure that it provided listeners with their favorite songs, and that any new songs it played would have similar qualities (e.g., the same beat, style, or rhythm), thus limiting the frequency of disliked songs. If you like Tears for Fears and other 1980s-style rock bands like U2, you're in luck—no more Justin Bieber. Pandora did not promote paid songs to its listeners, and listeners who paid for a subscription were spared any ads.*

* Pandora charges for value created by giving listeners the option of paying for an advertisement-free subscription service or using a free version that plays occasional advertisements.

This pervasive decoupling helped Pandora grow to 81 million monthly active users and earn more than $1.38 billion in 2016 revenues.[11] Not bad for a medium that many pronounced dying just a few years ago.

Take a moment to notice an object in the room around you. Who acquired it—you, a family member, an acquaintance, a hotel or airplane employee? Take the time to empathize with this person, and you will appreciate all that he or she went through in order to buy the object: identifying a need, evaluating vendors, comparing options, deciding, purchasing, paying, receiving, installing (if necessary), and eventually disposing of it. Whether an offering is a physical product or a service, consumable or durable, all of these activities can be classified as either value creating, value capturing, or value eroding. The person who bought the object was implicitly or explicitly trying to get more of the first, reduce the second, and avoid the third altogether. That is all customers do. Ever!

Can you envision a startup business mapping this chain of activities—the customer value chain—and choosing to deliver one (or a few) of these activities more advantageously than the original provider of the object? There could be dozens or even hundreds of entrepreneurs doing exactly this in an intuitive and unstructured manner. And guess what? They're doing it for the products and services that your company produces, too. If your customers discover an opportunity to accomplish any of the multiple activities in the customer value chain better with another incumbent or entrant, watch out. They just might take this opportunity. Paying attention to value from a customer's standpoint helps you understand what your customers really care about, and what they have to give up or part with in order to get it. But it also helps you do something else: understand the various ways that innovators in a market disrupt existing businesses.

THREE TYPES OF DECOUPLING

If you're a hardcore gamer, you've probably heard of a company called Twitch. Twitch has a website, Twitch.tv, devoted to live-streaming experienced people playing videogames. It turns out that some people love videogames so much that they are willing to spend countless hours watching others play online. And by "some people," I mean a *lot* of people. By 2018, Twitch had more than 140 million users, some of whom were spending an average of 95 minutes daily watching live gaming.[12]

Why would anyone spend time watching others play videogames, much less pay for the privilege? For some gamers, playing videogames and watching videogames are separate value-creating activities. Watching videogames can add value in its own right by giving gaming enthusiasts a chance to learn from other, expert gamers and by providing them with entertainment, a form of spectatorship similar to that offered by professional sports.

Just as customers acquiring a product or service engage in only three distinct types of activities, so only three types of decoupling exist. Twitch exemplifies a subset of disruptive businesses that decouple value-creating activities. Other disruptive businesses either decouple value-charging activities or decouple value-eroding activities.*

Value-creation decoupling includes businesses that break the links between two or more value-creating activities. The decoupler offers one of these value-creating activities, while the incumbent that has been decoupled retains another value-creating activity. Twitch took videogame spectatorship for itself, but it does not develop videogames to be played. It left that activity for incumbents like Electronic Arts. And that was Twitch's billion-dollar idea.

* I will use the term "value charging" as opposed to "value capturing" to highlight the fact that customers perceive this activity as levying a cost or "charging" them.

In *value-eroding decoupling*, disruptors break the links between value-eroding and value-creating activities. In videogames, Steam allows customers to stream videogames over the internet, just as Netflix does for movies and TV shows.[13] With Steam, players no longer have to get off the couch and go to a physical retailer (a value-eroding activity) in order to play a game (a value-creating one). For gamers, that's a pretty big deal, and Steam's success proves it. As of 2017, the company had more than 200 million users, with annual revenues of $1 billion and a value of as much as $10 billion.[14]

The third type of disruption, *value-charging decoupling*, includes businesses that decouple value-creating and value-charging activities. Mobile game developer SuperCell allowed consumers to play most of its games for free, charging value by selling digital goods (in-app purchases) to the company's most loyal players. In effect, SuperCell broke the link between buying a game (value charging) and playing it (value creating). SuperCell is famous for developing titles such as Clash of Clans, one of the world's highest-grossing mobile games by revenue, with 100 million users. In 2016, the company was sold at a valuation of $10.2 billion.[15]

FIGURE 3.2 **THE THREE TYPES OF DECOUPLING**

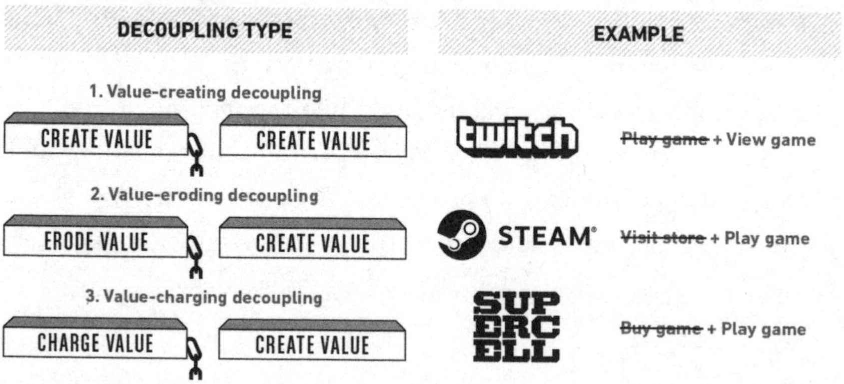

When it comes to classifying types of decoupling, the critical factor is not the kind of activity that the disruptor decouples and takes for itself. Rather, it's the activity that the decoupler *leaves behind* for the incumbent or someone else to continue providing.* In the videogame industry, Twitch leaves behind a value-creating activity—creating videogames. Steam leaves behind a value-eroding activity—the need to go to a retail store. And Supercell leaves behind a value-charging activity—charging customers a fee for using the product. That's what makes these forms of decoupling different. In each case, the decoupler takes for itself one activity that creates value for customers. Good thing, because otherwise the decoupler wouldn't attract any customers. Decouplers can also appropriate activities that allow them to charge for their services, but as we will see later, that is not strictly necessary. At the beginning of their life cycle, startups sometimes don't have a mechanism for generating revenue, or what is commonly referred to as monetization. Eventually startups have to develop such a mechanism or risk extinction. In its early days in 2008, the navigation app Waze offered value but didn't charge for its services. Four years later, the company started to sell location-based mobile advertising and license its real-time data to media companies and local governments. Today, Waze boasts 65 million active users in 185 countries.[16] The company was acquired by Google for $966 million in 2013.[17]

What Really Drives Decoupling?

Focusing on consumers helps us understand more deeply whether startups will succeed or fail at stealing customers from incumbents in existing markets. Simply because a disruptor *can* decouple the

* In a sense, this is a classification of types of disruption, not types of disruptors per se.

stages in a consumer's value chain does not mean consumers will rush to substitute the disruptor for the decoupled incumbent. Think of customer activities as train cars. *Integration forces* operating in consumers' minds cause the cars to become connected with one another. *Specialization forces* cause them to break apart. For decoupling to occur, the specialization forces must outweigh the integration forces. Consumers, in other words, must perceive that they benefit more from specialization—from turning to more than one provider for a set of activities—than from conducting the complete purchasing process with a single provider.

Consider the retail industry. Most large retailers deploy one of two pricing policies. Some chains, such as J. C. Penney or Sears in the United States, alternate between high prices and very low sale prices. Other chains, such as Walmart, price products more consistently at low prices, offering an "everyday low price" with little to no periodic deep discounting. Shoppers in the United States love everyday low prices, as evidenced by Walmart's dramatic growth in recent decades, because shopping in one place saves them time. Brazilian consumers see it differently. Earning only 18 percent of what the average American earns, they are more price sensitive, and thus less likely to buy all their groceries in one place. If they can find special deals on certain items elsewhere, they're happy to visit multiple retailers and forgo the convenience of one-stop shopping. This partially explains why Walmart is the market leader in the United States but is only in third place in Brazil, despite having similar stores. In other words, some shoppers will integrate all their shopping needs for the sake of convenience (an integration force), while others will separate them into specialized retailers for the sake of saving money, for example (a specialization force).

The same tension arises in decoupling. In the beauty industry, Sephora provides many benefits to customers by keeping their purchasing stages coupled. Consumers who visit a Sephora store can learn about different products, try them out, and buy them in Sephora stores. After an initial purchase, they can return and easily replenish their lipstick and mascara, buying additional products as needed.

Disruptors have sought to poach customers from Sephora by increasing the specialization forces between each stage of the beauty customer value chain. By sending customers a subscription box containing beauty samples, Birchbox allows customers to conveniently sample in the comfort of their own homes the same beauty products sold at Sephora. Amazon entices consumers with lower-priced, full-sized products, encouraging people to sample products in Sephora stores or with Birchbox but to buy them through Amazon. In response, Kiehl's, a division of industry giant L'Oreal Paris, allows extremely loyal consumers to "subscribe" to a given beauty cream or other product, paying by the subscription rather than the bottle. This service regularly replenishes consumers' beauty products by mail, ensuring that they will never run out. Although die-hard consumers might initially buy the product at Sephora, they later order from Kiehl's to guarantee replenishment. In other words, Kiehl's has decoupled the replenishment of beauty products, siphoning off repeat customers from Sephora.

We can represent the tension between integration and specialization forces in the beauty industry as a series of related benefits between stages of the customer value chain (*see Figure* 3.3). The incumbent, Sephora, offers benefits such as simplicity and expertise, both of which bind the entire customer value chain together. The three disruptors—Birchbox, Amazon, and Kiehl's/L'Oreal (the last of these an incumbent in manufacturing but a new entrant in retailing)—each offer benefits such as convenience, price, and assurance, which counteract the integration forces. Consumers who value convenience, price, and assurance more than they do simplicity and expertise will tend to decouple these three consumption activities.

FIGURE 3.3 **THE INCUMBENT'S INTEGRATION FORCES AND THE DECOUPLERS' SPECIALIZATION FORCES**

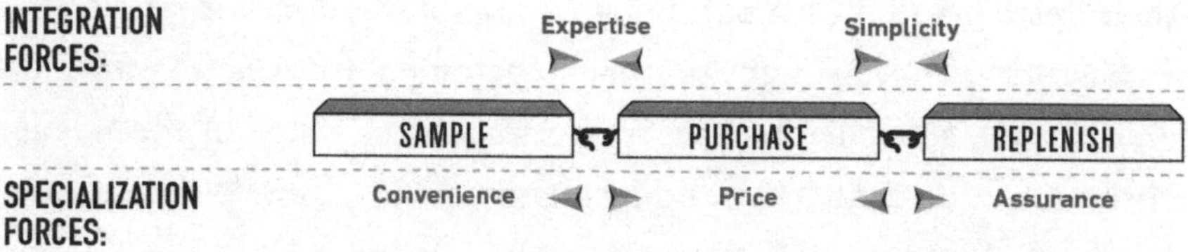

A word of caution. In assessing how competitors deliver on specialization and integration forces, it is important to perform an apples-to-apples comparison. In standard competition, company A will seek to claim market share by offering a significantly better (or different) product than company B. Tesla's success at claiming market share from big auto companies didn't involve decoupling. Rather, Tesla attempted to compete by offering a qualitatively different product: a high-end electric car. By contrast, I've assumed so far that decouplers and incumbents offer activities of essentially the same quality.* For instance, using Turo or Uber to ride in a Toyota Prius instead of purchasing and driving your own Prius *is* decoupling, if we assume that the end goal for the customer is to get from point A to point B and that the actual rides in these cars are of roughly similar quality. Likewise, if the quality of a gaming experience or beauty product purchased from an incumbent or disruptor is not materially different, these are cases of decoupling. If the difference in the quality of a product or service is large enough to account for the customer's choice, then decoupling might not be the sole phenomenon at play.

COSTS TO THE CONSUMER

Given the variety of customer benefits that result from integration or specialization forces in a given industry, we might wonder what

* This is not to say that the overall customer experience of the product or service needs to be exactly the same. Rather, each activity of the same type (e.g., sampling a lipstick, riding in a car) has a similar quality of experience, cost notwithstanding.

determines the customer's final decision. The answer is *cost.* Consumers incur costs in every stage of the CVC. Costs include not just the item's price but also such non-monetary costs as the effort required to identify and select items (*search costs*), the effort to order and receive items (*purchase costs*),* and the effort to use and dispose of items (*usage costs*). Amazon lowers search costs. It has built its website around the notion of facilitating search, offering a search box, algorithmic recommendations, and voice-, image-, and barcode-based searching features. Dollar Shave Club, a subscription service, lowers purchasing costs, telling consumers, "It doesn't get more convenient. We make and deliver the grooming products you need to look, feel, and shave like a million bucks. All delivered in one monthly box."[18] Turo lowers usage costs. By renting someone else's car on demand, drivers can use the car when they need it and dispose of it after they are done (i.e., by returning it). They save the inconvenience and expense of buying and maintaining their own cars. Conversely, owners of cars who rent their cars out or drive for Turo or Uber, respectively, can reduce their own usage cost by earning money when the cars are not in use.

FIGURE 3.4 **COSTS BY STAGE IN THE CUSTOMER'S VALUE CHAIN**

Source: Adapted from Thales S. Teixeira and Peter Jamieson, "The Decoupling Effect of Digital Disruptors," Harvard Business School Working Paper no. 15-031, October 28, 2014, 6.

After mapping costs against the stages of the customer value chain, we need to measure these costs. We can calculate *monetary*

* Not to be confused with "purchase price," which is the actual monetary amount paid to acquire the product or service.

costs measured in dollars (price, loan fee, shipping charges, etc.), *time costs* in hours or days (e.g., time to delivery, time spent purchasing), and *effort costs* through elementary information processes (EIPs)—cognitive steps that account for how consumers evaluate their options, decide to pay, and so on.[19] For instance, typing in a product name in a search bar is an EIP when you are purchasing online. Adding a product name to the virtual basket is another, as is inputting your credit card information or typing in your shipping address. (Note that simplicity, convenience, and one-stop shopping all fall under the rubric of reducing effort costs.)

To understand how various kinds of costs come into play in a specific customer value chain, consider the banking industry. Customers can choose between bank accounts that allow them to deposit money, pay expenses, invest their excess cash, and borrow if they need funds. To accomplish these and other tasks, consumers must be able to view and transfer balances between their checking, investment, and credit accounts. Traditionally, large retail banks such as Bank of America (BofA) have provided all of these services to their clients. A couple of decades ago, PayPal entered this space to allow consumers to pay expenses via its online platform. Why not pay using BofA? Because it's easier to do it online with PayPal.

More recently, peer-to-peer lending firms such as Lending Tree and Zopa have made it cheaper for consumers to borrow or lend money on their platforms. Startups such as Yodlee and Mint.com have allowed consumers to see all of their financial accounts in one online location, even if the accounts are held by different banking institutions (*see Figure 3.5*). Such so-called fintech disruption has made it easier, cheaper, and faster for clients to manage their money. At the same time, consumers still use incumbents such as Bank of America to "park" their money in deposit accounts. The problem for BofA and other banks is that cash deposits are a highly regulated and increasingly unprofitable portion of the customer value chain when provided in isolation. Other activities have been largely unregulated to date, since they do not entail the actual deposit of money for a long period of time. If customers continue to decouple their banking services using fintech startups, BofA's problems will likely grow. Startups' ability to reduce costs for customers is simply too compelling for them to pass up. Remember, whatever business you are in, your customers *always* pay you with three "currencies": their money, their time, and their effort.

FIGURE 3.5 **EFFORT, MONETARY, AND TIME COST IN THE BANKING CVC**

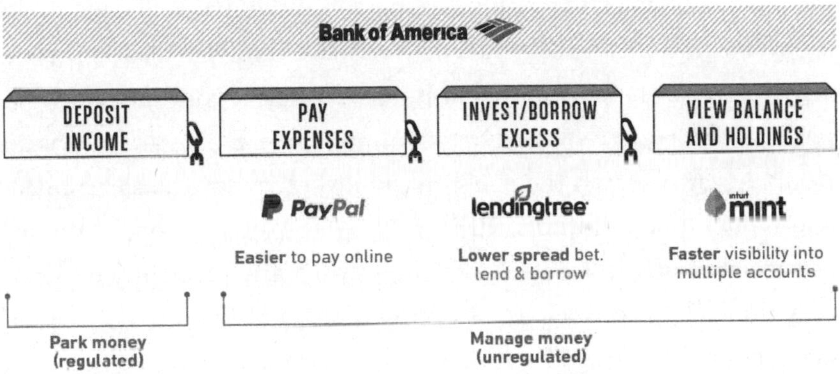

CALCULATING COST DIFFERENCES

We have examined the activities (e.g., evaluate, purchase, and use) that customers engage in and the types of costs (monetary, time, or effort) they incur in the course of procuring products and services. If we can understand precisely *where* customers experience costs, we can find places where customers might want to decouple. The higher the cost, the greater the motivation. Of course, customers need an alternative in order to do so, a startup that offers a distinct opportunity to lower customer costs. By comparing the differences in costs that customers incur during a coupled activity with those they incur during a decoupled activity, we can identify whether incumbents face a real risk of losing the customer activity to a disruptor, and whether disruptors see a genuine opportunity.

Imagine you're at a Walmart store, and you've selected a refrigerator.* You're debating whether to buy it from incumbent Walmart or from disruptor Amazon. You first consider the monetary costs. At Walmart, the LG fridge will run you $2,188. Amazon is selling it for only $2,048. Advantage to Amazon. But wait, Walmart can deliver that fridge for free in a day. It will take Amazon three days. Advantage to Walmart. But what about the effort that purchasing at either vendor will require of you? If you're at Walmart and chose the fridge (one elementary information process), you have already gone through the process of engaging with a salesperson. What you still need to do is pay for the item and schedule delivery (two more EIPs). To practice showrooming on Amazon—that is, to decouple—you would have to perform the equivalent activities online (three EIPs), and you also would have to search the site's online inventory for the same make and model (one additional EIP). Buying at Walmart, once you are already standing in front of the fridge you want, is slightly easier—only three EIPs to navigate as opposed to four.† In sum, the cost of decoupling (choosing the fridge at Walmart but going to Amazon.com to buy it) is –$140 + 2 days + 1 EIP.

So, will you buy the refrigerator from Walmart or from Amazon? Well, that depends on what you value most as a consumer. How sensitive are you to price, time, and effort? A price-sensitive college student who is looking to pay as little as possible may opt to buy the product on Amazon. But a less price-sensitive and deeply time-sensitive working mother might decide to pay a premium to have the new refrigerator delivered as soon as possible. The calculation clarifies the trade-offs that customers make when purchasing goods and services in a coupled or decoupled manner. Customers intuitively or

* We assume that the refrigerator evaluated on Amazon is identical, or very similar, to the corresponding one on Walmart.

† Let's assume that each of these steps requires the same effort regardless of where they are completed. We're also assuming that disruptors and incumbents are offering materially similar products or services.

FIGURE 3.6 **CALCULATION OF THE DIFFERENCES IN COSTS WHEN PURCHASING A REFRIGERATOR**

COSTS			
	Walmart	amazon	DIFFERENCE (AMAZON - WALMART)
MONETARY	$2,188	$2,048	-$140
TIME	1 day	3 days	2 days
EFFORT	3 EIPs	4 EIPs	1 EIP

deliberately assess the monetary, time, and effort costs they would accrue when dealing with disruptors or incumbents. Of course, they may not consciously assess their options in this way, but if you are the incumbent company, you should. Adopt your customer's point of view, and compare the options open to her. Unless you know all the small, subjective considerations that might influence this customer, your best bet is to perform the comparison in a simple, objective, and systematic manner. How much money, time, and effort must your customer expend to do business with your company? How much must she expend with a disruptor? Does the difference run in your favor or against you?

You might initially resist performing this analysis, given that many customers will not compare options and costs as carefully and methodically as I've described here. While procurement offices in large firms compare costs in a comprehensive way, individual consumers are more likely to check prices and leave it at that. Still, the point of this analysis isn't to determine what any given customer will do. It's to understand whether your offering at any stage of the customer value chain will prove more or less costly to customers than what a startup in your market might provide. If your fridge, say, is more or less costly, you would respond differently to a new entrant trying to disrupt your market. In the short term, you might win customers *despite* having a higher total cost than an entrant, or lose a sale despite having a cheaper cost. Eventually, though, customer decisions catch up to the reality of the underlying costs. The purpose of this analysis is to shed light on this reality. If you calculate the costs, you'll know early on how vulnerable you are to that disruptor on your home turf.

BEYOND THE THREE COSTS

The three costs I've mentioned—money, time, and effort—are not necessarily the only costs to consumers. Another common cost is risk-related costs (e.g., trust, reliability, transparency, and uncertainty). Consumers might know and trust Four Seasons Hotels and Bank of America, but do they trust that a property owner on Airbnb will guarantee their booking, or that a borrower on LendingTree will repay their loan? If they don't, that uncertainty might dramatically affect their decision to decouple or not. One well-established way to measure the trust, reliability, and uncertainty of a company's offerings is to consider the company's brand equity. Incumbents might enjoy a higher brand perception than a newly formed startup does. On the other hand, smaller brands sometimes enjoy an advantage over larger ones. When urban millennials in the United States shop for packaged food in established grocery stores, they have started to favor relatively unknown, upstart brands rather than major, well-established ones.[20]

Of course, brands and brand equity only go so far. As I've discovered when advising large companies, senior marketing executives tend to hide behind the brands they manage and their overhyped value. As established global brands see it, customers would never "fire" them for some unheard-of startup, because they, the incumbent, have spent hundreds of millions of dollars building their brands. Furthermore, in many cases, an incumbent's well-regarded brand does indeed reflect consistently lower monetary, time, or effort costs to the customers. You might not shop at Walmart, ship with FedEx, or bank with JPMorgan Chase were it not for cheaper, faster, less effortful transactions.

When in doubt, ask customers what they value most. Learn the costs they care about when making purchase decisions—not just some of the costs, but all of the important ones. Beyond the money, time, and effort they invest in making their purchase, luxury car buyers might tell you that reputation matters to them. Low-end car buyers, on the other hand, might claim that the vehicle's reliability is critical. Clients of low-end financial services might say they care about access, whereas high-end banking clients are looking for exclusivity. In assessing additional classes of costs beyond money, time, and effort, scrutinize them closely. Make sure they really do impact the customer's decision, and that you can measure these additional costs for both your offering and the disruptor's offering. Finally, make sure that you aren't double-counting. Additional costs must not overlap with any of the three discussed here.

Markets Through the Customer's Eyes

As we've seen, customers really do drive a great deal of the disruption we see unfolding all around us. And it's important to take them into account when formulating a strategy for responding to potential disruption. In the hospitality industry, who really matters most when it comes to disruption—Airbnb, or the customer's changing habits? If Airbnb ceased to exist, wouldn't another startup arise to take its place? In other words, the underlying customer trend would remain intact. A similar argument holds in any number of other industries where disruption has occurred. In the case of physical retailers, shoppers were testing and choosing electronics in-store and going home or elsewhere to compare prices even before Amazon entered this space. In the beauty category, women were collecting and using beauty samples well before Birchbox was founded. In the videogame industry, players were going to one another's homes to watch their friends play videogames before they began to subscribe to Twitch. Only when entrepreneurs recognized this desire and introduced an offering that attempted to satisfy it did a successful disruptor unsettle the market. To get ahead of disruption, executives of established companies need to focus more attention on customers and less on the startups they regard as their competitors.

Companies have much to gain by conducting the kind of customer-focused analysis I've laid out. Map the stages of your customer's CVC to discover where you create value, where you charge for it, and where you sometimes erode it. Then ask yourself three questions: (1) Can you deliver more value in the value-creating activities without charging more? (2) Can you afford to capture less in the value-charging activities, everything else being equal? (3) Can you reduce eroded customer value without diminishing what you're offering or capturing?

FIGURE 3.7 **EXAMPLES OF CHANGING CUSTOMER BEHAVIOR**

Be patient as you perform this analysis. You might feel tempted to consider at once all of the activities you provide, but you can find yourself overwhelmed, lost in a thicket of hypothetical adjustments to your business model. Think: "If I want to change this, I'll need to change that as well. And that. And that. And that." Do what disruptors do and consider one activity at a time. If you were Sephora, for instance, you might ask yourself whether you could eliminate value erosion at the sampling stage by launching a subscription box of your own. Or you might explore whether you could reduce the value charged at the first purchase stage—say, by price-matching Amazon. Or you might consider how to increase value created at the replenishing stage, perhaps by automatically replenishing the products your customer frequently uses, the way Kiehl's does.

As you ponder options in your own company, be prepared for pushback. Paul, the executive who oversees physical stores, might complain that subscription boxes will cannibalize foot traffic. Ann in accounting might argue that price-matching will erode profitability. And Jim from logistics will cry foul about higher costs of automating replenishment. How should you respond to them? Each of their separate analyses is correct, but all of them implicitly assume that your customer base will remain the same whether or not you embrace any of the above changes. When your customer has the option of decoupling a piece of your business, this assumption no longer holds. We'll analyze this in more detail in subsequent chapters.

For now, consider this: why have I focused so much on just a few industries? Chances are your business has little directly to do with any one of them. Do the lessons gleaned from such examples apply to your own industry? Participants in workshops I've led have raised exactly such questions. And here is the answer I give: The customer of Kiehl's, decoupling Sephora, is actually your customer, too. She buys cars, entertainment, financial services, and so on. And while she can choose from different options in each case, she does not have a different thought process for choosing. She does not have a perfume-buying brain, or a separate car-buying brain.

Decoupling might seem like an industry-specific phenomenon,

but as we saw in Chapter 1, it isn't. Not only is the basic process of decoupling and its application to business model innovation the same everywhere, but the primary force driving it—customer costs—is pervasive. Consider this: in 2016, 72 percent of American adults used at least one of eleven different shared or on-demand services such as Airbnb or Uber. The Pew Research Center found that about one in five Americans routinely incorporated four or more of these services into their daily lives. The same group of consumers is decoupling across industries.[21] To deeply understand the dynamics of this disruption, we must look first outside our industries for helpful illustrations before we look inward.

It pays to understand your customer's buying and usage behaviors across *all* of his or her primary purchasing choices. Now, you might wonder whether anyone can really look at the hundreds of thousands of purchase decisions that customers make during their lifetimes. The good news is you don't have to. In subsequent chapters I'll offer a shortcut. For now, just remember: it all starts with the customer. So you too should start with the customer.

Of course, this broader cross-industry understanding helps us only up to a point. When it comes to the disruption of a particular business, we don't know exactly what individual customers will decide to do. What we do know or can discover is how, as a group, customers will perceive a business's offerings and compare them to other options. As I've suggested, they'll consider the costs of specialization and compare them with the costs of integration, either deliberately or unintentionally. To avoid unpleasant surprises, you too should determine the costs incurred by your customer in each stage of the CVC, whether these are monetary, time, or effort costs. Then do the same for your competitors and new entrants, determining which company's offerings fare best in the eyes of the customer. Ultimately, most customers will favor the option they perceive to cost less—not just in terms of price but in total. Is it yours? Or is it your upstart competitor's?

This chapter and the two preceding it have sought to help you understand the new reality of disruption—what it is, how it works, and what causes it. There is a common pattern to the latest wave of digital disruption. It is driven not by technology but rather by customers' desires to reduce the costs of acquiring goods and services. It's not that technology is unimportant, but that it often serves as the enabler of disruption rather than as its primary originator. In Chapter 4, I'll offer a road map that entrepreneurs and incumbent executives can use in virtually any industry to disrupt via decoupling.

4

HOW TO ENGINEER DECOUPLING

Justin Kan was standing on the grounds of a medieval castle in Tuscany, attending the wedding of one of his company's cofounders, when he checked the Bank of America app on his phone. What he saw made him drop to his knees and break into laughter. The deal to sell his company to Amazon had gone through. Amazon had just wired the purchase price into Kan's corporate account—almost a billion dollars.[1] A billion dollars! "I did not even know one could put that much money in Bank of America," Kan recalled. "All the cofounders were like: 'Holy sh#%$!' "

How in the world had Kan and his partners pulled off such a brilliant success? The story began ten years earlier, in 2004, when Kan and his childhood friend Emmett Shear graduated from Yale. Unlike some of their peers, the two had no clear idea what to do with themselves. One option seemed promising: they could start a company. Silicon Valley was hot, startups were popping up everywhere, and founders were making millions—like that Harvard undergraduate who had started Facebook in his dorm. Why not give the entrepreneurial life a shot?

Emmett and Justin's first business idea—a web calendar app that would work as well as desktop software, but which users could access through a web browser—didn't take them very far. The two friends spent months creating the code, but, as they would later admit, the product wasn't very good. They didn't use calendar applications very much, and had no idea what they were doing. They didn't even know enough to ask calendar users for feedback.[2]

By 2006, they didn't know what to do next. For two months, they sat on the couch, playing videogames and chatting about their failed business and the new apps they could build. Then Justin had a crazy idea: The conversations they were having while playing their games were interesting. Wouldn't it be awesome to record their conversations, or even better, to live-stream them on the internet? And why stop there? Maybe they could live-stream *their entire lives.* Nobody had tried that before.

Others they spoke with thought that turning their minute-to-minute experience into an endless, uncut reality TV show was a truly dumb idea. Why would people want to watch Justin's boring daily life? But to everyone's surprise, some tech investors were intrigued. One liked the weirdness of the project and the ambition of disrupting traditional television entertainment.

In 2007, with a few tens of thousands of investor dollars in their pockets, Emmett and Justin moved to San Francisco and launched a new website called Justin.TV.[3] Joining them were two other friends: Michael Seibel, a fellow student from Yale, and Kyle Vogt, an MIT undergraduate whom Emmett and Justin had hired to figure out the hardware. Technology proved to be the biggest challenge—Google Glass wasn't yet available, nor were Snap's Spectacles, video cameras on smartphones, or cheap bandwidth. But the four aspiring media moguls figured it out. To secure bandwidth for streaming and to avoid delays or breaks, Justin and his friends used three cellphones at once to connect to the internet. Justin wore a webcam that was attached to his head and linked by cable to a laptop. In a backpack, he carried batteries that afforded him twenty-four hours of power. The webcam recorded as Justin ate, played videogames, hung out with friends, and occasionally got drunk. When Justin wanted to sleep, he put the camera on a tripod and turned it toward his bed. The show's slogan was "Waste time watching other people waste time."[4]

The media loved the novelty—"A new star is born," the *San Francisco Chronicle* announced—and soon Emmett and Justin boasted both viewers and advertisers.[5] It wouldn't last. A few weeks later, viewers grew bored watching Justin waste time. The founders were bored of Justin.TV, too. They noticed that users kept emailing them asking how they could create their own live streams. Why not modify their business plan, allowing users to stream their own video on Justin.TV?

In the autumn of 2007, Emmett, Justin, and their team relaunched Justin.TV with the support of their investors. They quickly attracted users who live-streamed everything, from home cooking demonstrations and singing performances to playful pet antics and videogame playing. Once again, their success was short-lived. Sports fans figured out how to run the signal from cable boxes into computers, and they used Justin.TV to stream NFL games and pay-per-view UFC fights for free. Traffic spiked to millions of users, but broadcasters and rights holders sued, and a public controversy arose around so-called pirated content. Although the courts found Justin.TV not guilty of "stealing cable," advertisers and investors grew wary of live, user-generated video given its unpredictability.[6]

With money drying up, the founders had to figure out what to do.[7] They asked themselves: Who would miss Justin.TV if it were gone? Was there anything worth watching on the website? Emmett thought there was. He loved watching other people playing videogames, like World of Warcraft, StarCraft II, or Minecraft. Although gamers represented just 2 percent of streamers, they had distinguished themselves as a loyal and engaged audience. Interviewing forty power users, Emmett learned that the best gamers were like sports stars—other fans wanted to see them play. As Emmett remarked, "If you don't love video games, just imagine something you do love. Don't you like watching people who are the best in the world at this play and talk about it?"[8] That's the kind of pleasure that Twitch offered for videogame fans.

Believing that he had stumbled upon an opportunity in the market, Emmett convinced Kevin and others to relaunch the startup to serve this niche community.[9] In 2011, the company did precisely that, giving the website a new name: Twitch. The company focused on building a vibrant, global community of players and viewers, and on improving the quality of the streaming. Five years after embarking on the entrepreneurial life, Emmett and Justin finally struck gold. Soon tens of millions of people were watching videogame streams on their site every month. Amazingly, Twitch ranked just behind Netflix, Apple, and Google in volume of peak internet traffic in the United States.[10] Advertisers including Riot Games, Paramount Studios, HP, Netflix, and Kellogg's found gaming streams brand-safe and friendly, and viewers were so engaged that they were ready to pay $4.99 for subscriptions to watch their favorite gamers. By 2014, some elite gamers were earning $300,000 a year, and Twitch was grabbing an estimated 43 percent of revenues in the $3.8 billion gaming content industry.[11] Finally they had a business model that worked. Later that year, Emmett, Justin, and their friends sold the site to Amazon. When Emmett checked his bank balance, there it was: $970 million.[12]

How had these entrepreneurs done it? The answer wasn't especially clear, not even to Kan. Years later, he still struggled to explain the success that he and his cofounders had achieved. "Anyone could do it really," he said. "We are not like Mozart or something."[13]

Much of the time, entrepreneurs take long, circuitous routes to success, with many missteps along the way. Success is anything but straightforward or formulaic. But that doesn't mean that a more predictable, streamlined approach to disruption isn't possible. In my study of dozens of would-be decouplers, I've identified several steps in the entrepreneurial journey that successful startups have in common, and others that lead unsuccessful startups to fail. It turns out that the critical steps and ingredients for successful decoupling are few, are remarkably consistent across industries, and address the key drivers of decoupling that I outlined in Chapter 3.

The existence of this underlying pattern carries enormous implications for both startups and incumbents. Whether you're an incumbent looking to preemptively disrupt your business or industry through decoupling or an entrepreneur looking to build a successful startup, you don't have to tread the sort of winding path that led to the Twitch founders' billion-dollar payday. You can *deliberately engineer* business model innovation and decoupling. In other words, there is a "recipe" that will help keep risk to a minimum. Far from the haphazard or uncertain activity that many people commonly take disruption to be, business model innovation can become rigorous and methodical. Let's examine how.

Layers of Innovation

As an advisor to incumbents and startups, I've had a chance to watch many entrepreneurs in action and to follow their thinking as it has evolved. Some entrepreneurs conceptualize their new business model all at once, in a single, grand epiphany. They proceed intuitively, rather than methodically. Twitch's founders are a good example. They began with a single, "big" idea—allowing people to live-cast on the internet their day-to-day activities—that was centered on technology. After many twists and turns, they arrived at their eventual business model of allowing gamers to decouple playing games from the activity of viewing top players playing them. Other entrepreneurs are more deliberate than this, beginning by analyzing the existing model in their industry and then layering their own innovation on top. But they still proceed largely by feeling their way, reacting opportunistically to circumstances as they arise.

What if entrepreneurs could proceed far more methodically? What might that look like? In my years of working with entrepreneurs who are building businesses from scratch, and executives rebuilding existing businesses, I've developed a way of thinking that is more deliberate, and hence replicable. I typically recommend that entrepreneurs or executives embrace the customer's vantage point and organize their thinking in terms of three layers. The first layer is to articulate the current or standard business model. After all, most startups need to pull customers away from existing businesses or activities (e.g., dry cleaning versus do-it-yourself clothes washing). Customers evaluate the startup *in comparison* to what they already have. If you want to thoroughly understand a new business idea, you must take the current reality as your foundation.

The second layer is to develop the *digital equivalent* of the standard model. Almost all young entrepreneurs I meet today incorporate the internet into their business ideas. When comparing their innovative products to the best options that are currently available, the less elaborate ideas tend to focus on simply translating or "porting" a traditional business model onto the internet. As an example, homeowners traditionally hire housekeepers, gardeners, and others to help with common household chores. TaskRabbit, the digital equivalent, lets you hire people, but do so over the web. Likewise, the startup company Washio created a mobile app that allowed you to request digitally that your dry cleaning be picked up and delivered, saving you the trouble of going to the dry cleaner's yourself.[14]

With this digital equivalent layered on top of the standard business model, the third and final layer for entrepreneurs and executives is to determine how to *innovate* on top of digital business models. Some entrepreneurs I've met understand that the mere porting of a business model online isn't enough. It might benefit users, but it creates downsides, too. TaskRabbit accelerates the process of choosing people to perform chores for you, but it's also riskier, since it requires that you allow complete strangers inside your home. Washio offered convenience, but at a price. Considering the benefits and costs, smart entrepreneurs try to layer on top of their digital business idea an innovation that transcends mere digitization, and that produces a functional benefit for customers. Founders of Hello Alfred innovated upon the TaskRabbit model by outsourcing the management of TaskRabbit workers to personally assigned butlers, or "Alfreds." For users, the presence of a butler on the scene allowed for a more trustworthy and reliable service.[15]

Many of the entrepreneurs I've worked with find that this three-part structure allows them to distinguish clearly between the novel and non-novel aspects of their business idea. It also forces the more intuitive thinkers to articulate, test, and validate their assumptions, rather than to just plop an idea out on the table and have others react to it. Finally, the format clarifies for all interested parties—including advisors, investors, and employees—the incremental value of the proposed business idea relative to the traditional approach. Further, it reveals the hidden assumptions, as well as the incremental value, of any innovative technologies and business model components being proposed (*see Figure 4.1*).

FIGURE 4.1 **THE LAYERS OF DESIGNING INNOVATIVE BUSINESS MODELS**

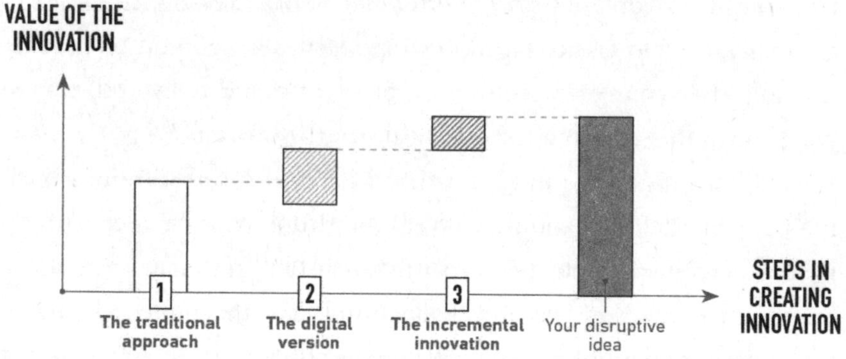

To understand better how this model might work in the real world, let's apply it to Twitch. If you had told me a few years ago that people from around the world would pay to observe others play games from the comfort of their homes, and that top players would as a consequence draw six-figure salaries, I would have said you were delusional. But when you view Twitch through the lens of the three layers, their business idea doesn't seem so crazy. In the past, kids discovered new games, learned to play them better, and entertained themselves by going to their friends' homes and playing games together. That was the "traditional approach," under my framework (layer one). When a number of kids got together, they had to wait their turn to play a game. While waiting, they chatted about what they were seeing onscreen, learning from the best players, and hearing about games they didn't currently own. That low-tech solution solved the problem for most kids quite effectively. But if a gamer had no close friends nearby, or if it was late at night, he or she was out of luck. The traditional approach didn't work.

Twitch had the solution. It ported the traditional model online (layer two), offering a digital equivalent of the five kids sitting around the living room watching one another play and talking about their experiences. Now gamers of all ages, anywhere, at any time could go online, learn about new games, and discover better playing strategies. Still, a problem remained. Viewers found Twitch useful to the extent they saw a wide variety of games being played live. But how would Twitch get the most interesting and skilled gamers to play for others to see?

Hiring skilled players to play around the clock for others' pleasure would cost too much. Fortunately, Twitch's founders arrived at a business model innovation (layer three), one that would let skilled players *monetize* their favorite pastime. If skilled players made enough money, they would stick around. Twitch founders created financial opportunities for players, giving them a cut of any advertising revenues generated on the site. That added up to a lot of money. In 2015, 14,000 high-profile streamers, or elite gamers, generated an estimated $60 million in revenue through ads and subscriptions, with top players earning $300,000 a year.[16] Players could also land sponsorships from videogame makers, and compete in tournaments for multimillion-dollar prizes. In 2016, five Chinese pro gamers earned $9.1 million by winning a single competition of the game

Dota 2 in Seattle.[17] Have you ever heard of Dota 2? Neither have I. This business model innovation of creating huge monetary value for players has allowed Twitch to retain its best players, further attracting more viewers, advertisers, and game developers to their site. And that is the final but critical element that enabled gaming enthusiasts to decouple playing (performed by a few skilled players) from viewing (performed by millions of users) (*see Figure 4.2*).

FIGURE 4.2 **THE LAYERS OF DESIGNING INNOVATIVE BUSINESSES APPLIED TO TWITCH**

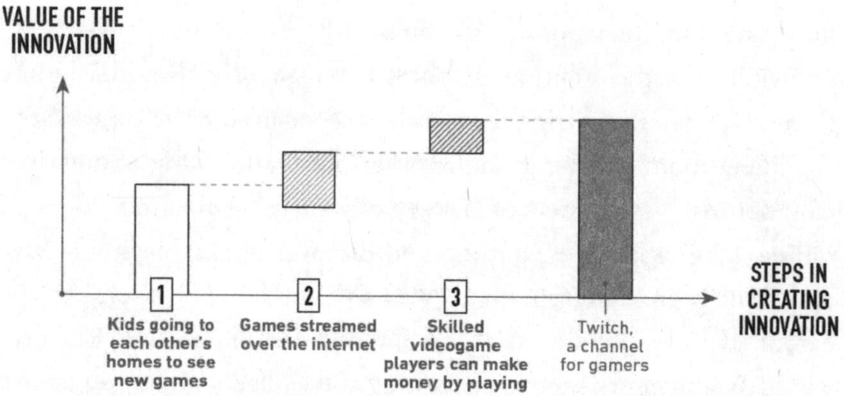

When a new business idea works out right away, it doesn't matter how you arrived at it. Unfortunately, most business innovations are not instant successes. They require many minor or even major tweaks before they begin to work, if they work at all. The layered approach to engineering innovation can help. It's much easier to figure out why your business model isn't working, and to change out the faulty pieces, when you can look at it layer by layer, as opposed to one big, monolithic problem. In attempting to innovate via decoupling, the last layer, the incremental innovation piece, is the critical one to build. Without it, purely digitized versions of traditional business models tend to contain many downsides, not just benefits. How can would-be decouplers go about engineering that last layer of innovation?

A Recipe for Decoupling

Most cases of successful decoupling originate with entrepreneurs creating startups (like Twitch). But there are also cases of incumbent companies decoupling their industry (for instance, Amazon). After research into decouplers of all types, I've come to realize that successful decouplers perform five key steps, either deliberately or instinctively, that unsuccessful ones don't. These steps were remarkably consistent across decouplers in a wide range of industries, including retailing, telecom, education, transportation, media, and financial services. Collectively, these steps address a key customer need—namely, a desire to specialize—by reducing the customer's costs of acquiring products and services. To disrupt markets through decoupling, successful decouplers must do the following:

Step 1: Identify a Target Segment and Its CVC

In Chapter 3, I pointed out that customers disrupt markets, shifting their behavior in the course of trying to satisfy their changing needs and desires. When customers decouple their consumption activities, they implicitly decide that they no longer wish to perform all of the activities required to acquire a product or service with the same company. Customers might still want to do business with the incumbent, but one or more of the CVC activities is now up for grabs. Aspiring decouplers thus must identify opportunities to snag one or more of the customer's value chain activities before other competitors do. The way to do that is to first understand a group of customers with similar needs—a target segment—and map out all the activities in that group's typical customer value chain.

Decouplers often trip up on this step in two ways. First, they are overly generic in articulating the CVC. When mapping the process of buying a car, auto executives tend to describe it as: feel the need to buy car > become aware of a car brand > develop an interest in the brand > visit the dealer > purchase the car. This is a start, but it is not specific enough. Decouplers must ask: When do people actually need a new car? How exactly do people become aware of car brands? How do people become interested in a make or model? And so on. The generic process of awareness, interest, desire, and purchase isn't specific enough to help.

Decouplers also flounder by failing to identify all the relevant stages in the value chain. For the car-buying process, a better description of the CVC might be: become aware that your car lease will expire in one month > feel the need to purchase a new car > develop a heightened interest in car ads > visit car manufacturers' websites > create a set of two or three brands of interest > visit third-party auto websites > compare options of cars in the same category > choose a model > shop online for the best price > visit the nearest dealer to see if they have the model in stock > see if they can beat the best online price > test-drive the cars > decide about financing, warranty, and other add-ons > negotiate a final price > sign the contract > pick up the car > use it > wait for the lease to expire again. With this far more detailed CVC, we can fully appreciate the complexity of the car-buying process, and how many options for decoupling exist.

It's so important to get this first step correct. In fact, I often spend 50 percent or more of my time working with companies on this single step. The CVC is the blueprint of digital disruption, and it must be fleshed out so that it is both accurate and comprehensive. Otherwise, your attempt at decoupling likely won't succeed.

Step 2: Classify the CVC Activities

As we've seen, customer activities can be either value creating, value charging, or value eroding. Disruptors need to snatch an activity that creates value for the consumer, such as negotiating price or test-driving the car. They can also aim to take over a value-charging activity, such as selling the financing and warranties or signing the contract. If the decoupler takes both a value-creating activity and a value-charging one, it might have a profitable business. If it takes over only a value-creating activity, it will have to introduce an entirely new, value-charging activity in order to remain viable. An entrepreneur or executive interested in creating a business that allows car buyers to test-drive cars from different brands in one place could decouple this function from traditional dealers. But this decoupler would need to find a way to make money, either charging car buyers directly for this value-added benefit, charging manufacturers, or selling something else to customers, such as financing or service contracts. All of these are value-charging activities.

Step 3: Identify Weak Links Between CVC Activities

Consumers might fulfill some of the eighteen activities involved in the purchase, usage, and disposal of a new leased car with the same company. They might well wish to stick with a single company when determining if a local dealer has a model in stock and when test-driving that model. It's simply more convenient than going to an entirely different company to test-drive a car. In contrast, customers might wish to work with different companies when comparing cars of a similar category across brands and when choosing their desired models. Ford knows a great deal about its cars but little about GM's cars. And customers wouldn't want to use a Ford website when comparing a Ford Mustang and a Chevy Corvette, for fear of bias. Third-party websites such as Edmunds, TrueCar, Cars.com, and other car information aggregators have snatched away the activity of comparing cars for themselves—many car buyers now search extensively online before ever setting foot in a car dealership. Prospective decouplers should consider all of the important stages in the CVC and identify those that customers currently fulfill all with one single firm but, in some cases if given the opportunity, might choose to fulfill with another company. The activities that these weak links bind together are prime candidates for decoupling.

Step 4: Break the Weak Links

The fourth step is to actually break the weak links and make it worthwhile for customers to decouple their activities from the incumbent. Successful decouplers achieve this by increasing the specialization forces that I discussed in Chapter 3. They reduce the money, effort, or time it takes for the consumer to fulfill each activity so that the combined costs fall below what consumers currently encounter with the incumbent. In our example, car dealers don't usually charge customers for the privilege of test-driving their cars. The chief costs shoppers bear are time and effort. For shoppers interested in test-trialing multiple cars from different makers, these costs might prove significant. Startups could lower these costs by, for instance, creating a space with multiple cars by different manufacturers available for test-driving. They could also bring cars to the buyer's home for a test trial. In Japan, dealers do precisely that. Can a startup offer this service and turn a profit? That's an important question, but not one that need concern startups at this early stage. For now, they're simply evaluating opportunities for successful decoupling.

Step 5: Predict How Incumbents Will Respond

Disruptors that decouple activities away from traditional competitors should anticipate how incumbents might respond, and then take preemptive action. As we'll see in Chapter 5, while competitors might respond in a thousand different ways, we can broadly classify these responses into two major categories: recoupling what the disruptor decoupled and preemptively decoupling, directly offering their customers the chance to decouple.

FIGURE 4.3 **THE FIVE-STEP PROCESS FOR DISRUPTING WITH DECOUPLING**

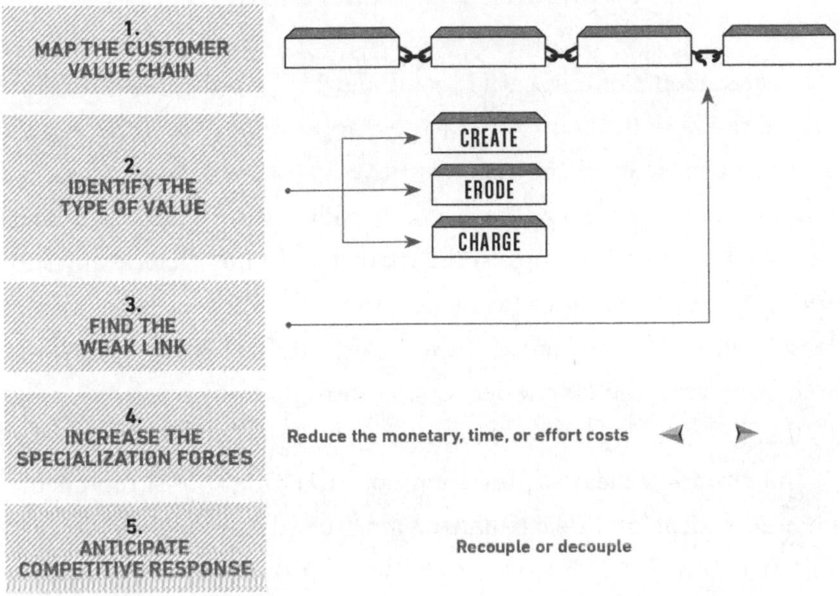

These five steps capture what successful decouplers actually do in developing and honing their disruptive business models. Entrepreneurs looking to disrupt a market have used this framework to craft business models more thoughtfully and deliberately. For executives at incumbent firms, this framework serves as a way to get at the underlying logic behind decouplers arising in an industry. Even better, this framework yields insights that incumbents can use when evaluating possible threats. I'll explain the framework's utility as a defensive strategy in a moment, but first let's work with these five steps a bit. As any amateur chef knows, trying out a new recipe is never as straightforward as it seems. If you're not careful, you'll overcook the ingredients or fail to prepare them properly. It helps to watch others before you attempt it yourself. Likewise, in business it helps to see how startups have worked with decoupling in their own industries before you apply it to your own.

Two Real-Life Case Studies

Former students of mine at Harvard and MIT have applied the five-step formula with their own startups, and I've borrowed from their stories in presenting the following two industry case studies. The stories I tell depict only the initial version of the business models deployed by these startups in the market. I do not include any subsequent alterations to these models that may have occurred. In at least one case, I should note, the founder(s) did not consciously know that they were applying a decoupling formula until I pointed it out to them.

In presenting these stories, I am not validating the entrepreneurs' choice of ideas and decisions, nor am I testifying to their success. A startup's ability to succeed over the long term depends on many factors beyond the five-step decoupling paradigm, including people, money, skills, execution, and adaptability. With these caveats in mind, let's consider how entrepreneurs used the decoupling formula to develop their own disruptive business models in the real estate and fashion industries.

REAL ESTATE

Let's say you're starting a new retail bakery, and you want to showcase your products for customers. You have to lease or buy a retail store. That means finding the right real estate, and possibly even paying for a space that's larger than you need. Traditionally, you would have had to acquire commercial real estate from companies such as Prologis, one of the largest incumbents in this industry, with almost 700 million square feet of commercial real estate space in eighteen countries.[18] In 2012, a San Francisco–based startup called Storefront sought to solve this problem by creating an online platform that allowed store owners with unutilized space inside their store to connect with and rent that extra space to vendors of non-competing goods who lacked access to commercial real estate.[19] Using a matchmaking website, Storefront decoupled the link between owning space and showcasing products.[20] The makers of goods could now do the latter without needing to do the former. Applying the five-step formula for decoupling in Storefront, we have the following:

Step 1: Identify a target segment and its CVC. The target customers in this instance are small shops seeking to sell their goods. In order to accomplish that objective, they must perform four activities as part of their CVC: acquire merchandise > acquire (buy, rent, or lease) commercial retail space > showcase their merchandise > sell merchandise.

Step 2: Classify the CVC activities. The activity of acquiring retail space provides no real value to shops. It is a value-charging activity, a means to the end of showcasing and selling merchandise. The latter two are the real value-creating activities.

Step 3: Identify weak links between CVC activities. As retail studies show, the weak link in the CVC is that between acquiring retail space and showcasing products. The former is a major cost to small shops, and they would gladly do away with this activity if they could.

Step 4: Break the weak links. Storefront allows some shops to rent unused space in their stores to other shops. In exchange for a modest fee, these renters can fill the formerly unused space with their merchandise. By lowering the cost for small shops to acquire real estate space, Storefront decouples the owning of retail space from the showcasing of merchandise. It takes away a value-charging activity from traditional commercial real estate developers such as Prologis, and reduces that expense for its clients—both the shop owner and the merchant seeking retail space.

Step 5: Predict how incumbents will respond. How might Prologis react if Storefront catches fire and many retailers use the service to rent spaces in their stores? Prologis might decide to force its retailer lessees to sign a contract forbidding them from "subletting" their space in total or in part. Apartment owners have done this to prevent tenants from listing their apartments on sites such as Airbnb. Prologis might also raise its rents or sales prices to reflect the new income stream that retailers might receive from Storefront, capturing some of the incremental revenue Storefront's clients generate by renting out part of their space. One way or another, Storefront must figure out how to address these possibilities before they occur.

FASHION APPAREL

In the clothing industry, online personal stylists such as New York–based Keaton Row and Chicago-based Trunk Club are decoupling the link between assembling a complete outfit and purchasing individual pieces of the outfit.[21] Traditionally, consumers have had to visit a department store to select the items that comprise an outfit. Some people enjoy this process; others, not so much. Keaton Row and Trunk Club have reduced the burden for unenthusiastic shoppers by either advising them on which items to purchase and where or assembling and shipping to them complete outfits prepared by in-house stylists.[22] These companies have increased the specialization forces and decoupled the link between choosing and purchasing outfits. To break down the underlying logic here, let's run through the five steps:

Step 1: Identify a target segment and its CVC. People don't just need to buy clothing items. They need outfits. And in order to use an outfit, they need to do the following: visit a retailer that sells multiple items that can be combined into an outfit > choose an initial item (e.g., a blouse) > choose a second item (e.g., a matching skirt) > choose a third item (e.g., shoes) > . . . > purchase all the items > use the items together in an outfit.

Step 2: Classify the CVC activities. Choosing items might be a value-creating activity for some, but for others it erodes value. Macy's captures value as customers buy items. Using the outfit—the end goal—creates value for shoppers.

Step 3: Identify weak links between CVC activities. Some people love visiting department stores such as Macy's to choose and coordinate items in an outfit. Others regard it as a colossal waste of time. Surveys have shown that a considerable minority of shoppers would do away with the item-by-item shopping for outfits if they could. Thus, we have a weak link.

Step 4: Break the weak links. Keaton Row and Trunk Club decouple the act of choosing the items in an outfit from the acts of buying and using the outfit. Using personal stylists (Keaton Row) and algorithms (Trunk Club), these decouplers discern their clients' styles and do the work of searching online for all the items in an outfit on behalf of their clients. The services either send clients links to the items for purchase (Keaton Row) or deliver the actual items to their homes (Trunk Club), thus reducing the time and effort it takes to choose items that go well together in an outfit.

Step 5: Predict how incumbents will respond. How might Macy's react if this trend grows? The trend could result in fewer store visits from customers. Or it could result in stylists browsing online or visiting stores on behalf of clients in lieu of actual shoppers. Because Macy's does not lose a value-charging activity, the company might not see this as a huge threat to its business model. Consequently, it might decide to adapt slowly to the new clientele of professional stylists and buyers, changing the format of its stores or catering to this clientele with a special section on the Macy's website. Alternatively, Macy's might see this as a major threat to their business model, which hinges upon shoppers buying items in multiple departments. In this scenario, Macy's might launch its own Keaton Row–like stylist shopper program or Trunk Club–like outfit subscription service. Decouplers would need to prepare for this eventual competition.

These are just a few examples of how startups have applied the decoupling recipe to forge their business models in a more deliberate, systematic way. Entrepreneurs and incumbents can apply this five-step recipe in virtually any industry, in both consumer-facing businesses (e.g., Keaton Row, Trunk Club) and business-to-business cases (e.g., Storefront, Shelfmint). These five steps can be applied to virtually any situation in which you have customers who perform a series of activities in order to acquire a product, service, or idea. As long as a single company currently provides more than one activity to customers, an opportunity exists at least in theory for an entrant to come in and decouple those activities for customers.

THREE VARIATIONS, THREE MARKET VALUES

Suppose a startup threatens to decouple your business. This might not pose much of a threat if the startup lacks sufficient funding. How do we determine whether entrepreneurs are likely to get that funding? It turns out that we can roughly assess the likelihood of investor interest in a more rigorous way based on the type of decoupling a startup has chosen to use in order to disrupt markets.

In order to identify the most promising type of decoupling from an investment perspective, I assessed 325 startups based in the United States for which I had up-to-date market valuations.[23] Out of those, I identified fifty-five as decouplers focused on a single type of disruption: value creating, value charging, or value eroding.* I discovered

* With the others, either they employed all types of decoupling in multiple businesses (e.g., Amazon, Google, or Facebook), they used no decoupling at all, or I could not judge on the basis of their business description. In very few cases (e.g., Dropbox, Skype), a dis-

that the investor market seems to value the three types of decoupling quite differently. Investors assign much higher market value to value-creating decouplers. They assign the lowest market value to value-eroding decouplers, and they assign a value somewhere in the middle to the value-charging decouplers (*see Figure 4.4*).

Markets treat decouplers of value-creating activities most generously, as evidenced by the lucrative deals landed by the online communications company Skype (acquired by Microsoft in 2011 for $8.5 billion), the messaging and voice-over-internet-protocol (VoIP) company Viber (acquired by Rakuten in 2014 for $900 million), and Twitch (acquired by Amazon for $970 million in 2014).* Although these valuations vary widely, the decoupling of value-creating activities correlates with a median valuation of around $600 million (and an average of $2.7 billion, due to the aforementioned outliers).[24]

Investors regard a second category of decouplers—value-charging—less highly, giving them a median value of $350 million (on average $1.6 billion). These companies include the cloud storage company Dropbox (valued at $10 billion when it raised money in 2014), the digital music service Spotify (valued at $8.5 billion in 2015 before its IPO in 2018), Zynga (a $2.1 billion market capitalization in 2016), and JetSmarter, a marketplace that offers instant pricing and availability for private jets worldwide (valued at $1.5 billion in 2016).[25]

Decouplers of value-eroding activities are the least valuable to investors among the three categories. Rent the Runway, a company that rents designer clothing online, thus eliminating the need for customers to visit clothing boutiques and purchase expensive items, was valued in excess of $600 million in late 2016.[26] Online grocer

---

ruptor might be classified as pursuing two types of decoupling. In these cases, we chose the one most prominent to consumers, that which was explained front-and-center on the companies' websites. Further details are available in the endnotes.

* Note that while Skype does not charge for IP-only talking, it does charge for IP-to-telephony talking. Thus, it is not classified as a value-capturing decoupler via-à-vis telecom operators.

FIGURE 4.4 **MARKET VALUE BY DECOUPLING TYPE**

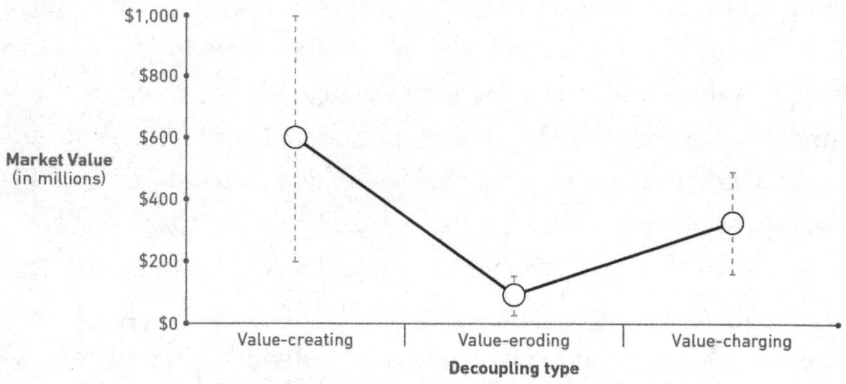

Note: N = 55 U.S.-based business-to-consumer startups using decoupling to disrupt markets, identified among 325 U.S.-based startups with investors' valuation of $10 million and higher that had their last funding round in 2016 (see endnotes for more details). Jagged vertical lines represent half of one standard deviation.

Fresh Direct, which allowed consumers to shop without going to the supermarket, was valued at $480 million as of mid-2016.[27] A notable outlier, Dollar Shave Club, was acquired by Unilever for $1 billion in 2016.[28] Value-eroding decoupling has a median market value of $100 million (with an average of nearly $500 million).

What accounts for these huge differences in valuations across types of decoupling? I can't say definitively. Digital decoupling is a very recent phenomenon, a new wave, and there are not enough examples in each of the three categories to perform a rigorous statistical analysis of valuation drivers. The lack of publicly available data prevents me from even controlling for other well-known sources of valuation such as growth rate, profitability, number of employees, and so on. When I've spoken before senior executives at large companies, some have conjectured that the lower average valuation for value-eroding decouplers owes to the more limited upside potential that exists for investors. A firm can eliminate only so many value-eroding activities until it runs out of opportunities or begins to eliminate value-creating activities as well. Executives have also pointed out that this type of decoupling is easily copied by other startups as well as by incumbents. For instance, after Birchbox eliminated the need for people to go to the store in order to get samples of beauty products to test, dozens of sample and subscription box startups copied its model.

Executives sometimes explain the higher average valuations of value-charging decouplers by noting that these firms can grow quickly and acquire customers, as they provide clear and compelling reasons for customers to switch. Fast growth is highly valued by investors. At the same time, there is no guarantee that the decoupler will find an alternative source of revenue to justify the business. This uncertainty in monetization is reflected in the large variation in observed valuations.

To explain the high valuation applied to value-creating decouplers, executives have pointed to the larger upside that arises when a startup steals customers from incumbents while at the same time still counting on incumbents to deliver value from them. This upside seems more sustainable and monetizable, and less likely to be copied (thanks to the startup's technology or high switching cost advantage). Investors thus see major upside potential, and they value these startups more highly. Audience members often cite Skype, Twitch, and WhatsApp, all of which had huge initial growth rates, as examples.

As a caveat, my observations about market valuations are based on an analysis of only fifty-five U.S. firms that vary in terms of industry, profitability, time of market entry, and size. Also, I included in the above analysis only disruptors that were performing a single and identifiable type of decoupling at the time. For that reason, I excluded large tech firms such as Amazon, Alphabet, and Facebook (owner of WhatsApp, Instagram, and Oculus). It is thus best to treat this analysis as only an early indication of possible differences in investor preference by type of decoupling. As more disruptors decouple in different ways, we'll be able to better assess the relationship between market value and type of decoupling. Still, it seems likely that the type of decoupling matters to venture capital markets. And if it does, then incumbents have a useful tool at their disposal. The more valuable the type of decoupling is to investors, the more capital a startup is likely to amass, and the larger the war chest it will have at its disposal when coming after your business. Be especially wary of value-creating and value-charging decouplers. Value-eroding decouplers will likely pose less of a threat and can be dealt with differently.

How Incumbents Can Respond

Ask entrepreneurs how they go about disrupting a market, and you'll hear that startups seem to succeed on the basis of trial and error, stumbling upon innovation. But as we've seen, there is more than this to a successful startup when the startup in question is a decoupler. Having observed many startups at close range, I've distilled a formula that all successful decouplers follow in one form or another, often without realizing it. Entrepreneurs intent on decoupling tend to zigzag furiously, and not every twist and turn can be explained rationally (nor is that even necessary). But the underlying logic of the successful ones is sound, and it forms the basis of a recipe to decouple. While never a guarantee of success, it is possible to engineer it.

I began the chapter by showing that we can engineer business model innovation by stacking three layers.* The first layer is the traditional way of doing things, the standard business model. Here, incumbents enjoy an advantage relative to startups, since you know this layer better than they do. While they might certainly know how your business works, in many instances they will never know it as well as you do. You should leverage this advantage, building on your

* We can use this approach in innovative product or technologies as well, but it holds the greatest potential in the designing of innovative business models.

strengths. In the next layer, digitization, you might enjoy an advantage if you replicate your business online and deliver more benefits to customers than downsides. Otherwise, startups performing the same process might hold an edge. In the last layer, incremental innovation can tip the advantage in favor of the player who comes up with the most innovative addition to the two previous layers. In some cases, the proposed innovation might be so dramatic that it completely alters the nature of the business. Wikipedia's last layer of innovation, using crowdsourcing to write and review articles, departs significantly from traditional print encyclopedias such as Britannica and even digital versions such as Microsoft Encarta.

When the incremental innovation is based on decoupling, all successful decouplers manage to perform the five critical steps outlined earlier: they identify a target segment and its CVC, classify the CVC activities, identify weak links between CVC activities, break the weak links, and predict how incumbents will respond. Entrepreneurs can use this formula to create innovative business models in a more systematic and structured way, thus reducing their risk. Incumbents can use the recipe to disrupt their own businesses, or those of other incumbents.

Whether decouplers consciously follow this recipe or just intuitively understand the reasoning behind the critical steps for success, incumbents should be prepared for the arrival of additional would-be decouplers. With a formula in hand, more entrepreneurs will become significantly better challengers. Unlike the Twitch founders, who stumbled their way to success, this new generation of decouplers will likely make fewer mistakes and succeed more quickly.

Instead of looking at the trajectory of each new threat, you might well need a "radar system" in place to monitor your space for threats, in order to keep track of the decouplers entering and operating in your market. You'll also need to consider more fully how your company should respond to any threats. I have begun to distinguish different levels of risk posed by different types of decouplers, based on their fund-raising capabilities. If the potential loss to your business is clear and their funding firepower is high—and in the case of value-creating decouplers, it is—then sound the alarm and prepare to respond. Incumbents have many options from which to choose in mounting a response. Fortunately, we can analyze potential responses by placing them in a few distinct categories, as I'll describe in Chapter 5.

PART II
Responding to Decoupling

As we've seen, a new approach to digital disruption has been taking over many industries, one characterized by the breaking or "decoupling" of links between adjacent customer activities. Many people assume that startups armed with new technology drive disruption. But decoupling generally arises from business model innovations designed to help satisfy shifting *customer* needs and desires.

Many startups have exploited the customer's changing needs and behaviors in a haphazard manner through decoupling. But we can actually identify a systematic process or roadmap that any business can use to deliberately engineer this class of disruption. Decoupling has a recipe. Like a culinary recipe, it doesn't guarantee success, but it is invaluable to new challengers entering various industries, as well as to defending companies who need to mount a response.

Chapters 5 and 6 cover the major avenues for responding to

decoupling. Regardless of the industry or the challengers that an established company faces, there are only a few broad avenues for responding, which I address in Chapter 5. Before deciding which one to take, you need to know the options, their upsides and risks. Chapter 6 shows you how to determine what's at stake and how to decide when it is time to respond to decoupling. A meticulous analysis of risks (e.g., risk of loss due to the wrong action versus the risk of loss due to inaction) is paramount when deciding how incumbents should respond to the rise of decoupling in their industries.

5

AVENUES OF RESPONSE

It was a summer morning in 1895, and a forty-year-old Pennsylvania bottle cap salesman and serial inventor named King Camp Gillette had a problem. He needed to shave to get ready for work, but his razor was dull—"beyond the point of successful stropping," as he later wrote to his wife. Back in those days, the remedy for a dull blade was a visit to a barber or cutler, who would sharpen it using professional tools. But that was inconvenient, and there was no guarantee that the sharpening would succeed. If the blade was beyond help, Gillette would have to pay up to $1.50—about the price of a pair of shoes—to buy an entirely new blade.

By this time, Gillette had become obsessed with finding an idea for a product that would make him rich and famous. Watching his creative torments, his boss at Crown Cork and Seal Company offered a portentous piece of advice: "Why don't you try to think of something like [a bottle cap] which, when once used, is thrown away, and the customer keeps coming back for more?"[1] Traveling to clients by train, Gillette often pondered a long list of items that people used en masse and that could be made disposable.

On this particular morning, Gillette experienced a flash of insight. Why not make a *razor* disposable? If he could bring to market a cheap blade, men could use it to shave until it got dull, and then simply replace it with a new one. No more stropping. No more visits to barbers or cutlers.

"I have got it," Gillette wrote to his wife. "Our fortunes are made."[2]

Well, not quite yet. In the absence of a modern-day venture capital industry, it took Gillette eight years to get investors, figure out the technology, and start production. But Gillette persevered, and in 1903 he went to market, selling his razor, together with twelve blades, for $5, with additional packs of twelve blades selling for $1. During his first year, he sold 51 razors and 14 dozen blades. His second year, he sold 91,000 razors and 10,000 dozen blades. Sales grew steadily from there, reaching 1 million razors and 10 million blade sets by 1917.

One challenge that emerged was copycats. In 1921, with his initial patents expiring, Gillette filed a new application for an "improved" razor technology, and sold his "old" razors at a discount for less than a dollar apiece. Result: sales of his razors jumped to over 4 million. To the company's surprise, the bigger user base of razors drove demand for replacement blade sets, even though those were still selling at the initial price. Profiting from this realization, the company reduced the number of blades in its $1 packs, effectively increasing the price per blade. After subsequent price increases, the razor became cheaper than a pack of replacement blades.[3]

Without realizing it, Gillette had stumbled upon a powerful new business model for modularized products. Companies could build a user base by selling cheaply or even giving away the durable component of its product, in this case the razor, and make money by selling the disposable component, here the blades, at a high margin. For Gillette, this "razor-and-blades" model, as it is now called, served as a source of vast and sustainable profits. A century later, Gillette was the undisputed leader of the razor market with a share of around 80 percent in the United States and 66 percent worldwide.[4] The model had also taken hold and spread into unrelated industries, including printers and ink cartridges, videogame consoles and games, and e-readers and e-books.[5]

As powerful a disruptive force as the "razor-and-blades" model was, it was hardly invulnerable. In early 2011, a thirtysomething entrepreneur named Michael Dubin with no experience in the shaving industry built a website to offer razors online via subscription. To say the website caught fire is an understatement. By 2015, an incredible 51 percent of all online sales of razors came from Dubin's Dollar Shave Club (DSC), dwarfing Gillette's 21 percent in online sales.[6] How did an undisputed industry leader whose name was virtually synonymous with the category fall prey to an outsider with nothing but a website and a product outsourced to a manufacturer in Korea?[7]

Did DSC have a better product? No, the product was the same "lemonade," a standard plastic razor with two-, four-, or six-blade disposable cartridges. Did DSC market its products better? Some argued that the company took off after a video went viral with a memorable pitch from Michael: "Are the blades any good? No, our blades are f***ing great."[8] But Gillette was part of Procter & Gamble, the world's largest advertiser. In 2014 alone, Proctor & Gamble spent *$10 billion* on advertising. Gillette had access to the biggest wallet, the best ad agencies, and all types of media. So if it wasn't marketing, did DSC deliver more convenience to shoppers? Not even close. Both companies could ship razors to your doorstep with similar shipping services.

Then I posed the question to my students, most of whom had become DSC subscribers. Jonathan, one of my best students, had an answer. As a kid, he told me, he had watched his father shave frequently for his job. His father had bought Gillette razors because they were the best, and they were cheap. But his father also spent a big chunk of change on replacement blades. When Jonathan grew up and began to shave himself, he felt frustrated at how expensive it was to keep replacing Gillette blades. "Gillette has been holding us hostage," he remembered thinking, "forcing us to buy their expensive blades. These things can't possibly cost that much to manufacture."

Then an unknown startup named DSC came along, promising no more of the famous razor-and-blade pricing model that made you feel like a hostage. Its value proposition: "No hidden costs. Cancel anytime. You're never locked in."[9] After years of seeing his father locked in, suffering in what seemed like an abusive relationship with Gillette, Jonathan could finally break away. DSC offered him the transparency of a standard pay-as-you-go model. And he took it, a switch that has saved him hundreds of dollars in shaving costs over the years.

As Jonathan's story suggests, the razor-and-blades business model works well in two distinct situations. First, it works when a myopic consumer focuses on the short term at the expense of the long term. This consumer buys a cheap Gillette razor or Lexmark printer only to later unknowingly pay exorbitant prices for the replacement blades or ink. Jonathan, of course, was not one of these consumers. After watching his dad, he knew how costly Gillette's offering was over the long term. Unfortunately, before DSC appeared, the razor-and-blade model had reduced consumer choice in the market, displacing other options (apart from electric shavers and cheap disposable razors) that might have pleased consumers like Jonathan. Jonathan had no real choice—and that is the second situation in which the razor-and-blade model works. Like millions of other consumers, Jonathan was forced to endure the dearth of similar-quality alternatives.

Large companies such as Gillette with razor-and-blade-type models have captured so much excess value from customers that they have little incentive to adapt their business model to modern times. Frankly, it's the *last* thing they want to do. In 2004, before being bought by Procter & Gamble, Gillette reported a remarkable 60 percent gross margin.[10] To protect such high margins, companies like Gillette invest in patents for products as simple as razors. They justify those patents by arguing that they spend hundreds of millions of dollars on research and development every year, and their investment requires protection. As of July 2017, Gillette held almost two thousand patents, all of which had been granted since 1975. In 2012 alone, after DSC had come onto the scene, Gillette obtained 125 new patents. Remember, we're not talking about a jet engine or a complex new way of delivering a vaccine. We're talking about a razor! By comparison, pharma giant Pfizer received fifty-seven U.S. patents in 2015, and New York University's researchers—all of them—received a sum total of sixty-three. Mazda took sixty-three, Black & Decker seventy-four, and Airbus's helicopter division received seventy-five (in the United States).[11] How can a maker of disposable razors and shaving creams require so many more patents than makers of helicopters or pharmaceuticals?

During the early 1900s, Gillette used patents to protect a new and highly innovative product from copycats. But by the late 1900s, Gillette was using patents covering even the merest tweak to its razor or blades as a means of fending off any prospect of decoupling. Gillette was overserving the customer with ever smaller incremental innovations, and overcharging for them—all to protect its lucrative business model. And when that wasn't enough, Gillette—like other incumbents—turned to another tactic: acquiring companies that so much as hinted they would come to market with an alternative business model. In 2009, for instance, Procter & Gamble spent $60 million to buy high-end grooming brand The Art of Shaving.[12]

In the jargon of business, these incumbent companies create "barriers," "walls," or "moats" around their business models. But there's a big problem with creating these moats around your castle. It's not that the strategy doesn't work. Rather, it works *too* well—until one day it doesn't. For Gillette, that day was March 6, 2012, when DSC launched its Executive razor, a six-blade product that was just as good as Gillette's high-end razor.[13] From then on, Gillette's market share slid. Men told one another about DSC, and the product went viral.

Jonathan and other male millennials were the first ones to adopt. They then served as evangelists for the product, "contaminating" their fathers and grandfathers with the idea of switching over. Other grooming products startups such as Harry's joined the party in 2013, launching their own products online. And the rest is history.[14]

I asked my students whether they would go back to Gillette if the company reduced its replacement blade prices to match DSC's. Their response: a near-unanimous no. That's understandable. Just as people who leave abusive romantic relationships are loath to return, so, too, are customers in abusive commercial relationships. Going against the customer's desires can work for some time, but not forever. Eventually a new company arises to offer customers what they really need. The simple truth is this: there is no larger risk to your business than going against customers' needs and wants.

Now that you understand how decoupling works, and how to engineer decoupling, it's time to address the burning question: *How do I respond to this new wave of digital disruption?* Although it might seem as if incumbents have a dizzying number of responses from which to choose, in truth only two broad avenues exist as first-line responses (although, as we'll see, many possible actions or tactics can fall under each). This stark reality should come as some comfort. You don't have to sift through dozens of potential ways of responding. But you do need to determine which of the two primary avenues to pursue. And that, it turns out, is far from straightforward.

The Two Broad Avenues of Response

As we've seen, decoupling unfolds in a patterned way across industries. It occurs in situations where the incumbent company delivers two or more consumption activities to customers and then charges for the coupled activities. Unlike with bundled products, coupled activities can always be broken apart into at least two, an activity that creates value (for instance, watching a TV show, talking to a friend on the phone, or browsing in-store for the right product) and an activity through which the company charges for value (for instance, getting viewers to watch ads, pay a subscription, connect to a mobile network, or buy a product on the shelf).* When a new entrant decouples the two activities and attempts to deliver a value-creating activity without a value-charging one, and when the decoupler monetizes this either by charging others (such as advertisers, retailers, or heavy users) or by simply charging less, established businesses face a serious threat. If they are to survive, they must mount a response.

Most established businesses often attempt to respond in one of three ways: they imitate the entrant, they buy it out, or they attempt to suffocate it by drastically reducing prices. Yet these options carry unintended consequences for the rest of your organization, even if they prove successful. Incumbents that imitate startups might see dramatically reduced profits. Small startups might be able to make money on the significantly lower revenues or tighter margins that decoupling usually yields, but large organizations such as NBC, Telefonica, and Gillette lack the cost structure to support that. Buying the disruptor isn't risk free, either. Apart from such a purchase eating into its cash reserves, an incumbent might have trouble integrating a disruptor smoothly into its existing business. Many acquisitions of tech companies have flopped, most famously Time Warner's purchase of AOL (resulting in a $99 billion write-off), HP's purchase of Autonomy (an $8.8 billion write-off), and Microsoft's purchase of onetime tech darling Nokia (a $7.6 billion write-off). Finally, drastically reducing prices to stifle a disruptor also impacts profits, and it might carry legal ramifications if the U.S. Justice Department perceives it as an anticompetitive practice.

Given these concerns, managers of incumbent companies should

* As I explained in Chapter 3, in some cases a third type of activity exists, value-eroding activities.

refrain from responding too quickly. To the extent that decoupling is a local problem (in other words, affecting only a portion of the customer value chain and certain customers), incumbents should treat it locally. Best Buy saw that customers were showrooming in categories such as consumer electronics, electronic baby equipment, and electronic toys, but not in other categories such as media, appliances, and accessories. In crafting a response, Best Buy did not intervene by making changes that affected the entire store. They focused only on the electronics section.

Mimicking, buying, or launching a price war are not really local and isolated interventions; they potentially affect the incumbent's entire organization. Do other responses exist that focus only on the core problem? It turns out that the responses fall into two broad avenues. To develop an intuitive understanding of them, let's first consider a hypothetical scenario. Say you run a company that sells cakes with frosting. A new startup allows your younger customers to acquire only the frosting, leaving you to deal with mountains of unpurchased frosting as you continue to bake and sell cakes. What can you do? One option is to force all cake buyers to purchase both cake and frosting together. The other alternative is to let customers buy only what they want. In other words, you can *recouple* the cake and the frosting back together, or you can *preemptively decouple* your cakes, allowing each part to be sold separately.* These two avenues are available to all incumbents, irrespective of industry. Let's examine each one in turn.

RECOUPLING

In my experience, established companies faced with decoupling initially respond by attempting to recouple the two (or more) activities

* When we are talking about two products, as in frosting and cake, broken apart, the precise terminology is "unbundling." But I use the cake example for the purpose of explaining the intuition behind the options for decoupling, as it is easily relatable.

that have been split apart. They require customers to consume them jointly, even if customers prefer to fulfill only some activities with the incumbent and others with the decoupler. If others break apart your customers' value chain, the obvious first response is to glue it back together. Companies achieve this in a variety of ways: through contracts with customers, reducing product compatibility, controlling platform standards, using legal measures to enforce terms of use, and closing software systems.

Incumbents in the television industry, for instance, have deployed a number of recoupling tactics. In 1999, DVR manufacturers such as TiVo and ReplayTV developed hardware to allow TV viewers to record programming and then skip the ads. This hardware in effect enabled viewers to decouple the activity of viewing shows from that of viewing ads. In response, network broadcasters have shown ads during (not after) the programs, making use of product placements, pop-up ads around the edges of the screen, and brand-sponsored content. TV companies have also worked with DVR manufacturers like TiVo to limit how much advertising watchers can skip, suing other manufacturers that didn't comply.

These recoupling approaches have often appeared to work, yet their long-term sustainability remains in question. TV viewers who really hated advertising quickly embraced online video platforms such as Netflix, HBO Now, and Amazon Video that did away with commercials. Frustrated, these viewers stopped watching traditional TV and canceled their cable subscriptions. TiVo eventually had to choose between cozying up to broadcasters or appealing to its potential customer base of cord-cutting viewers. In 2015, the company decided to "give commercials the finger" (that's an actual quote from a TiVo press release), offering a Skip Mode that allowed users to bypass commercial breaks automatically.[15]

In the retail industry, we find many attempts to recouple customer activities. We've seen that showrooming—browsing products in a physical store and then comparing prices using a mobile app—has threatened physical retailers tremendously. Many stores can't compete with online-only merchants that don't carry the high cost of maintaining a physical footprint or sales staff. Small retailers face the greatest challenge. To meet it, one small retailer—Celiac Supplies, a specialty gluten-free grocery store based in Brisbane, Australia—decided to require every in-store customer either to make a purchase or to pay a $5 "just looking" fee for browsing. Figuring that the fee would compel many shoppers to make a purchase, Celiac saw the policy as a way of preventing online retailers from harvesting demand built at its store.[16] While extreme, the policy is an incumbent's clear attempt to glue back the browsing and buying activities that had been broken by Amazon and others.

Recoupling may work if a firm that has served its customers across multiple activities can either *increase* the cost to them of fulfilling these activities using multiple firms (thus reducing the specialization forces, as described in Chapter 3) or *reduce* the cost to exclusively serve the customers across all their CVC activities (thus increasing the integration forces). Celiac Supplies, by implementing this new $5 charge policy, tried to increase the cost shoppers would incur to specialize. Celiac Supplies was creating value for customers in showcasing novel and niche products not available elsewhere. Yet it wasn't capturing any of this value if a shopper learned in-store, bought online, and walked out the door empty-handed. Celiac Supplies needed to get paid somehow. So it took action to make that happen, albeit action that was extreme and ill-advised.

What else could Celiac Supplies have done to better implement recoupling? One approach is to reconfigure value-charging activities (which affect the monetary costs of integration) or to eliminate value-eroding activities (which affect the effort or time costs of integration). Other retailers have succeeded with such subtler forms of recoupling—for instance, charging membership fees (as Costco does), or charging ancillary fees for amenities such as onsite parking in major cities. However, these practices also carry some risk, as consumers can question the value of the core activity they seek and potentially elect to abandon the company altogether. Another alternative is to add value-creating activities. Ask yourself, "How can I increase the total value offered to my customer, incentivizing him or her to stick with me for the entire CVC?" In simple terms, recoupling involves either making it more worthwhile for customers to stick around or making it costlier for them to leave you, Gillette-style.

In both the Celiac Supply and television industry examples, incumbents quickly attempted recoupling via changes in value charging, for the most part. Incumbents can also recouple in other, more forceful ways. Telecom operators have used technologies such as SIM cards and software to block customers from switching telecom networks after buying a mobile device with them. They have also used two-year contracts to try to prevent customers from decoupling the purchase of a device from the usage of the network for mobile communication. Software developers such as Microsoft, Adobe, and Oracle have historically implemented end-user licensing agreements that buyers have to sign as a precondition for usage. Some clauses prohibit the adaptation, translation, and modification of their software or code for integration with other software. And lastly, incumbents can turn to legal and political lobbying as a means of recoupling.* Consider, for instance, the hotel industry's attempts in cities including New York, San Francisco, and Paris to prevent property owners from listing their homes for short-term rental on sites such as Airbnb. Likewise, U.S. news publishers have asked Congress for a limited antitrust exemption so that they can negotiate collectively with digital platforms such as Facebook and Google, digital media companies that decoupled creation from distribution of news content.

All of these attempts to recouple consumer activities are somewhat

* American firms reportedly spend $3 billion per year on lobbying, according to the *Economist* (April 15, 2017, 59).

dangerous for incumbents, if only because the company in question is going against the grain of customer desires. Customers wish to decouple, startups are providing an option for them to break free, and incumbents are trying to keep the floodgates closed. Any recoupling attempt should thus attend closely to two issues: how long can you, the incumbent, keep the floodgates closed? And how much is it going to cost you to do so? In this regard, the printer and ink toner industry offers a cautionary tale.

RECOUPLERS, BEWARE

Gillette's razor-and-blade model was so ingenious that other durable consumer goods manufacturers started to adapt it for their businesses. They lowered prices on the durable components to snare customers quickly, even if it meant losing money. And they made up for any losses by capturing high margins on the replenishable module, in effect subsidizing the durable component. Since customers could buy the durable components so cheaply, the model seemed to benefit consumers and manufacturers alike. Kodak used the razor-and-blade model to subsidize cameras, making up for it with high-margin film. Printer manufacturers such as HP, Canon, and Lexmark sold subsidized printers, making up for it by selling high-margin toner and ink. More recently, Nestlé adopted the model for its widely popular Nespresso business unit, selling high-end espresso coffeemakers at low prices and making most of their money on the coffee pods.

But the razor-and-blade model comes with a catch: it works for the company only if consumers couple their shopping process, buying the Gillette razor, Nespresso coffeemaker, or HP printer, and then subsequently and repeatedly buying the blades, pods, and toner from the same company. If customers buy the replenishable parts elsewhere, companies can't offset their subsidization of the durable component. It's for this reason that large manufacturers go to such great lengths to ensure that only the replenished products that they make are technically and legally compatible with their devices (think Gillette's thousands of patents). When upstarts threaten to decouple the purchase of durable and replenishable parts, these incumbents fight back . . . hard.

For years, a small family-run business called Impression Products has been buying used toner cartridges, filling them with toner, and selling them to owners of copiers and printers at prices 30 to 50 percent lower than Lexmark was charging for new toners. Impression Products was responding to abiding customer desires for cheaper toner. As a comedic writer put it: "Either printer ink is made from unicorn blood or we're all getting screwed [by printer manufacturers]."[17] In order to make sure the used toner cartridges would work, Impression Products disabled a chip in the cartridges that detected when they were being reused and blocked their usage. As a result, Lexmark printers didn't detect these refills, and customers could use them to print more cheaply.

Lexmark wasn't at all happy about Impression Products' toner cartridge business. In 2013, the company sued, claiming that the patent rights covering its printers allowed it to enforce unauthorized usage of its components, such as unapproved toner. Impression Products countered by claiming that patents of products should not restrict the customers' usage of the product *after* purchase. Once people buy a product, Impression Products argued, they should be able to do whatever they want with it. Observers realized that a verdict in the case would reverberate far beyond the printing industry. According to a *Fortune* article, if patent owners had the broad ability to assert control over a customer's usage of products after buying them, then "a [patent owner could sell] pharmaceuticals 'only to be swallowed whole,' or a radio 'only for use on Sundays,' and sue someone who splits his pills or forgets the day of the week for patent infringement." In the auto industry, manufacturers could scuttle the entire used car market by selling cars with a "no resale" proviso. Wherever you looked, the article noted, patent owners could claim that "a certain use of a product is unauthorized, and that the owner must pay damages."[18]

As the case worked its way up to the U.S. Supreme Court, companies in many industries lined up on both sides. Firms such as Costco, the phone maker HTC, and Intel supported Impression Products, while phone chip manufacturer Qualcomm and a variety of pharmaceutical makers and patent-holding companies supported Lexmark. It was, in the words of one news service, "a patent case that affects everyone"—a battle between decouplers and recouplers, waged over the question of whether consumers could decouple razor-and-blade-type business models. In 2017, after four years of litigation, the Supreme Court ruled seven to one in favor of Impression Products. As the Court's decision stated, Lexmark had exhausted its patent rights when it sold its printers and ink cartridges, and it could not impose any usage restrictions on consumers or third-party suppliers.[19] This ruling enforced the customer's right to decouple the purchase of a durable module (e.g., printer, razor, car) from the repair and usage of replenishable modules (e.g., ink, blades, car parts) from other providers. Power to the people!

If you are an incumbent, this ruling should serve as a wake-up call. Your customers might feel strongly motivated to decouple you. And that motivation might give rise to startups deploying new business models, technologies, or legislation to circumvent your recoupling efforts. Can you afford to hold the floodgates closed by force, against your customers' will? For how long? And at what cost? Before opting for recoupling, think through each of these questions. And don't underestimate the cost to your business of forcibly recoupling. Between 2013 to 2016, while Lexmark's lawsuit was pending, the company's total revenues on its printer business fell 7 percent while revenues of other major players rose. As Lexmark was busy trying to recouple printer and ink through legal means, major market competitors chipped away at its business.[20]

PREEMPTIVE DECOUPLING

Incumbents do have a viable alternative to recoupling that is also minimally invasive. They can do just the opposite, opening the floodgates themselves by *preemptively decoupling* two or more activities. Returning to our cake analogy, rather than forcing customers to buy and eat its cake with frosting, a baker can decide to sell customers only the cake, or only the frosting, as per the customer's wishes. Taking this to the extreme, incumbents in any industry could decide to allow customers to pick and choose any subset of the activities that it delivers in a customer value chain.

It may well be that your present business model doesn't support such a drastic change. If you decouple activities that create value from those that capture it, you run the risk of offering value-charging activities without value-creating ones to go with it. Why, for instance, would anyone want to turn on the TV just to watch ads? You also run the risk of offering value-creating activities without value-charging ones—an even worse situation. Why would any telecom company allow people to use its cellular network without paying for it in the form of a subscription or pay-as-you-go fee? Quite obviously, decoupling yourself does not always make sense.

To preemptively decouple in a way that rewards both customers and the company, and that is hence sustainable, you might have to change your business model. To understand how to go about doing that, let's perform a quick thought experiment. Say you are the owner of Wholeana, a fictitious, high-end restaurant located in Boston, Massachusetts. You fulfill four activities in the diner's CVC: making a reservation, occupying a table, consuming drinks and dinner, and accepting payment. In general, your customers perform all four in a coupled manner, that is, with you.

Let's imagine that a new startup disrupted the fine dining market in all possible ways. It created technology that allowed patrons to reserve tables anywhere, whether or not the restaurant allowed it. Lobbying politicians, it got laws passed allowing people to occupy restaurant tables without buying anything and to bring in any food they wanted from outside the restaurant. If this last scenario strikes you as fanciful, consider that legislation on a number of occasions has granted the separation of products and services. Examples include energy in the European Union (households are free to switch their energy supplier), textbooks in the United States (students are free to resell used textbooks, and buyers cannot be barred in any way from using them), and auto repair services in Poland (parts manufacturers and dealers can produce parts and perform maintenance services for any brand of car they wish).

In addition, imagine that this disruptor created an on-demand app that allowed customers to order food and drinks from any establishment with the touch of a button. A diner could reserve a nice table at your fine establishment using the app. He could arrive on the premises and sit there with his party. He could pull out an app and order drinks from one bar and dinner from another restaurant, all delivered to his table at Wholeana. His party could dine and enjoy, and when you, the owner, brought the check, this customer would pay only for what he and his party consumed from Wholeana's kitchen.

In this instance, technology and legislation prohibit you from recoupling the various customer activities. So instead you decide to decouple all four activities for your patrons so that they can freely pick and choose the activities they want Wholeana to fulfill. For that to even begin to make economic sense, you must follow one critical law of business model decomposition: rebalancing.

Rebalancing: Create value at every point where you attempt to capture value, and capture value at every point where you attempt to create value.

If Wholeana is going to allow people to reserve tables through its reservation system and then not order its own food, then Wholeana needs to charge for this value-creating activity. After all, customers benefit from having tables waiting for them when they arrive. If Wholeana allows its patrons to use another reservation system to reserve a table at Wholeana, or if it allows them to order drinks and food from outside vendors, then Wholeana must charge them for the activity of occupying one of Wholeana's tables. All of these activities create value for customers. In a totally decoupled CVC, Wholeana needs to charge for each value-created activity if and precisely when customers perform it.* As regards the last activity, paying the bill at the end of the meal, Wholeana can abolish bill-paying and redistribute this into value-charging activities throughout the restaurant experience. If it does decide to charge at the end, Wholeana needs to build some value for the customer into that final value-charging activity—for instance, by allowing the customer to enjoy live music or some other form of entertainment. This process of carefully marrying activities that create value with those that charge for them is what I call rebalancing.[21] It is a near foolproof way of avoiding value leakage, as I will explain in the next section.

EXAMPLES OF REBALANCING

You might wonder why preemptive decoupling requires rebalancing. Zynga, SuperCell, and other mobile game developers have decoupled the traditional videogame industry by allowing gamers to play games without paying the $60-plus up-front price to acquire them. Skype, Google Hangouts, and other VoIP providers decoupled telecoms by providing telecommunications for free or at prices much

* The customer does not need to physically pay at every instant she receives value, but rather eventually be charged for it.

lower than those charged by telecom companies, who still needed to build and maintain their networks. Amazon decoupled by allowing shoppers to benefit from browsing at physical stores and still get the cheaper deal at Amazon.com. These disruptors could provide highly valuable services and not charge for them as incumbents did because they operated under different business models that relied upon a combination of other revenue sources, lower pricing levels, and lower marginal costs. Incumbents that might have considered joining these decouplers and decoupling themselves couldn't just mimic their challengers. They needed to adapt their business models to decouple in an economically sustainable manner. *That* is what rebalancing aims to achieve.

For a successful example of rebalancing, consider Best Buy's response to decoupling. By allowing people to interact physically with products, retailers create value for them. In so doing, brick-and-mortar retailers accrue high fixed costs associated with maintaining and staffing a physical store. For Best Buy, simply matching Amazon's prices helped for a while, but it didn't provide a long-term solution. Best Buy moved instead to charge manufacturers for the right to display products at its stores. As Best Buy concluded, it had long been creating value for manufacturers (who didn't care where customers bought their products), but it hadn't been capturing this value. Best Buy thus *rebalanced* by capturing value via manufacturer payments (known as slotting fees) at the very moment this value was created (i.e., when customers experienced their products). This move departed drastically from Best Buy's traditional retailing business model, which formerly had relied on margins on goods sold. Now Best Buy makes money irrespective of whether customers buy a television set at its stores or not.

In adding slotting fees as a revenue source to its business model, Best Buy put itself in an enviable position. It didn't go against customers' desires, as it would have by recoupling. If shoppers valued touching and testing electronics before buying, then retailers should encourage them to do so. Barring them from using apps for online price comparisons would have constituted a stopgap solution at best. Also, Best Buy carefully adjusted its pricing policy to reflect new competitors, instituting an automatic and permanent price-matching policy. As a result of this policy, most products in the store sold at prices similar to those on any online store.* This policy ensured that Best Buy didn't lose sales to online competitors solely on the basis of price.

If a price policy shift in response to a new entrant translates into lower income, as it almost always does, incumbents must find other revenue sources. Although they may feel tempted to start by quickly launching new services, I advise companies to look instead for new revenues systematically by mapping out the customer's value chain and spotting activities that create value and for which incumbents are not yet charging.

In certain contexts, identifying unremunerated activities isn't a simple exercise. If you're a retailer, media company, or digital platform, you have more than one customer (e.g., consumer and supplier), and you should perform this analysis separately for each type of customer. Best Buy figured out that its suppliers were obtaining a "free service" when the retailer displayed their new electronics on the shelf and shoppers saw and tried them in-store, then bought them online. The retailer decided to transform this activity into one for which it charged value. In order to ensure it was abiding by the first part of the rebalancing rule, Best Buy figured out a way to further create value at the point where it wanted to capture value. It built high-end, freestanding shelves, located them in a central part of the store away from competing products, and drew attention to them with big, bright signage. In executing this tactic, Best Buy borrowed the "store-within-a-store" concept commonly used by department stores.

* In conversations with me, CEO Herbert Joly revealed that marketplaces such as eBay and Amazon Marketplace were excluded from the price-matching policy.

Profiting from the trend in showrooming, Best Buy effectively decoupled itself. It can now coexist somewhat peaceably with both new customer shopping habits and Best Buy's disruptor, Amazon. Best Buy is hardly alone in successfully rebalancing its business. In the mid-2000s, so-called over-the-top (OTT) mobile apps such as Skype, WhatsApp, and Viber were eating into revenues at the Spanish telecom company Telefonica. Many of Telefonica's subscribers signed up for a mobile plan, reduced their voice and text message usage to a minimum in order to lower their phone bill, and then used OTTs for their primary communication needs.* The OTT players had decoupled the connectivity that was necessary for any two parties to talk—an activity still provided by Telefonica—from the actual person-to-person communication, which mobile voice and messaging apps provided. Unfortunately for Telefonica, its original business model relied heavily on recurring revenues from voice-based communication services and not from connectivity, which Telefonica partially subsidized in some countries.

At first, Telefonica and other telecom operators around the world tried recoupling. They attempted to block OTT apps from using their networks, deploying technology to prevent subscribers from accessing Skype and WhatsApp. After subscribers found work-arounds, operators tried to get legislation passed to forbid the OTT's free-riding behavior. Most European governments declined to pass such laws, realizing that OTTs benefited consumers.

Coming to grips with the reality that neither the new customer behavior nor the OTT's would disappear anytime soon, Telefonica shifted its strategy to rebalancing. The company changed its pricing policy, charging more for connectivity, an activity that created value for the customers but that Telefonica had previously provided free or at highly subsidized rates. At the same time, Telefonica charged

* Unlike in the United States, in 2014 many countries still operated on a pay-per-usage basis for voice and text.

significantly less for voice and text communication, shifting it to a fixed fee rather than a charge based on usage volume. In a case study I wrote in 2012, I described how Telefonica implemented this pricing policy change differently for each of the twenty-four countries in which it operated, accounting for differences in usage behavior. In some countries with high OTT usage, Telefonica began charging a flat fee for unlimited talking or texting. This new pricing policy dramatically reduced consumers' monetary incentives to use OTTs. Customers still use them, but not nearly as much as some had. (Since then, telecoms have had trouble matching the constant innovation of OTT services, accounting in part for these services' continued growth.) By creating value for the consumer (reducing the costs of calls and messaging) and charging for value elsewhere (connectivity), telecom operators like Telefonica rebalanced their business models, a move that in turn allowed them to coexist profitably with consumers' new behaviors and the industry's savvy decouplers.

Rebalance Your Business Model

Recoupling differs fundamentally from decoupling yourself in that it causes your company to go against prevailing customer desires. Sometimes your customers *want* to specialize. They don't want an established company—yours—to force them to fulfill all of their CVC activities with the same firm. I like to think of customer decoupling desires as akin to the concept of entropy in physics. Physical systems such as electrons, stars, and my daughter's bedroom naturally become more disorganized over time. Its level of entropy, a measure of a system's disorganization, rises. You can resist the law of entropy, but only by expending energy (in the case of my daughter's bedroom, a lot of energy) to render a given system more orderly and to reverse the tendency toward disorganization. Likewise, decoupling renders a market more chaotic, in the sense that customers now rely on multiple companies to perform a variety of activities they formerly performed neatly and profitably with a single company. Companies can push back against customers' desires, but it takes effort—all that precious time, attention, and money devoted to developing new recoupling technologies, devising and enforcing restrictive contracts, lobbying politicians, and so on. Going against the customer will certainly cost you. Alternatively, going in favor of the customer by rebalancing may not if done right.

Let's examine a tool you can use to help understand *where* to rebalance in case you do decide to pursue preemptive decoupling.

LEAKAGE

When advising established companies on rebalancing, I like to begin by first mapping out the entire CVC of my client's customers in as much detail as possible. I specify all the activities I can discern that bear on how a customer actually learns of my client's product or service, evaluates it, compares it with other products or services, chooses it, pays for it, uses it, reuses it, and disposes of it (if it is a physical product). I think of the CVC as one big oil pipeline, with each segment of the pipeline a CVC activity. In a coupled process, all the segments are tightly welded together, and oil (i.e., value) flows continuously from the beginning of the pipeline to the end.

I then seek to understand how my clients can break up these segments of the pipeline and still ensure that value flows evenly and constantly from one end to the other. That can only happen, of course, if there are no leaks at any point in the pipeline. If leakage does occur, then the company has created an opportunity for a competitor to come in, put a bucket under the leak, and capture much of the value without having to build the expensive drilling and pipeline infrastructure that my client has built.

It behooves us to understand leakage in more detail. Formally, we can define it as follows:

$$\text{Leakage}_t = \text{Value created}_t - \text{Value charged}_t$$

Before advising companies to decouple, I look for activities in the CVC where I can spot a difference between the value being created at some point in the CVC and the value that the company is charging up to that point. That's what I call "leakage." When it exists, decouplers have an incentive to barge in and capture some of the as-yet-uncaptured value. Amazon did precisely this with retailers such as Toys "R" Us, Circuit City, and Radio Shack—it captured showrooming leakage. Likewise, Skype captured mobile connectivity leakage from Telefonica, Impression Products captured printing leakage from Lexmark, and TiVo captured program-viewing leakage from NBC. Each of these disruptors spotted a section in the value delivery pipeline where value was created but only charged for at some later point in the process. Leaving money on the table is what feeds these opportunistic decouplers. The only way to coexist with them, without expending huge resources to squash each and every one as they appear, is to minimize their incentives. Rebalancing achieves this, allowing you to capture value at every point in the CVC where you create it. So, before preemptively decoupling, and as a precondition for successfully changing your business model through rebalancing, be sure to calculate the leakage that exists in your business model. Figure out what you're leaving on the table, and claim that value before decouplers build a business around it.

CALCULATING LEAKAGE

To see how we might calculate leakage, let's go back to our hypothetical restaurant, Wholeana. Assume that Wholeana's patrons have to reserve a table to dine there, and that in order to discourage no-shows, the restaurant charges customers a $4 booking fee. Customers gain some value—let's assume $5 worth—in knowing that a coveted table will be at their disposal. They also gain value in occupying a table, let's say $25 worth. The value of drinks and a dinner entrée amounts to $70. This isn't the price customers pay, but rather the monetary value a meal has for them. When the bill comes, Wholeana charges $75 for the entire service, apart from the $4 reservation fee.

Figure 5.1 describes value-creating and value-charging activities that arise when a diner chooses to fulfill all four activities with Wholeana. With this figure in mind, why do people with these particular values for the four activities dine with Wholeana? Objectively, customers receive $100 worth of value but pay only $79. The difference, $21, is what economists call "consumer surplus." Conceptually, a person will buy a good or service only if the value to that person exceeds its price.

FIGURE 5.1 **EXAMPLE OF VALUE CREATED AND CHARGED IN WHOLEANA RESTAURANT**

	RESERVE TABLE	OCCUPY TABLE	DRINKS & DINNER	PAY BILL	
VALUE					**TOTAL**
Created:	$5	$25	$70	$0	**$100**
Charged:	$4	$0	$0	$75	**$79**
SURPLUS					**$21**

Now let's assume that new legislation grants diners at a given establishment the right to order and eat any meal from another restaurant. If that sounds strange, please bear with me. In this scenario, disruptive startups might take notice and offer on-demand meal delivery to restaurant-goers using a mobile app. This would allow a patron of Wholeana to reserve a table and occupy it, but order food and drinks from another establishment, consuming nothing else from Wholeana apart from, say, a glass of water (*see Figure 5.2*). Is Wholeana at risk of being decoupled? Let's determine that by calculating its leakage. Wholeana's leakage in the last two activities of the dining CVC can be calculated as value created minus value captured at that instant before a possibility of a decoupled activity occurs:

$$\text{Leakage}_{\text{Occupy table}} = \$30 - \$4 = \$26$$

FIGURE 5.2 **DECOUPLING AT WHOLEANA**

Since leakage here is sizable, disruptors have an incentive to build a business that allows restaurant patrons to decouple their CVC: "Reserve a table and go to any restaurant, but order the food with us, and we'll bring it to your table." Naturally, the food and drinks that a disruptor offers either have to be of much better quality at the same price compared with Wholeana, or of the same quality at a lower price. Let's assume the latter case—that a disruptor sells comparable quality food and drinks at $35 instead of Wholeana's $75. Since the disruptor doesn't have to pay expensive rent or maintain staff to wait on tables, the decoupler can still make money by charging less. Does this represent a risk for Wholeana? Well, only if a sizable portion of the restaurant's patrons ultimately choose to decouple. But how can we know that in advance?

It turns out that we can infer whether a decoupler might steal our customers before it builds out its business and enters the market by comparing surplus values. Let's calculate the consumer surplus for a patron who chooses to decouple, comparing that to the original surplus she would get via a coupled process. By using Wholeana's reservation system and occupying a table, the patron garners $26 of surplus (\$30 – \$4). By using the decoupler's app to order food and drinks, the patron receives another \$35 in surplus value (\$70 – \$35), for a total of \$61.

$$\text{Consumer Surplus}_{\text{(Wholeana + Decoupler)}} = \$26 + \$35 = \$61$$

$$\text{Consumer Surplus}_{\text{(Wholeana only)}} = \$100 - \$79 = \$21$$

Since their surplus was only \$21 if they chose to couple all activities with Wholeana, many patrons looking for a deal will likely decouple, other factors being equal (*see Figure 5.3*). Consumers now have an additional incentive to decouple, receiving \$40 in incremental value if they do. Decouplers also have an incentive to offer this service, since they can tap into the \$26 in leakage. Collectively, these two conditions—higher consumer surplus and sizable leakage—spell trouble for Wholeana.

FIGURE 5.3 **COMPARISON OF CONSUMER SURPLUS IN COUPLED AND DECOUPLED OPTIONS**

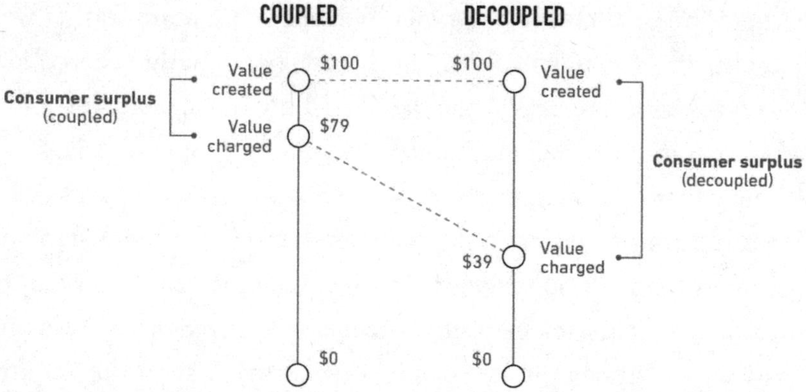

Note: If the CVC is fulfilled by a single business, leakage at the end of the CVC equals the consumer surplus.

If you're an incumbent in a situation analogous to Wholeana's, you can respond, as we've seen, by recoupling, or by decoupling and rebalancing (*see Figure 5.4*). No need to create a long list of possible responses, or to tirelessly debate the pros and cons of each. With only two avenues, you can consider each of them quite diligently by assessing the costs of implementation, the challenges of execution, and the degree of risk involved. Generally, rebalancing is the most sustainable approach, as it tends to eliminate the outstanding incentives for decouplers, whereas recoupling merely defends against the decoupler's current plan of entry without negating those incentives. So, which should you choose? To answer that question, let's pick up with the story of Celiac Supplies.

FIGURE 5.4 **THE TWO RESPONSES TO DECOUPLING: RECOUPLING OR DECOUPLING AND REBALANCING**

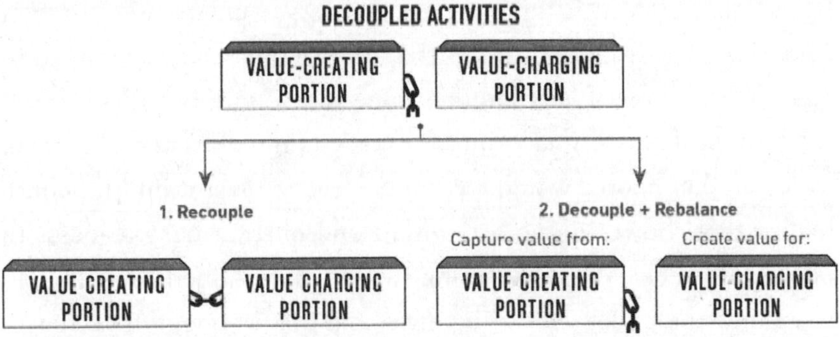

Source: Adapted from Thales S. Teixeira and Peter Jamieson, "The Decoupling Effect of Digital Disruptors," Harvard Business School Working Paper no. 15-031, October 28, 2014, 8.

To Recouple or Rebalance?

As Celiac Supplies teaches us, you don't need to be a large corporation to be considered the market incumbent. This tiny retailer was seeing its well-established business threatened by decoupling. As owner Georgina Fatseas-Sano noted, she arrived at her initial response—charging a $5 fee for "just looking"—by noticing that other local stores were facing similar problems related to showrooming. She pointed to one local clothing company that had decided to charge shoppers for trying on shoes and clothing if they subsequently left and didn't buy anything. "It's not my own idea," Georgina said. "I have heard of other shops doing it, but they haven't put a sign up at the front door. I have to wake people up, everything in life is not free."[22]

A flat $5 fee for showrooming seems like a punishment levied on shoppers, and quite an unorthodox one. You probably wouldn't condone Georgina's value-charging tactic. But look at it from Georgina's point of view. Is it fair for her to set up a store, hire salespeople to help shoppers, dispense specialized advice, and then receive no compensation in return? Is it fair for any business to create value and not capture a dime from consumers that receive that value? Her need to capture a portion of this forgone value was sound, but the way she went about it was arguably not. Yet as Georgina relates, she never expected that people would pay the $5 fee. She just wanted them to realize that showrooming was unfair and hurting her business. In fact, a few weeks after instituting the fee, she claimed that she had to enforce the policy only four times, and that in one of those cases the customer proactively asked to pay.

How else might Georgina have captured some of the leaked value she created as a small shopkeeper? Best Buy faced the same challenge and charged suppliers. But Best Buy is a dominant player in the electronics industry. Could Celiac Supplies have forced its suppliers to pay for slotting fees? Probably not. Nor can small shops pull off charging membership fees to enter their store, as Costco does. Unfortunately, Georgina did not consider the consequences her new policy might have on traffic to her store. The number of people willing to enter Celiac Supplies plummeted. In 2016, the store closed.

But Georgina is a fighter. When recoupling didn't work, she realized that she was adding value for customers by providing them with advice and recommendations. So, she decided to revamp her business model. First she began to charge for the value of the education that customers received, offering courses and personal consultation sessions for individuals with celiac disease, gluten intolerance, or related conditions. In other words, she rebalanced her business model by having customers pay up front to book a session. Eventually concluding that retailing didn't mesh well with a consultative-type service, Georgina abandoned her retail business altogether, reopening Celiac Supplies as an "educational center."[23] Now she's in the business of providing dietary advisory services to people with celiac disease.

Georgina learned the hard way that recoupling wasn't the right answer for her business. If decoupling poses an imminent threat to your business, don't turn to recoupling as a permanent solution. Instead, devise both a short-term recoupling plan and a plan for preemptive decoupling. If you choose to proceed with recoupling, treat it as a way of buying more time so that you can conceptualize and experiment with a new and rebalanced business model. When recoupling becomes too costly to maintain or too technologically impracticable, you'll then have another plan to fall back on, a way ahead that potentially *will* be sustainable over a longer period.

If decoupling doesn't pose an imminent threat to your business, you're in a somewhat different situation. Rather than trying to buy more time, you can play offense, anticipating how your market will change and modifying your offerings *before* a challenger appears to fill the void. Doing so may require both external and internal transformations to your business, revamping the products you bring to market as well as your business model. Only if you can't create a new business model that is profitable should you resort to recoupling.

Notice that I've refrained from offering a single, straightforward answer about how to respond to decoupling. I do not believe there is one. I have quite purposely used the word "avenue" instead of terms like "solution" or "answer." As I see it, recoupling and preemptive decoupling constitute two classes of responses, each implementable in various ways. They are avenues that transport the company to different places. And just as drivers know their cars and driving conditions better than anyone else, you know best the market conditions and organizational constraints that you face. Whichever route you choose to take, only you can best judge how to drive along it.

The framework I've suggested is ultimately a *filtering* guide, designed to help you eliminate the least probable solution. Which solution you go with hinges on various contingencies, such as costs, legal and technological environments, leakage opportunity, and, most important, your willingness to go along with customer desires (decoupling) or against them (recoupling). Further, note that a company's response doesn't depend on the disruptor's intrinsic characteristics—whether it is a big tech company such as Google and Amazon or a small startup such as Impression Products or Dollar Shave Club. As we've seen, decoupling is a *wave* of business model innovation. By their very nature, these waves are pervasive, drawing in many new players from inside and outside the industry. Most of these players are small, nimble, and unpredictable in their trajectories. But you can track their collective trajectory if you study their general motivation, dynamics, and range of options. Don't focus just on the particular startup or tech disruptor that is coming after you. Broaden your perspective, observe the entire incoming wave, and respond to that.

Before deciding on a course of action, you might also consider whether you should respond at all. After all, gluing, breaking, or fixing your business isn't easy. It requires considerable investment in money and managerial time. Would you be better off waiting? To answer that question, you'll want to take into account the cost of action, as well as the risk of loss due to inaction. The cost of action will depend on the specifics of your firm's market, approach, and resources. It's a fairly standard calculation that established firms can easily perform. The risk of loss due to inaction, however, is trickier. In Chapter 6, I'll provide a framework and set of tools to help you assess the two major risks you potentially accrue by *not* responding. First, what is the risk that, by doing nothing, you will be decoupled anytime soon? Second, if a new entrant tries to decouple your business, what's at stake?

6

ASSESSING RISK AND DECIDING TO RESPOND

In April 2017, luxury electric carmaker Tesla achieved a market cap of more than $53 billion, surpassing General Motors to become the most valuable carmaker in the United States.[1] Industry insiders were stunned—and for good reason. General Motors had operated for over a century and was home to popular brands including Chevrolet, GMC, and Cadillac. In 2016, it churned out some 10 million cars, earning $10 billion in profits on revenues of $166 billion. Tesla sold just 76,000 cars in 2016, losing $1 billion on revenues of just $7 billion.[2] "It's totally inexplicable," said Mike Jackson, CEO of AutoNation, the biggest auto dealer in the United States. Even Tesla's CEO, Elon Musk, was surprised. "I do believe this market cap is higher than we have any right to deserve," he said.[3]

In driving up Tesla's stock, investors were betting that all-electric, increasingly connected, and self-driving cars would soon disrupt GM and other carbon-reliant auto manufacturers.[4] GM itself was aware of this risk. As early as 2013, the company had committed itself to catching up with Tesla, with its CEO regarding Tesla as potentially "a big disrupter if we're not careful."[5] By 2016, GM had caught up in at least one respect, bringing to market the affordable all-electric car that Tesla had promised before Tesla managed to deliver it.[6]

Yet GM still couldn't rest easy. As long as people bought new cars, either gasoline-powered or electric, the company would have a business. But it was conceivable that more people would soon forgo buying cars of any kind. Studying shifts in people's mobility habits, GM's executives discovered that millennials had a lower rate of car ownership than previous generations of consumers, and that they were buying cars more pragmatically. Younger consumers who lived in heavily populated, traffic-clogged cities regarded cars as burdens rather than symbols of freedom. In their minds, transportation was increasingly not a product requiring a huge up-front investment but a service available on demand using mobile apps.[7] By June 2017, the biggest of the car-as-a-service companies, Uber, had collected $12 billion over fifteen rounds of investment and reported a valuation of nearly $70 billion.[8] Customers drove with Uber in 633 cities across seventy-six countries worldwide.[9] What if Uber was eventually more disruptive to GM than Tesla? What risk did the rise of transportation as a service pose, and how should GM respond?

If you assessed the risk on the basis of asset utilization rates, it appeared quite high. The average private car in the United States was used fifty-six minutes per day, or less than 4 percent of a twenty-four-hour period.[10] This represented a very low utilization rate considering that professional fleet operators such as Avis rented their cars 66 to 76 percent of the time, and that the hourly rental company Zipcar utilized its cars 32 to 48 percent of the time.[11] In many industries with expensive assets, companies compete by optimizing utilization rates. In the airline industry, Ryanair keeps its planes in the air for almost ten hours per day, or 40 percent of the time, while Lufthansa, British Airways, and Air France have utilization rates of 34 percent, 28 percent, and 26 percent, respectively.[12] In the hotel industry, the average occupancy rate in the United States was 66 percent, more than three times higher than at properties listed by Airbnb (20 percent).[13] In light of these numbers, it seems that business models in the automobile industry based on consumers' individual ownership of automobiles—the dominant model for the past 115 years—are the worst possible models of all, as judged on an asset utilization basis.

Car-sharing or ride-hailing services challenge that inefficiency head-on. These companies allow owners of private cars to put their underused assets on the market, and then to manage their cars like professional fleets. These customers effectively double the utilization rates of private car ownership in the short term.[14] Uber hopes to further increase utilization rates by rolling out self-driving technology. In 2016, it deployed a fleet of autonomous Ford Fusions in Pittsburgh, Pennsylvania, each car outfitted with 360-degree lidar, or light radar, and twenty cameras to help detect obstacles. Software instead of drivers controlled the cars.[15] In theory, self-driving software would never need to go to sleep, as drivers do, and the ride-hailing startup could have its fleet operating twenty-four hours per day, making possible near 100 percent asset utilization rates after discounting yearly maintenance and weekly refueling downtimes.

By driving down the total number of cars needed, these higher utilization rates would disrupt the automotive industry on an unprecedented scale. But how big was the risk? The U.S. Transport Research Board estimated that each car-sharing vehicle took fifteen private cars off the road. The European Parliament's report claimed that full adoption of car-sharing could reduce the number of privately owned cars in European countries by between 63 and 90 percent. Germany, the world's largest car exporter and fifth-biggest new-car market, would see the largest potential reduction.[16] Seemingly unbeknownst to some auto executives, transportation-as-a-service puts the incumbent model of private car ownership at risk of near extinction.

Rather than debate whether transportation-as-a-service or electrification posed the greater threat, GM executives decided to hedge their bets by taking action across the board. In 2016, the same year GM got ready to produce all-electric cars to challenge Tesla, it invested $500 million in an 11 percent stake in Uber's biggest U.S. competitor, the ride-hailing company Lyft. GM had tried to buy Lyft, but the company turned it down.[17] That same year, the Detroit giant launched a new car-sharing service called Maven, which allowed customers to rent cars for hours or weeks, both for private use and for money-making gigs with services like Lyft or Uber, akin to a taxi fleet manager. GM didn't disclose how much it was investing in Maven.[18] GM placed its biggest bet of all in 2016 by paying almost $1 billion for a small startup called Cruise Automation.[19] Cruise worked on software running self-driving cars. At the time of the acquisition, the startup was two years old and employed just forty-six people. It made a number of demos on fixed routes but didn't yet have a viable commercial product, nor had it figured out an innovative business model.[20] Explaining the move, GM's CEO, Mary Barra, said: "We see it all fits together: electric, autonomous, and sharing. People still need to get from point A to point B, and we believe autonomous will be a big part of it."[21]

In 2017, Ford, the second-largest U.S. carmaker, invested $1 billion in Argo AI, a previously unknown startup built by two self-driving technology engineers who had worked at Google and Uber. The size of these deals by GM and Ford surprised competitors. In a lawsuit against former employees, Tesla issued its own commentary on the merits of such deals: "In their zeal to play catch-up [with autopilot features by Tesla], traditional automakers created a get-rich-quick environment. Small teams of programmers with little more than demo-ware have been bought for as much as a billion dollars."[22] These are multiple huge bets made because executives at incumbents feared being disrupted by new technologies.

Time will tell whether GM's strategy of responding to multiple startups by means of acquisitions is a good idea. For many incumbents, however, snapping up startups simply isn't an option—the financial burden is too great. Even companies that do have the resources might want to think twice before following GM's example. Firms often don't need to respond to decouplers if they don't threaten a significant portion of market share. Before mounting a response, in line with the discussion in Chapter 5, it's important to consider if you need to respond at all. This decision entails balancing the cost of responding (financial and management's time) with the risk of loss to the established business if you don't respond. As regards the latter, executives at incumbent companies must consider two types of risk: the risk that a decoupler will enter the market, and the risk that it will steal a significant portion of your customers if it does enter. Let's consider each in turn.

Assessing the Risk of Entry

Is a startup poised to enter your market and attempt to decouple your business? Executives should stay alert to the threat, continuously monitoring their risk of being decoupled. In particular, executives should constantly ask themselves three questions. First: Does their company require customers to co-consume any of the company's activities (e.g., browsing and buying)? In the unlikely case that the answer is no, the business need not worry, as there is nothing to decouple. If the company does require co-consumption, then managers should pose a follow-up question: Can a disruptor conceivably *separate* the value-creating piece from another value-charging, value-eroding, or value-creating activity (for instance, using technology or business model innovation)? If not, managers should monitor for new innovations that could eventually make separation possible, but they need not worry about responding immediately. If the answer is yes, then new entrants might consider disrupting the incumbent by decoupling. In this scenario, managers should start taking that risk seriously and assess it objectively.

Taking the risk seriously leads managers to pose a third question: Does leakage exist that a disruptor might exploit in separating the co-consumed activities—as Amazon, for instance, did with traditional retailers? If not, managers should continue to monitor the situation but take no action. If leakage does exist, the incumbent should sound the alarm. The decoupling risk is real and a response via one of the two major avenues we described in the previous chapter is warranted (*see Figure 6.1*).

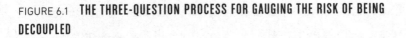

FIGURE 6.1 **THE THREE-QUESTION PROCESS FOR GAUGING THE RISK OF BEING DECOUPLED**

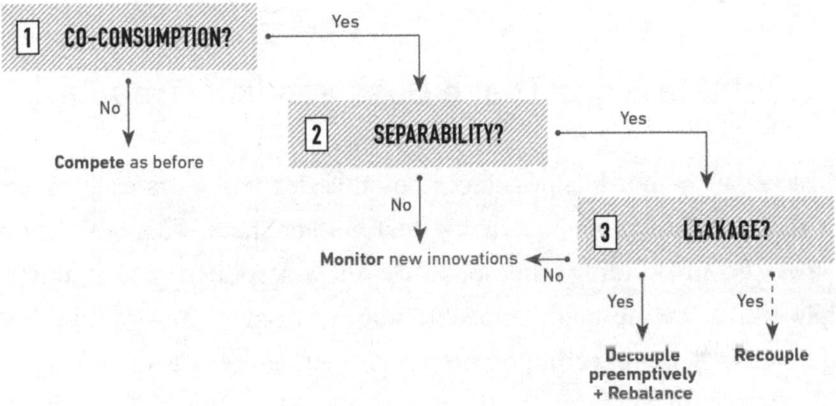

To illustrate how you might use this three-question process, let's apply it to gauge Gillette's risk of being decoupled circa 2012:

Question #1: Is there co-consumption? Yes. The razor giant forced the purchase of the razor and that of the replacement blades, two separate consumption activities, on its customers through tightly controlled patents.

Question #2: Is there separability? For decades, there wasn't. More recently, though, consumer frustration mounted. The link between the purchasing of a cheap razor and replenishing expensive blades with the same manufacturer weakened commensurately.

Question #3: Is there leakage? Yes. The leakage potential was high before the purchase of replacement blades, as is the case in any razor-and-blade business model.

A Gillette executive performing this analysis around 2012 would have understood the heightened risk of disruption. Even before Dollar Shave Club cropped up, Gillette should have been ready. But could they have predicted the extent of the market share they could lose? Let's now move from assessing the risk that a disruptor will enter to assessing the risk that a company will lose customers.

Telltale Signs That a Business Is in Trouble

Just because your business faces possible decoupling doesn't mean that a given startup will actually steal market share. Therefore, your next step in deciding whether to mount a response is to evaluate how well a startup might appeal to your customers. You can do this qualitatively by reflecting on how customers go about making their purchase choices.

Customers always have a choice as to what to purchase. In many categories, they have more choices than ever. How do customers select a car, say, when faced with dozens, even hundreds of options? They can't possibly compare every car across dimensions such as price, miles per gallon, design, comfort, or accessories. Even buying a simpler product such as yogurt entails making decisions about the packaging, flavor, added sugar, taste, and other features. In the face of such complexity, customers tend to simplify the task of choosing, employing a two-stage approach. First, they use quick and simple filtering techniques to eliminate undesirable options. They then perform a slower, more elaborate comparison of the remaining options. For instance, consumers choosing which yogurt to buy might first eliminate all options that are not major known brands or that cost too much. This leaves them with what marketers have called a "consideration set," a group of brands that customers actively consider before selecting one to purchase.[23]

The consideration set is one of the most important marketing concepts of the past few decades.[24] It posits that brands in consumer products don't compete by vying at once for each customer in one big match-up. Rather, the competition resembles the Olympic Games, where swimmers, say, compete head-to-head for the gold medal in stages. There are preliminary races for each distance, and only eight or so swimmers make it through to compete in the finals. Swimmers competing in the finals are akin to a consideration set, and the number eight is the size of that set. When it comes to consumer purchases, each customer chooses his or her own set members and size.

How exactly do customers do that? As academic research in marketing has shown, customers compose consideration sets on the basis of their awareness of and preferences for various options, as well as based on brand image, product differentiation, and category-specific factors. Consideration sets can vary greatly by the person, category, and even country.[25] For instance, research has found that typical yogurt buyers keep three to four brands in their consideration sets. Typical U.S. car buyers keep eight make-and-model combinations (brands) in their consideration set, whereas the typical Norwegian car buyer includes only two brands.[26] When selecting where to open a checking account, customers typically have only one or two banks in mind before making their choice.[27]

What does all this have to do with disruption? *Everything*. The consideration set is where the competition for customers begins (and ends) for some brands. If your customers decide that your company no longer resides in their small consideration set, then you won't make the sale. As an incumbent, your company registers as an ongoing part of the consideration sets of many loyal customers. When a new competitor enters the market, big or small, disruptor or not, your goal is always twofold: to remain part of your customer's consideration set, and to keep the new entrant out of that set. If loyal customers dropped you from their consideration set and added the new entrant, that would represent a worst-case scenario. There is no greater disruption than that.

So how do you determine if such a switch represents a serious risk? Well, either you ask customers directly or you observe their choices and infer whether you are in or out. By assessing the composition of your customers' consideration sets, asking about or inferring which options customers are considering for their next purchase occasion, you can understand the changing nature of the competition among alternative options, discerning the degree of risk that new entrants pose to your business. Changes in your customers' consideration sets are the first telltale signs of impending disruption to your market, and possibly to your business as well.

DEGREES OF DISRUPTION RISK

Suppose you are General Motors, a maker of automobiles that run on gasoline or diesel to power an internal combustion engine. You ask current owners who are shopping for a new midrange car about the options they are considering. They tell you that they are considering models marketed by Chevrolet (a GM brand), Ford, and Chrysler (an FCA brand), all gasoline-powered. This consideration set suggests that they are asking themselves an underlying question: "What midpriced gasoline-powered car should I purchase?" GM faces the lowest degree of disruption among those customers. For any given customer, GM may win that person's business or lose it to a direct competitor, but market shares are unlikely to change dramatically, as the market is split among longtime competitors. Competition will hinge on traditional brand rivalry between manufacturers, and customers won't stray anytime soon beyond the established category (i.e., midrange internal combustion engine cars). That would not constitute disruption.

Another, smaller group of GM customers might be debating whether to buy an electric car or one with an internal combustion engine. In this case, the potential for disruption still remains fairly low since Chrysler, Ford, and Chevrolet are all working on both types of cars. In a scenario in which customers ask (or behave as if asking), "Should I buy an electric car or a gas-powered automobile?" their consideration sets have changed slightly. They may now incorporate new brands such as Tesla, which has rolled out its midpriced Model 3. GM can offer electric car options such as the Volt, but it doesn't "own" this part of the market. GM's risk thus runs slightly higher, since new entrants are now more likely to steal some market share due to electric-powered cars.[28] Considerably fewer GM customers might pose this question as compared with the previous question, but their number could grow quickly.

What if an even smaller group of car buyers began to choose from a consideration set that included both autonomous, self-driving cars and traditional cars? Since existing carmakers haven't yet built and marketed a fully autonomous car as of 2018, the appearance of customers who seriously considered these two modes of transportation could disrupt traditional automakers. Still, this would constitute a technological disruption rather than a business model disruption. It wouldn't constitute decoupling. In 2019, very few individual customers, if any, were posing the question "Should I buy an autonomous car?" But as semi- and fully autonomous cars come to market, we might see a sizable shift in the consideration sets of current GM customers as they add brands such as Google's Waymo and other contenders. GM might market its own autonomous vehicle, but autonomous cars could still emerge as a disruptive technology, posing high levels of risk to traditional American automakers.

As I explained in Chapter 2, the most profound disruption often originates in business models rather than in technological innovation. The automobile industry would see business model innovation—and decoupling in particular—if car buyers were considering whether to purchase a car or to use modes of private transportation such as Turo, Uber, or BlaBlaCar. In this case, traditional car manufacturers would run the highest risk of being disrupted, in the sense of abrupt and meaningful changes in market shares. GM in particular would run the highest risk if a sizable portion of its current customers suddenly began asking the question "Should I even buy a car?" These customers would be altering their consideration sets significantly, adding ride-hailing or ride-sharing startups at a first stage and potentially bumping GM quickly from their sets at a second stage (*see Figure 6.2*). That is disruption in its strongest form.

FIGURE 6.2 **CUSTOMER CONSIDERATIONS AND POTENTIAL FOR DISRUPTION**

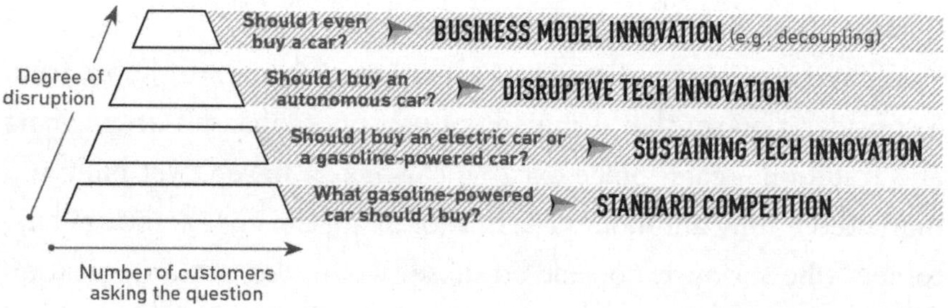

Business model innovation is considerably more disruptive than technological innovation in two respects. First, since business model innovations often don't require that customers adopt a costly new "hardware" technology, the impact they have on a market tends to unfold more quickly. Innovative technologies sometimes allow firms—new entrants or established competitors—to steal a sizable portion of the market. And the nature of the technology will determine whether that market reshuffling happens quickly or slowly. Clayton Christensen has called certain abrupt changes "disruptive" innovations, as compared with "sustaining" innovations that lead to gradual market share shifts.[29] The challenge, of course, is to predict in advance whether any given technology will prove to be disruptive or sustaining. Ultimately, a technology will disrupt a market only if many customers pay to have it. (To understand more about the main differences between these two theories, refer to "Note on Differences Between Decoupling and Disruptive Innovation," located at the end of the book.)

The other important distinction is that in almost all cases, the choice to pursue technological innovation remains largely under a firm's control. It is true that some patented technologies have no practical alternatives, but usually firms can determine how forcefully they wish to develop a specific technology. In the automobile example, companies such as GM can decide whether and how quickly to develop electric cars and autonomous vehicles. Even in the case of intellectual property (IP) held by other firms, companies can keep pace through some combination of building, acquiring, or partnering with IP holders of the core technology. Established companies exercise much less control in the case of business model innovation, and decoupling in particular. Here *consumers* are the decouplers. *They* determine whether to ask themselves "Should I even be purchasing a product in that category?" The decision to pose that question is largely outside management's purview.

When aggregated for all customers in a market, the questions individual customers ask themselves and the associated changes to their consideration sets dictate the type of market competition that your company faces and, consequently, the degree of possible disruption. Paying close attention to consideration set composition can thus help you gauge not merely the chances that a disruptor will enter the market but also the risk that it starts racing neck and neck with you, eventually seizing a significant chunk of your market share.

Market Share at Risk

Both the three-question process and the concept of the consideration set afford a qualitative assessment of risk. Sometimes, however, qualitative assessment isn't enough. In these cases, we have to delve further into the consideration sets of individual customers to measure the risk of market share erosion more precisely, in a quantitative fashion. By mapping out customers' value chain and then aggregating their likely decisions, we can identify market-level (i.e., share) disruption. To do so, let's first take the disruptors' point of view, identifying their potential gains *as they see them*. We'll then switch to the incumbents' point of view, assessing their risk of loss. Both vantage points are instructive.

The standard approach for assessing how much market share a new disruptive entrant stands to capture is to review its sales and forecast its growth. Yet many executives at incumbent companies can't perform these analyses, as they can't access a startup's sales and growth rates. Other methods to estimate potential growth based on business valuation approaches (e.g., cash flow analysis, balance sheet valuation, market comparables) are problematic for our purpose in that they confound the *impact* of the business idea or model with its *execution*, which is hard to predict. Luckily, we don't need to consider execution to gauge decoupling's potential impact on an incumbent's business. If Four Seasons Hotels wanted to determine the potential impact of home sharing on its business, its analysis would rightfully regard the role of Airbnb founders, executives, and employees as secondary. It would also largely disregard the abilities of employees of HomeAway, VRBO, and the dozens of other vacation rental websites that appeared before Airbnb. While generally important, executional capabilities are beside the point here—it's the business model and its potential impact that matters. To determine how much market share incumbents like Four Seasons risk losing, incumbents need foremost to assess how their current customers will respond to new offerings in the market.

That response in turn hinges on costs—especially monetary, effort, and time costs (see Chapter 3). We should note that individual customers tolerate these various costs differently. As consumer research has shown, younger people and those with lower incomes tend to be more price sensitive, while older and higher-income individuals tend to be less so.[30] Comparable findings apply to effort and time.[31] Research has also revealed that consumers who are more price sensitive tend to be *less* effort sensitive. My past research employing online field experiments has shown that online shoppers of a fashion e-commerce player who seek items with the highest discounts will expend more effort browsing and clicking in order to find them.[32] Less price-sensitive shoppers, on the other hand, tend to be highly sensitive to effort. They don't want to browse the online store for very long just to save a few dollars on promotional items, so they tend to buy higher-priced, less-discounted items. A colleague and I used this insight with our client to deliberately "hide" high-discount products on their e-commerce website, so that visitors had to perform extra clicks to find them. This way, price-insensitive customers purchase full-price, high-margin items, while effort-insensitive customers take the time to find and purchase low-price, low-margin bargains. By doing so, the online fashion retailer gets the best of both worlds: more customers, without the need to reduce the number of items sold at a healthy profit margin.

The trade-off between costs to customers matters to both decouplers and incumbents. Rarely will a business offer the same quality of product or service as its competitors but at a significantly lower price and with less commitment of time or effort. Something has to give. Either the business will lose money or it will require higher customer costs of some kind. For instance, some private car transportation options might be cheaper for customers, but they'll also be harder to use (e.g., Turo). Others might be easier to use but more expensive (e.g., Uber Black). Such differences create what academics call "self-selection mechanisms" in the market. Some consumers will prefer the cheaper option, as they are highly price sensitive, while others, being less sensitive to price but highly sensitive to effort, will prefer the more expensive option. The bottom line is that executives should incorporate customer sensitivity to different costs into any cost comparison analysis of incumbent companies and disruptors.

To quantify the customer's inclination to decouple an incumbent, we begin by calculating the cost differential of a decoupler's offering vis-à-vis incumbents, and then accounting for the degree to which the target market population values money, time, and effort. This analysis will reveal what portion of customers the decoupler will likely win away. Factoring in the incumbent's market share, you'll arrive at the potential market share that the decoupler gains, and conversely, the potential share that the incumbent loses. Summing up this potential, calculated for the decoupler vis-à-vis all established businesses in a certain market, you'll arrive at the total market share that a decoupler can potentially steal from all players—and that all incumbents with traditional business models can potentially lose. Whether this "change of hands" of market share will occur quickly or take a decade is important, but beside the point here. What matters when determining whether to respond to decoupling is the incumbent's market share that is at risk. Let's examine how to perform this calculation step by step.

Calculating Market Share at Risk (MaR™)

Salary Finance is one of the UK's fastest-growing employee benefits financial technology (fintech) companies. Cofounded by Dan Cobley of Google UK, Asesh Sarkar, and Daniel Shakhani, its social purpose is to help people who have jobs pay off their debt faster. Most employees carry some form of personal loan in the form of credit card debt, personal loans, payday loans, or bank overdrafts. Salary Finance developed an employee benefits platform that employers can adopt cost-free and offer to employees, allowing them to consolidate personal loans into a single, low-cost loan with an interest rate averaging 7.9 percent per year, about half the average bank rate. Other benefits to employees include speed and convenience: applications take five minutes to complete and are reviewed within forty-eight hours. When applications are approved, Salary Finance releases funds immediately, deducting payments automatically from the employee's paycheck. Employers benefit, too: they can offer Salary Finance as an extra perk, freeing their employees of the financial distress caused by high interest rates.

Analyzing Salary Finance's business model, we find that it decouples steps in the customer's process of taking out a personal loan and paying it back. This process unfolds as follows: you go to the bank > you apply for the loan in person > you provide documents requested by the bank > the bank assesses your risk and ability to repay the loan > the bank approves the loan > the bank deposits the funds > you incur interest > you secure funds to pay the principal > you go to the bank to pay, or to transfer the money > the bank deems the loan fully repaid. With Salary Finance, your employer verifies your employment and makes loan repayments through payroll deductions, which reduces the risk of default, as well as the effort customers must expend in applying for a loan. It also lowers customers' interest payments. Up to this point in the process, Salary Finance offers some benefits but doesn't actually decouple anything. The employer enables the loan to be repaid by automatically deducting the monthly payments from its employees' paychecks. It is here—the value-eroding activity of having to go to the bank or send a check—where we find decoupling. As Salary Finance claims, "We take the hassle out of repayment."

Salary Finance is a great example of decoupling, because it implements a business model innovation without significantly altering the final product. For consumers, a personal loan is largely the same product, regardless of where they obtain the money. The costs of securing this loan, on the other hand, can vary dramatically. The major cost consumers consider is the interest rate that they will need to pay on the loan, which is often measured on a yearly basis as the annual percentage rate (APR). APRs vary by loan size and loan agent (mostly banks and credit card companies). *Table 6.1* compares three of the United Kingdom's largest consumer lending banks, providing their APRs for average medium and large loans of £4,000 and £8,000, respectively.[33] Column five shows Salary Finance's APR minus that of major banks. Column six translates that into actual cost to the borrower, in pounds per year. The figures here are negative (a saving) if they are cheaper with Salary Finance, positive if they are cheaper with the incumbent. Obviously, these figures represent average cost, a simplification that doesn't factor in credit rating or the possibility that the bank will reject an applicant.* But consumers would compare figures akin to these *before* choosing to apply to an individual institution for a loan. In most cases, Salary Finance stands as the less costly option. In others, particularly for large loans, incumbent banks are cheaper.

TABLE 6.1 **COST DIFFERENCES FOR TOP THREE INCUMBENT BANKS COMPARED TO SALARY FINANCE**

INCUMBENT	TYPE	LOAN SIZE	APR	APR DIFFERENCE	COST DIFFERENCE
HSBC	Medium loan	£4,000	18.9%	-11.00%	-£440
	Large loan	£8,000	3.3%	4.6%	£368
Barclays	Medium loan	£4,000	22.9%	-15.00%	-£600
	Large loan	£8,000	4.9%	3.00%	£240
Lloyds	Medium loan	£4,000	26.3%	-18.40%	-£736
	Large loan	£8,000	4.6%	3.30%	£264

Source: HSBC Bank, Personal Loan, https://www.hsbc.co.uk/1/2/loans/personal-loan; Barclays Bank, Personal Loans, http://www.barclays.co.uk/Howtoapply/BarclayloanPersonalloans/P1242591272078; and Lloyds Bank, Flexible Loan, https://www.lloydsbank.com/loans/personal-loan.asp, all accessed June 15 and 21, 2017. The APRs given for Lloyds Bank are for its flexible loan option. Lloyds Bank also offered an "online exclusive" personal loan with a lower possible representative APR than its "flexible" personal loan option.

* Therefore, adverse selection is not factored into this calculation.

But monetary cost isn't the only type of cost that can affect consumers' decision-making. Explicitly or implicitly, customers also consider the time and effort involved in procuring, buying, and using products and services. A complete assessment of the cost to customers of decoupling the banks that hold their checking accounts must factor in these additional costs, assessing how much easier (or harder) and quicker (or slower) it is to obtain a loan elsewhere. In sum, we must assess whether the customer sees a lower (negative) or higher (positive) total cost of decoupling.

Because employers partially support its process, applying for, securing, and paying off loans at Salary Finance require less effort compared with typical banks. This is also accounted for. As for time savings, it would be quite hard to determine how many days it would take to secure an approval from each bank for purposes of a comparison with Salary Finance. For simplicity's sake, let's assume that all lead times are the same. If time costs are known and not identical, then you should incorporate those into your calculations.

Let's now factor in cost sensitivity. In the consumer loan industry, as in the retail sector, customers who are highly price sensitive tend not to be very sensitive to effort, and vice versa. Some people take out credit card loans even when their average APR is very high, precisely because it's easy. What consumers don't find so easy is comparing all the options in order to choose the cheapest bank loan. Those who do take the time tend to care more about price.

So how do we assess price sensitivity in the United Kingdom's consumer loan industry? Well, we can ask people seeking loans to make trade-off decisions on loans involving different levels of effort and price (e.g., APRs). On that basis, we can determine their implicit sensitivities to these costs. A survey of 208 people conducted by Salary Finance revealed that 85 percent of consumers with outstanding personal loans were willing to consider Salary Finance, and 15 percent were not, regardless of terms. Of the 85 percent who had added Salary Finance to their consideration sets, 14.7 percent would consider switching loan providers to achieve any reduction in their APR. These, in other words, were highly price-sensitive and minimally effort-sensitive consumers. Another 61.7 percent of respondents were somewhat price and effort sensitive. They wouldn't change lenders unless they could reduce the APR by at least two percentage points.* Anything less and they would stick with their current option. The fourth customer group, representing 8.6 percent of the sample, ranked very low in price sensitivity and high in effort sensitivity. Loyal to their banks, they demanded a reduction in APRs of at least four percentage points to switch—a tough demand to meet (*see Figure 6.3*).

FIGURE 6.3 **DISTRIBUTION OF SENSITIVITY TO LOAN INTEREST RATES (APR)**

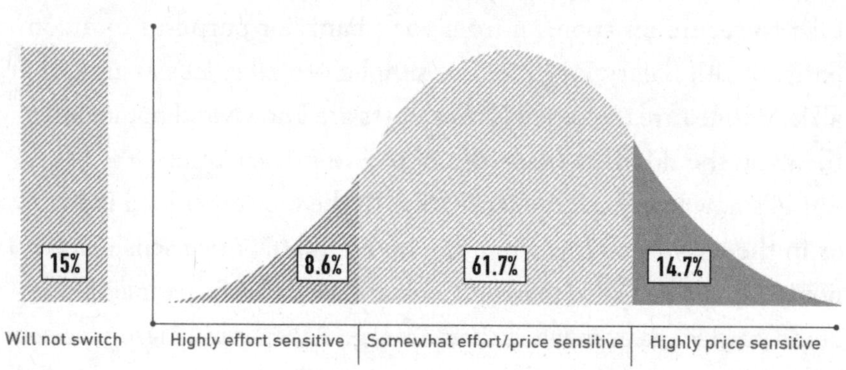

Now that we've calculated the monetary and effort cost differential for Salary Finance relative to each incumbent, and now that we know customers' cost sensitivity (that is, what it would take to capture each segment of customers), we can calculate the decoupler's potential to steal customers away from a given incumbent.

Take Barclays's medium loan product, with a higher APR rate of 22.9 percent. For a £4,000 loan, customers would pay an annual

* The exact APR differences have been calculated based on a survey conducted by Salary Finance and are disguised here.

monetary cost of £916, compared with Salary Finance's £316. Since it's cheaper and easier to go with Salary Finance, this decoupler could eventually hope to persuade all but 15 percent of customers—those in the price-insensitive groups. Barclays thus risks losing up to 85 percent of its medium-sized loan business to Salary Finance for employees of participating companies. Given that the bank captured 15.6 percent of market share in 2016, and assuming that its consumer loan portfolio was equally split between medium and large loans, its potential loss amounted to 6.6 percent of the entire market.[34] Barclays's large loans carried a more competitive APR of 4.9 percent versus Salary Finance's average of 7.9 percent. On the other hand, Salary Finance's automatic payment via salary deduction made it easier for customers to use. Barclays's APR advantage of three percentage points will allow it to keep the 15 percent of customers who would never switch, the 14.7 percent of customers who were highly price sensitive, and the 61.7 percent of customers who were somewhat effort (and price) sensitive. Salary Finance would be able to steal only the 8.6 percent of customers who were highly price insensitive and effort sensitive, putting only 0.7 percent of Barclays's market share at risk.

Obviously, these calculations represent an upper limit of a new challenger's disruptive potential. In 2016, the United Kingdom's eight largest banks collectively accounted for 65 percent of the market for consumer loans. Salary Finance's business model had the potential to steal a whopping 28.9 percentage points of market share. This result owed partially to the lower APR Salary Finance offered compared with large banks (in the case of medium loans for most banks), as well as to the relative ease with which consumers could secure and pay off loans using the service (*see Table 6.2*).

If you think this potential market share theft is a lot for a single fintech startup to pull off when facing giant incumbents, hold on, there's more. When I began to talk with Salary Finance, its cofounders were

TABLE 6.2 **POTENTIAL LOSS AND MaR™ BY INCUMBENT BANK**

INCUMBENT	TYPE	POTENTIAL LOSS	MARKET SHARE	MARKET SHARE AT RISK
HSBC	Medium loan	85.0%	31.4%	13.4%
	Large loan	0.0%		0.0%
Barclays	Medium loan	85.0%	15.6%	6.6%
	Large loan	8.6%		0.7%
Lloyds	Medium loan	85.0%	5.7%	2.4%
	Large loan	8.6%		0.2%
Next five other banks	All loans	45.1%	12.2%	5.5%
Total			65.0%	28.9%

Note: Assume the market shares in column four are equally split between medium and large loans. Source: Calculated by the author from data in "Consumer Loans [FY 2016] (£GBPmm, Historical Rate)," Capital IQ Inc., a division of Standard & Poor's, accessed July 19, 2017, and Bank of England, Bankstats, A Money & Lending, A5.6, "Consumer Credit Excluding Student Loans," Excel workbook, "NSA Amts Outstanding" worksheet, last updated June 29, 2017, available at http://www.bankofengland.co.uk/statistics/pages/bankstats/current/default.aspx, accessed July 2017.

striving to position the startup as a cheaper and more convenient alternative to loans than established banks.* In a sense, my analysis put numbers to their intuition. I decided to perform a final analysis, this time adding credit card companies as incumbents. How would Salary Finance potentially impact the card companies' small-loan business?

Since credit card companies often make smaller loans than banks, let's assume that the average customer carries a £1,000 outstanding balance month to month. In the United Kingdom, the average credit card APR in 2016 was about 22 percent, translating to an annual cost of £220—much higher than Salary Finance's £79.[35] On the other hand, obtaining a loan from a credit card is quite easy. All

* Disclosure: I have no financial stake in Salary Finance.

you have to do is decide not to pay the total balance, and you automatically are taking out a loan. So, obtaining a Salary Finance loan requires more effort than obtaining one from a credit card. Under these two assumptions, Salary Finance can expect to eventually take the 14.7 percent of customers who are highly price sensitive and the 61.7 percent of customers who are somewhat price and effort sensitive. Given that credit card loans in the United Kingdom represented 35 percent of the entire consumer loan market in that country in 2016, by stealing a bit more than three-quarters of it Salary Finance has the potential to take in 27 percent of the market share from this single source. Based on this insight, Salary Finance should attempt to position itself as a significantly cheaper yet almost as convenient alternative to obtaining a credit card loan (*see Figure 6.4*). For simplicity, these calculations do not account for total market growth, just change of shares. However, one can easily account for any expected increase in market size. For details of how to calculate Market and Total Market at Risk, see "Note on Calculating MaR and TMaR" at the end of the book.

FIGURE 6.4 **SOURCES OF TOTAL MARKET AT RISK (TMaR)™**

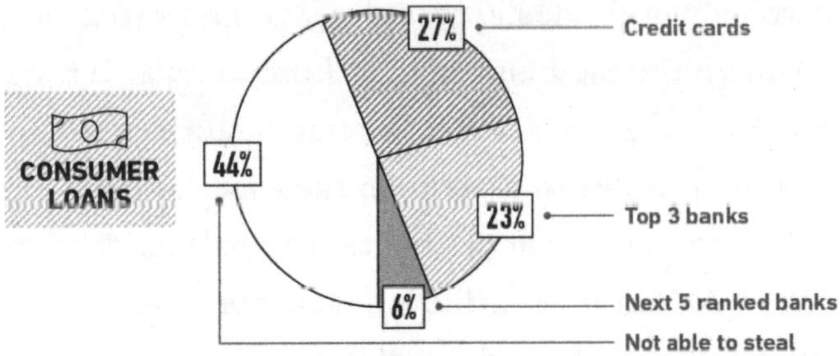

Source: Salary Finance's survey of 208 consumers; market share data calculated by the author from "Consumer Loans [FY 2016] (£GBPmm, Historical Rate)," Capital IQ Inc., a division of Standard & Poor's, accessed July 19, 2017; Bank of England, Bankstats, A Money & Lending, A5.6, "Consumer Credit Excluding Student Loans," Excel workbook, "NSA Amts Outstanding" worksheet, last updated June 29, 2017, http://www.bankofengland.co.uk/statistics/pages/bankstats/current/default.aspx, accessed July 2017.

Where does this analysis leave banks and credit card companies? First, and most obviously, it reveals how Salary Finance's business model can disrupt incumbent lenders if the incumbents do nothing. As I mentioned, from the incumbent's point of view the appropriate unit of analysis is the business model, not the startup. In calculating its total market at risk, each incumbent is determining its own potential market share risk due to the type of decoupling that Salary Finance is undertaking. It's not calculating its actual loss to Salary Finance. If HSBC, the bank with the highest potential losses, were to acquire Salary Finance and either let it wither or shut it down, it wouldn't completely avert this risk. Another decoupler with a similar business model is likely to appear in Salary Finance's place. Incumbents can harness or use market share potential, but never trap and eliminate them. Small personal loan incumbents in the United Kingdom thus have a great deal at stake.

Putting It All Together

What are the early signs that doing nothing might put your business at risk? You generally can't see them very clearly by looking inward at your own products, technologies, and processes. And if you can, it might already be too late. Look outward, toward your customers. As we've seen, executives at incumbents can deploy two distinct approaches to determine their market risk due to new entrants. Performing an initial qualitative analysis of current customers' consideration sets can reveal whether your customers are considering purchasing from new entrant(s). At the extreme, decouplers that cause your customers to question the need to purchase *any* product in your market engender the highest level of risk. A follow-up quantitative analysis can help clarify the extent of the risk that your company faces. Of course, putting numbers to the market at risk calculation requires a great deal of data, both at the level of the firm and within the market, from current customers, prospective customers, and competitors. If some of this data is available, the calculations provided in this chapter can help incumbents assess just how much market share a disruptor can potentially steal, as well as which incumbent will lose the most. If your business faces a low risk of loss, then you might want to forgo a response, at least for now. In that case, monitor the market for other decouplers on an ongoing basis using the three-question process that I outlined earlier in the chapter.

If a quantitative market at risk analysis reveals a high risk of potential market share losses due to decoupling, consider responding. You will need to decide upon the nature of the response and how many resources to allocate on a case-by-case basis. If the best response remains too costly relative to the risk, you can always decide not to respond. If the risk justifies the cost, then evaluate the appropriate responses, among those described in the previous chapter. Putting all of these steps together help you to decide whether and how to respond to decoupling (*see Figure 6.5*):

1. Calculate the market share at risk due to decoupling (i.e., all similar decouplers).
2. If the risk is high, calculate the cost of responding and weigh it against the risk. This calculation will allow you to decide whether to respond to decoupling or not.
3. If you decide to respond, decide whether to recouple or decouple.
4. If decoupling, decide whether to change the business model by rebalancing or not.

This decision tree can help incumbent companies respond more efficiently to disruption. In my work with large companies, I've often seen executive teams exhaust themselves working toward *the* best

FIGURE 6.5 **DECISION TREE TO AID IN DECIDING WHETHER TO RESPOND AND HOW TO RESPOND**

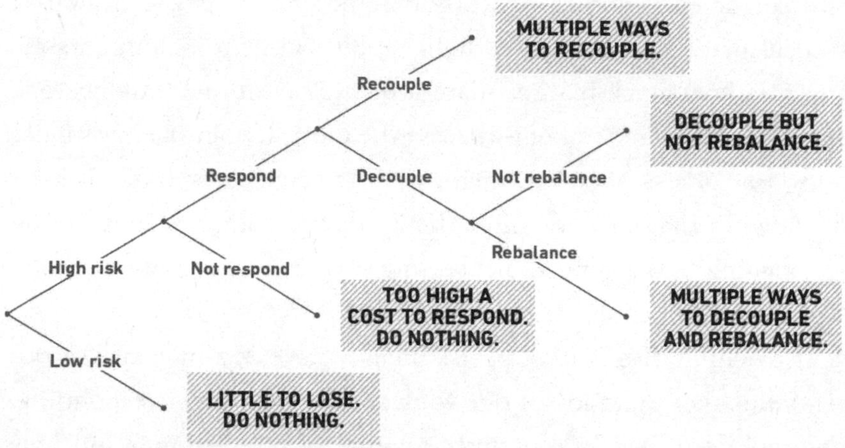

response, only to have to perform their analyses all over again when their initial response didn't yield the intended results. Decision trees help decision-makers by laying out all the major avenues available, as well as their contingencies. These trees also make it easier to revisit the decision when the team chooses an incorrect or ineffective option. In large organizations, such decisions don't happen quickly, as they involve many stakeholders. Hopefully, after months of deliberation involving key stakeholders, you will have arrived at the best option for responding to decoupling. But sometimes this doesn't happen. If you have to revisit a decision, having previously organized the available options in a tree-like structure makes reassessment much quicker and more straightforward.

Suppose a company has performed a market risk analysis and concluded that the risk of loss is too high to bear. It has decided to act. Between recoupling and decoupling, it chose the former. If attempts to recouple—say, by lobbying for a change in regulations—have failed, what should it do next? The company need not start from scratch. If other internal or external environmental factors haven't changed, the company should try another form of recoupling, say technological or contractual. Similarly, if the company exhausts all of its recoupling options, it should pursue a decoupling path, possibly without rebalancing. If that doesn't work, it should attempt rebalancing. Last, if none of these options work, the company might revisit whether it is worthwhile to respond at all. In general, as options fail, decision-makers should work backward from right to left in the decision tree. There is no need to redo the analysis all over again.

Implications of Risk Assessment

Companies in a low-risk situation should continue to monitor the market for threats. The brands that compose your customer's consideration set change very quickly in some categories. As my previous research has shown, for instance, consumers, particularly young ones, can prove very fickle when consuming ready-to-drink beverages, confectionary, and alcoholic drinks. Exposure to even one television commercial can convince consumers to include a new brand in their consideration set.[36] In many other categories, the entry and exit of brands require considerably more time. As a result, incumbents must constantly monitor their customers' consideration set via surveys and other market research tools. In categories such as snack foods, incumbents should do so monthly. In other categories, such as apparel, cars, or banking, they can do this quarterly, yearly, or even every two years.

Monitoring consideration sets will tell you which brands have a shot at stealing your customers and which don't. Obviously, a given brand's odds of success depends on many factors. As a general rule, sizes of consideration sets in the United States for consumer package goods are about one-tenth the number of brands in the category overall.[37] In less competitive markets, the chances that a brand is part of a customer's set tend to be higher. Of course, merely being considered by consumers doesn't guarantee sales. It's critically important to monitor the brands and startups entering your market, as well as those in adjacent markets. In principle they all can enter your customer's consideration set. But it is important to monitor the set, rather than all of the startups that appear. Monitoring the consideration set is always manageable, whereas it can be much harder to keep track of every startup. CB Insights, a research firm, likes to create so-called digital landscape maps containing all the new startups in an industry. Their 2017 beauty disruption map included more than seventy startups backed by venture capital. Their healthcare maps listed more than five hundred startups. And the banking space was crowded with more than a thousand would-be disruptors.[38] Even the most analyst-heavy incumbents will have trouble monitoring that many startups and tracking their progress. So don't try. Stick to monitoring the consideration set.

Also, be sure to think outside the market. When a startup makes it into your customer's consideration set, they become competitors, even if they don't offer a directly competing product. Many families place cable television providers in the same consideration set as movie theaters, the ballet, or weekend trips. When it comes to Father's Day gifts, as my strategy colleague Bharat Anand likes to point out, neckties occupy the same consideration set as power and gardening tools, electronic gadgets, and even restaurant meals.[39] And for certain people, ride-sharing services are now in the same consideration sets as automobile ownership.[40] You need to define your competition as your customers see it, not on the basis of how physically similar your products might appear on the surface.

Try using the market at risk calculation to quantify the upper bound (or potential) of a decoupling business model. Early on, when it's hard to project a startup's future risk to large established businesses, this calculation can help you to measure the disruptive potential or risk of business ideas, as opposed to the risk posed by a specific business. The startup's potential gain is your potential loss.

The higher the loss, the more motivated an incumbent must be to invest in a strong response *before* the risk takes hold and affects its market share.

But beware: mounting too large a response also carries negative consequences. Not every entrant deserves diligent consideration and a response. When business model innovation is on the rise, as is the case of decoupling, responding to all startups would constitute a huge economic burden. Yahoo offers a cautionary tale. By 2012, when former Google executive Marissa Mayer became its CEO, Yahoo was an incumbent in the search engine space, the third-most-popular search engine in the United States in terms of market share, after Google and Microsoft. Worried about a continuing decrease in its rankings, Yahoo went on a multiyear shopping spree. As of 2016, Mayer had acquired fifty-three digital and tech startups, spending between $2.3 and $2.8 billion, not to mention countless hours of her top executives' time for M&A due diligence. Yahoo eventually shut down thirty-three of these startups, discontinued the products of eleven startups, and left five to their own devices, failing to assimilate them. In all, Yahoo fully integrated only two of these startups.[41] In 2017, unable to grow, Yahoo was acquired by Verizon for $4.8 billion, a far cry from Yahoo's peak valuation of $100 billion.[42] Overresponding can kill companies, just as failing to respond can.

The tools provided in this chapter help you to approach disruption risk from multiple vantage points. To spot early signs that customers are considering decoupling, examine their changing consideration sets. The second vantage point is that of the decoupler. As I discussed in Chapter 4, the decoupler's motivation to enter and the financial war chest that it is awarded in financial markets reflect the opportunity it perceives to snatch away markets from incumbents. Try to see what they see, and you will better understand what is at stake. The way to do that is to calculate the decoupler's potential gain. After looking at decoupling from the customer's and decoupler's vantage points, next assess the situation from your own vantage point, calculating the market at risk. Ultimately, the customer savings, the decoupler's potential gain, and the incumbent's risk are the exact same thing: they represent a transfer of value. The difference is who gains and who loses when this value changes hands.

Collectively, the market at risk calculation, the three-question process, and monitoring consumers' consideration sets can serve as a "radar system" to detect incoming threats. In conjunction with the decision tree, these tools can help you assess multiple types of risk, allowing you to decide if, when, and how best to respond to the threat posed by decoupling.

PART III
Building Disruptive Businesses

In the book's first section, we looked at what's really disrupting businesses: the decoupling of activities done by customers. The second section delved into whether, when, and how established companies should respond. Incumbents can respond in two distinct ways when confronting a decoupler: either they can glue various customer activities back together (recoupling), or they can find ways of accepting the rupturing of these activities and coexisting peacefully with it (rebalancing). To decide what to do before or after a disruptor has entered your market, you must assess the multiple risks involved in taking action or in failing to do so. In-depth analysis of customers' choices, preferences, and associated costs will reveal how incumbents should approach the threat of decoupling in their industries.

With this foundation in place, we can now proceed to tackle the task of building and growing disruptive businesses and, in the process, revisiting and rethinking established paradigms. How do you start a disruptive business? How do you grow one? How do you prevent one from declining once it has become mature? Whether you're starting a new venture inside your established business (an "intrapreneur") or you're an entrepreneur starting a new, innovative startup, applying the basic precepts of decoupling theory can yield intriguing new answers to the major challenges you will likely face along the way.

I've organized the chapters in this section to follow the general contours of a company's life cycle (*see the figure below*). All businesses, large and small, traditional and disruptive, hew to a similar pattern in their journeys toward increased market penetration. During the initial phase, revenues and market share gains are typically slow. If companies survive this phase, they tend to progress into a second phase of much more rapid growth. Some companies flounder during this phase. Those that survive it eventually reach a third phase: a tapering off, slowing, or declining growth. The challenge here is to sustain growth as long as possible, or to jump-start new growth.

THE LIFE CYCLE OF A BUSINESS

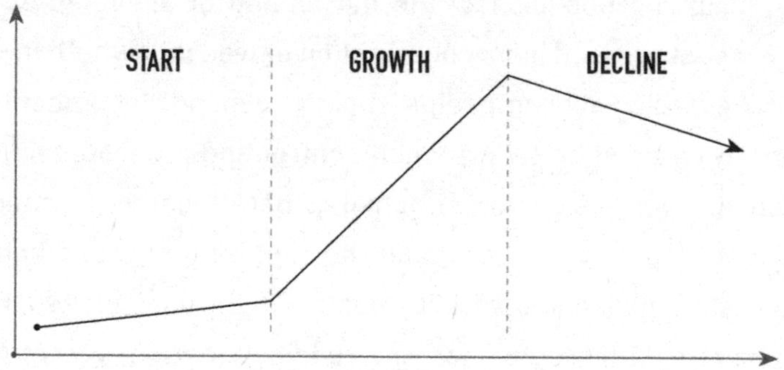

Of course, different companies will linger in each phase for varying lengths of time, and they'll achieve varying levels of revenue or market share in each phase. But they all follow this trajectory. Moreover, when you observe companies of different sizes and ages and in different industries, from airline services to zipper manufacturing, you tend to find firms in a given phase experiencing the same underlying business challenges. People tend to think that big businesses have big-business problems, whereas smaller businesses have different business problems. This is only partially the case. Life stages define the "experience" of a business. Companies in the start phase all grapple with the challenge of acquiring their first customers in a cost-effective way, whereas businesses in the growth phase tend to focus more on deciding which new products to develop and markets to conquer, as well as how to organize people and processes to support these new initiatives. During the third phase, companies tend to focus more on how to counter a stall in growth and innovate themselves in or out of markets in which they have lost market share.

Each of the next three chapters covers a stage in the life of disruptive companies, applying lessons learned from decoupling theory. By shedding new light on the challenges companies face, I hope to deepen and broaden leaders' and managers' thinking, so that they can find their ways to new solutions and their businesses can thrive. Let's start at the beginning, with the creation of a disruptive business. As we move from early stages to growth and finally to decline, never lose sight of the real prize: the customer.

7

ACQUIRING YOUR FIRST ONE THOUSAND CUSTOMERS

In 2014, a young entrepreneur named Charles-Albert Gorra had an intriguing idea for a business selling secondhand high-end dresses online. Before going all in, he decided he wanted to test his idea cheaply, so he purchased some dresses from acquaintances, had them dry-cleaned, and tried selling them on eBay. He discovered that although a market for used high-end apparel existed, the margins on luxury dresses were too slim, regardless of the volume, to sustain a business. But Gorra wouldn't give up on his idea just yet. He thought he might still build a viable business if he ventured into another category of durable goods with relatively high price points.

Researching offline secondary markets, he realized that large, profitable resellers tended to sell goods with low utilization rates, as measured by the percentage of time the product remains idle in consumers' hands. The less owners used their products, the more willing they were to try to monetize it. Products that people used frequently, such as eyeglasses and mobile phones, didn't give rise to successful secondhand reselling businesses, since their owners relied on them every day.* Gorra noticed something else: traditional,

* Most secondhand phone resale markets in the United States are for refurbished or outdated phones.

profitable resellers tended to sell goods that also had low depreciation rates, as measured by the natural decrease in the product's market value over its lifetime. Technology products became obsolete quickly, so while their owners might have sought to dispose of them by reselling, a reseller might earn only modest commissions. Goods such as luxury handbags, gold jewelry, and motor homes seemed ideal for reselling, since they had both low utilization and low depreciation rates. They kept their value, and owners didn't use them very often.

Gorra subsequently tried reselling luxury handbags online, and this time he succeeded. The original owners received a high enough price to motivate them to part with their bags, and Gorra managed to keep sales prices on eBay and other online marketplaces low enough to attract buyers while still securing a healthy commission for himself. The opportunity, he felt, was enticing. According to the NPD Group, American women between the ages of eighteen and forty-five owned thirteen handbags from seven different brands, on average. Gorra's own field market research revealed that "north of 80% of women's closets [were] essentially untapped," and that these closets contained high-quality, slightly worn bags that their owners had never thought of reselling. After confirming that he could create value for both sides and still charge for a portion of the value created, Gorra set out to raise seed venture capital in order to build his startup. Within a year, he and a cofounder raised $4.8 million to create Rebag, an online website that purchased used luxury-brand handbags from women.

At this point, Gorra confronted a problem facing all would-be disruptors: Where should he start? How might he get his company off the ground, taking what seemed like a great business idea and building a truly innovative company that would thrive? How should he spend his seed money?

Successful entrepreneurs and others in the startup universe have exhorted entrepreneurs to address a whole slew of issues all at once in starting up their businesses, including attending to the product, technology, channels, and so on. A mantra in Silicon Valley holds that entrepreneurs should aim to build a proprietary offering that is "ten times better" than what is currently on the market. The logic seems sound: make a ten-times-better product and you will attract all the customers you can handle, all the venture capital investments you need, and all the talented employees you want to work for you. Experts also counsel entrepreneurs to harness network effects early on. When customers join a network, such as a telecom service or a communication channel like email, Skype, or a messenger app, they glean increasing value from the network as more customers join, which in turn makes new users more likely to join. And according to the experts, entrepreneurs shouldn't forget to build out their technology infrastructure. Many of the fastest-growing companies in recent years have been tech startups. If you want to build a new business and quickly get it growing, it seems to follow that you must do what Google, Facebook, and Amazon did and build your technology infrastructure right away. Finally, experts tell entrepreneurs to own the customer experience end to end when they're starting out. After all, customers generally want to "hire" businesses to solve an entire problem for them.

These are just a few of many pieces of advice budding entrepreneurs receive, and none of them is necessarily wrong. Each has led disruptive startups to take root and grow. Yet collectively, they comprise a mishmash of advice that entrepreneurs find overwhelming to follow. It's not easy, for instance, to create a product that is ten times better than others in the market. Pick any market and select the leading product or service in that market. Can you come up with an idea for a product that is ten times better than that? Can you then manufacture this product and build a business around it? Remember, you're a new venture. You don't have the best engineers or salespeople, unlimited funding, and other critical resources. Network effects are likewise notoriously difficult to engineer, particularly in a company's early days. Before such an effect can kick in, a startup must entice a critical mass of customers to sign up. But startups and new ventures generally don't have all the resources and capabilities to make that happen, or for that matter, to build out their technology infrastructure. As for creating an end-to-end user experience, delivering even one sliver of the customer experience better than established companies in the market is hard, let alone attempting to create a better end-to-end solution.

Now, try building network effects, creating a product that's ten times better, putting a technology infrastructure in place, aiming for an end-to-end customer experience, and addressing any number of other challenges *all at once*. It's practically impossible for the typical startup. Those who try will likely encounter perpetual frustration, distraction, and, all too often, failure. Entrepreneurs and managers of new ventures would do far better to focus on one goal and to achieve that goal as best they can.

But what would that goal be? Decoupling theory points toward an answer. As we saw earlier, the theory emphasizes customers' critical role as drivers of innovation. Applying that insight here, we arrive at a focused approach for starting a disruptive business. Rule #1: Acquire customer activities. Rule #2: Revert to the first rule.

Startups in their earliest days struggle mightily to acquire enough customers to support their operations. This task is so difficult, in fact, and so vital for a company's success, that entrepreneurs should make customer acquisition their primary focus. If you can't attract customers, how much of a future does your business really have? Most potential decouplers fail either because they didn't acquire enough customers or because they couldn't profitably serve those customers who had signed on. This raises a question: how should disruptive new ventures acquire their first customers?

Specialization and the Growth of Markets

To understand generally how new businesses with no history or reputation can steal customers from established businesses in mature markets, let's step back and review how markets develop. Most markets originate with businesses that sell a mass or undifferentiated product appealing to all customers to some extent. Spotting an opportunity, a company develops a single, unique offering to capture most of the market. It does so by identifying the main dimensions that customers care about and positioning its new offering to capture the largest part of the market, roughly in the center of those dimensions. In 1858, Macy's saw an opportunity to offer multiple categories of good-quality consumer goods conveniently delivered in one large store at reasonable prices. In its early days, it was not the cheapest store, nor the most high-end, nor the most convenient. It did reasonably well across each of these dimensions, and attracted many shoppers willing to compromise on one dimension or another.

As the first business in a fast-growing market, mass offerings eventually attract competitors. Those considering entering the original incumbent market could do so by building another mass offering to compete with them. But that would be foolish, as customers would not clearly distinguish the new offering from the established one. So instead, new entrants usually specialize. That is, they choose one or a couple of dimensions that they know customers might value more, and they create so-called niche offerings that are appreciably stronger in those dimensions. That allows new entrants to quickly win new customers—for instance, those that value low prices, high quality, or convenience more than they value assortment or customization. For mass merchant incumbents, this means that some of their customers defect to niche players.

Over the years, niche players appeared to challenge the domination of Macy's and other department stores. After growing dramatically to achieve leadership in the groceries category in the United States, Walmart started introducing brand name apparel at lower prices. Nordstrom started selling higher-end and some custom-made clothing. And smaller, franchised or individually owned mall stores such as the Gap attracted customers with trendy and conveniently located stores in shopping malls. To serve customers' desire for specialized offerings, new entrants arose, each choosing a small subset of key dimensions at which to excel.

As more entrants crowded onto the field, the original mass player became the middle offering: not the cheapest, nor the one with the most assortment or the highest quality. It became, as consultants say, "trapped in the middle." And with that, the market share of the middle player eroded. By 2018, large department stores such as Neiman Marcus and Sears were stuck in this position, and at risk of bankruptcy. Other stores, too, including J. C. Penney and Macy's, have struggled as well, stuck in the middle with nowhere to go. As more niche players enter the market, incumbents that fail to respond decisively lose market share to specialized players that "eat around the edges." *Figure 7.1* depicts the evolution of markets as seen from the perspective of a mass merchant, with the niche players attacking from the boundaries.

In yet another, subsequent phase of market specialization, a new batch of entrants offer a product that is significantly stronger in one or two dimensions, using digital tools to reduce the customer's costs. To stay with our retail example, the last few years have seen new apparel disruptors enter the market. Startups such as clothing brand Bonobos and eyeglasses brand Warby Parker gained prominence by offering customers the ability to acquire custom-fit wearables in the convenience of one's home, without having to visit a physical store. Indochino grew at the extremes by offering reasonably priced, custom-made suits and shirts. Stitchfix customized the

FIGURE 7.1 **EVOLUTION OF MARKET LANDSCAPE OCCUPANCY IN CLOTHING**

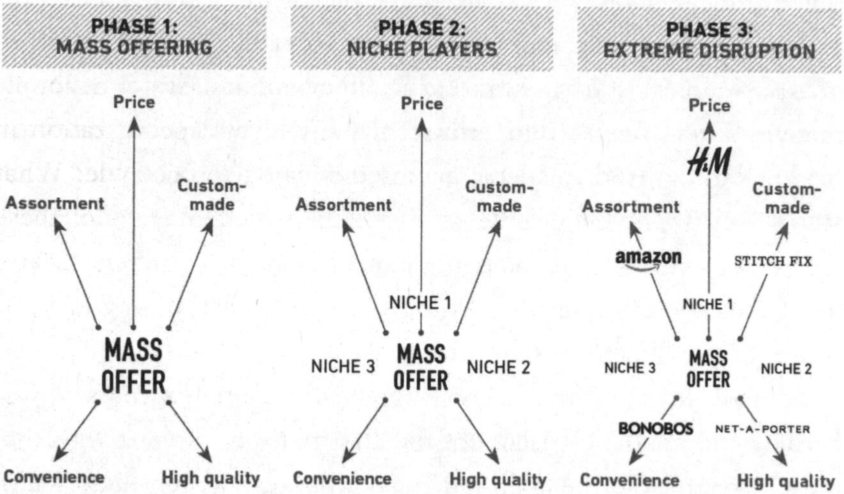

subscription of apparel. Even Amazon, no longer a startup, has adopted this approach and created Amazon Fashion, a quick-delivery clothing startup within the everything-store e-commerce giant. From the moment it was born, Amazon Fashion boasted one of the largest assortments in the market, and at very reasonable prices.

By entering at the extremes of an important dimension for the customer, and by also featuring an offering strong in a secondary dimension (e.g., low price, effort, or time), these fashion disruptors appeal to a small group of shoppers who care deeply about that dimension. In fact, these shoppers care so much about the dimension that they'll quickly switch from one of the established players to a startup. After these startups have secured a position as the extreme provider in a certain dimension, they move on to conquer adjacent dimensions. Collectively, these multiple disruptive startups further trap and suffocate both the established niche players and the original mass offering incumbent.

Decoupling, too, tends to follow this dynamic. In that sense, it is really a theory of specialization. As I mentioned in Chapter 3, sometimes your customer wants to specialize, and that offers startups a chance to enter. But instead of specializing on the basis of the type of customers or the types of products, decoupling entails specialization in activities that make up the customer value chain. If you're starting a disruptive business, especially one that seeks to decouple activities, you need to understand the history of specialization in the market. Who are the customers motivated to decouple? What are their dimensions of interest? How can you steal some of these customer activities for yourself? That must be your primary set of questions from the start.

Double Decouplers

To answer these questions, let's consider a special class of disruptive businesses: online marketplaces. These marketplaces are notoriously difficult to start, but when they do become established, they become among the most valuable startups around. Analyzing how the founders of these companies started yields valuable guidelines for other disruptive startups.

We can define online marketplaces as digital platforms that attract and match two very different types of customers. Uber matches car drivers with car riders; Airbnb matches homeowners with short-term renters; eBay matches sellers with buyers; Etsy matches crafters and artisans with buyers. But these are hardly the only online businesses that function as two-sided marketplaces. Job sites match employers with employees. Media companies essentially serve as platforms that match consumers with advertisers. Even a retailer that doesn't own its inventory but rather showcases third-party products on its website functions as a marketplace or platform that matches manufacturers with shoppers.

In *The Wealth of Nations*, Adam Smith described the "invisible hand" that animates markets by helping to match the demand for goods with their supply. Prior to the internet, drivers and riders had long been free to transact in the market for taxi and car rides, just as rental property owners had been free to rent to short-term renters, and makers and buyers of crafts had been free to find each other and transact. In theory, the "invisible hand" helped these vendors and producers find one another automatically. In practice, of course, this matching often didn't happen. A person needing a ride might have stood on a street corner miles from any available driver. Or a person wishing to rent a house might have overlooked an attractive listing just a few blocks away. Pure market-driven matchmaking frequently proved challenging, cumbersome, and opaque. What online marketplaces did was displace the "invisible hand," decoupling the act of offering to sell (or to buy) goods and services from the actual delivery (or receiving) of these products. Matching supply with demand, marketplaces convinced prospective users that their websites would soon rank among the largest gatherings around where buyers and suppliers could meet and transact.

Let's say you need to buy a unique item, such as a hard-to-find piece of sports memorabilia, a used computer, or organic heirloom tomatoes. Disregarding traditional mass retailers, you might think of visiting a specialty store. But since not many stores carry these items, and you don't want to waste time driving from store to store, you might also choose to visit a marketplace such as a flea market, a used goods fair, or a farmer's market. There you might inspect all sellers' stalls, select one, and choose an item from that stall to purchase. This activity of "going to the market" can take place at either physical or online marketplaces, and it constitutes a central step in the buyer's value chain (starting at the lower left-hand corner of *Figure* 7.2).

Makers or suppliers also serve as customers of online marketplaces, such as Amazon or Uber. To get off the ground, such online marketplaces must acquire suppliers and create value for them,

FIGURE 7.2 **SUPPLY-SIDE AND DEMAND-SIDE CVCS AT EBAY**

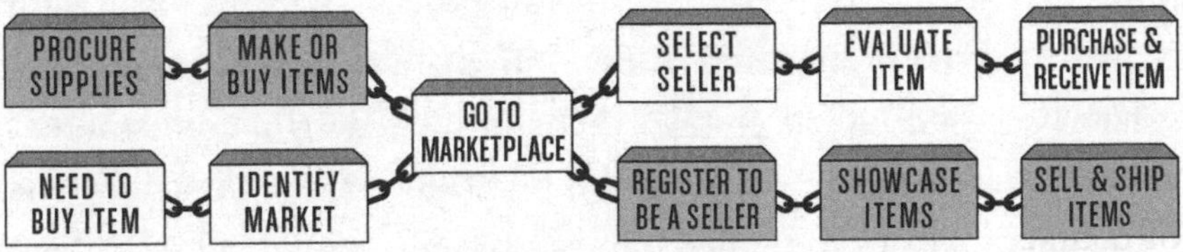

just as they do for buyers. Suppliers also have their own value chain (starting at the upper left-hand corner of *Figure* 7.2), which involves procuring their own suppliers (e.g., garments in the case of clothing manufacturers, seeds in the case of tomato growers), making or buying the item, choosing a market(place) to offer their goods, signing up to be a seller, showcasing their merchandise, and selling it. Take eBay, which serves as an online marketplace for various kinds of goods. As a two-sided platform, eBay does not produce the products it sells. Rather, it brings supply and demand together and facilitates a transaction, decoupling the activity that exists at the intersection of the maker and buyer's CVC. In this respect, eBay decouples the matchmaking role of traditional markets. It can also serve as a complete substitute for physical marketplaces at which buyers and sellers meet one another and do business.

When you think about it, decouplers such as eBay, Etsy, Uber, and Airbnb have helped resolve a number of innate inefficiencies of traditional physical marketplaces. By using technology, data, and the web, online marketplaces better balance supply and demand, enhance the trust participants feel in one another and in the quality of goods sold, and reduce the monetary, time, effort, and transaction costs. As a result of the value they add, online marketplaces create markets that can grow significantly larger than their offline counterparts, reducing further inefficiencies for both sides.

Two-sided marketplaces are more challenging and complex to launch than other disruptors. It's hard enough to acquire one type of customer in an online business. Two-sided marketplaces must acquire two distinct types of customers to their platforms, each with a distinct value proposition. Riders on Uber want cheap and convenient access to a car to take them to their destination, whereas drivers want to earn money on the platform. Trying to attract one set of customers or the other leaves entrepreneurs facing a chicken-and-egg problem. How do you entice employees to join a professional networking website if you don't have many job seekers on the site yet—and vice versa? If you do succeed in acquiring both groups of customers, you must go further and prompt them to pair up quickly and efficiently. If you don't, customers won't remain on your platform. As an entrepreneur, if you can understand how to acquire and retain two kinds of customers from scratch, chances are you will know how to acquire customers for a typical (one-sided) business, too.

How Airbnb Acquired Its First One Thousand Customers

We can glean some basic principles of customer acquisition by examining how one of these marketplaces got its start.[1] Let's consider how Airbnb acquired its first one thousand customers. In 2008, three friends—Brian Chesky, Joe Gebbia, and Nathan Blecharczyk—were living in San Francisco and working as designers. There was a big design conference coming up in the city, and hotel space was limited. So Chesky, Gebbia, and Blecharczyk decided to try to make some extra money by renting out their loft. They set up a simple website featuring pictures of their loft, promising to provide a home-cooked breakfast to guests in the morning. That first weekend, three renters stayed with them, each paying $80 for the privilege. Shortly after that, Chesky, Gebbia, and Blecharczyk began receiving emails from people around the world, and they knew they were on to something. Three months later, they launched their startup, timing it to coincide with the 2008 Democratic National Convention, held in San Francisco. That event allowed them to secure multiple hosts and guests for their website.

Initially, the Airbnb site had very few listings. The founders weren't sure how to overcome the chicken-and-egg problem. They needed accommodations—initially rooms and then entire houses—in order to attract individuals to browse the site. However, to get owners to create a listing of their properties, they needed consumer traffic—people looking to rent. Nobody would go to the trouble of listing or searching for rentals on a sparsely trafficked site. As it turned out, the supply side was the harder side to grow: many people felt uncomfortable at first with the idea of opening their homes to strangers. Potential renters felt reluctant to take the first step and advertise their properties far and wide. So, the founders decided to do this work for them. Airbnb offered users who listed properties on Airbnb the opportunity to post them to Craigslist as well, even though Craigslist offered no sanctioned way to do this. Airbnb also automated a way to contact property owners on Craigslist to ask them to post their listings on Airbnb.

In mobilizing Craigslist, Airbnb worked hard to distinguish itself from the incumbent's online classified listings. But Craigslist possessed an asset that Airbnb lacked: a massive user base. Airbnb knew that travelers who sought more than the standard hotel experience clicked on Craigslist. Craigslist represented an attractive "feeder" for Airbnb because Airbnb's listings tended to be more personal than listings for other properties on Craigslist, with better descriptions and photos. Standing out to Craigslist users, Airbnb's more detailed listings lured them over to the Airbnb site. Once there, they tended to book directly through Airbnb the next time around.

Airbnb's founders experimented with many tactics for attracting renters to their website, recognizing that what worked in one city or country might flop in another. In France, one of Airbnb's first non-U.S. destinations, Airbnb employees set up an A/B test in several localities. In half of the French cities or towns, they physically visited and promoted Airbnb using low-tech, non-scalable tactics. Teams of two or three people talked to the few users already in that market to understand conditions there. They threw parties and held information sessions, set up booths around town, posted flyers, and obtained contact information from everyone they met who showed interest in hosting. They then followed up with more information, an offer to create a listing for prospective renters to review, and the like. In the other half of French localities in the selection set, Airbnb targeted prospective hosts using Facebook ads, a standard online mass marketing customer acquisition approach. In the first set of cities and towns, Airbnb kept meticulous track of what it cost to send prospective hosts to the Airbnb website (including the cost of throwing parties, setting up booths, and other "on the ground" activities) and the listings that resulted. They compared those costs to those of the Facebook ads, tracking the listings that resulted from each. It turned out that the cost per acquisition was five times lower in the cities and towns where Airbnb had deployed the low-tech, non-scalable tactics.

By the summer of 2009, Airbnb was growing quickly in some local areas, but it hadn't gained much traction in the important New York City market. To understand why, Gebbia and Chesky flew out and booked rooms and homes with twenty-four hosts (the two used their own service when traveling). The founders discovered that users weren't presenting their listings on Airbnb very well. As Gebbia noted, "The photos were really bad. People were using camera phones and taking Craigslist-quality pictures. Surprise! No one was booking because you couldn't see what you were paying for." Gebbia and Chesky generated a low-tech but effective solution to this problem. According to Chesky, "A web startup would say, 'Let's send emails, teach [users] professional photography, and test them.' We said, 'Screw that.'"[2] Chesky, Gebbia, and Blecharczyk rented a $5,000 camera and went door to door, snapping professional pictures of as many New York listings as possible. This approach generated two to three times as many bookings on New York listings.[3] By the end of the month, Airbnb's revenue in the city had doubled. Better-quality pictures from hosts prompted a flurry of other local hosts to step up their game and take better pictures of their properties, or risk not renting them quickly. Importantly, it set the standard for quality photography that future property owners would have to match in order to compete.

By using such tactics to secure a minimal number of listings to their site early on, Airbnb founders bolstered their supply side. This allowed them to attract and sustain demand, which in turn slowly attracted an even greater supply of homes for rent. The flywheel of success started spinning—slowly at first, and then faster. The result, ultimately, was tremendous growth for Airbnb for years to come.

Airbnb's story is especially interesting because the company didn't generate demand solely on the basis of a new and innovative idea. Many online businesses already offered short-term home accommodations, among them HomeAway, VRBO, and Couchsurfing. Yet only Airbnb grew its user base rapidly from zero to thousands, and then to millions—a testament to its prowess at cultivating its first customers.

So what can entrepreneurs learn about early customer acquisition from Airbnb and, by extension, from other fast-growing marketplaces such as Etsy and Uber?[4] Analyzing Airbnb's story, we can discern the following seven principles at work:

1. **"Buy" customers in bulk.** Acquiring users one by one takes too much time. A small startup needs to acquire customers in bulk, as Airbnb did during oversubscribed conferences and by

tapping into Craigslist's user base. Uber and Etsy pursued this strategy as well early on. Uber made itself available to customers at the conclusion of sports events and concerts, when masses of people sought rides.[5] The founders of Etsy visited large crafts fairs to promote their site, signing up entire groups of artisans at each fair.[6]

2. **Don't confront competitors directly.** A startup must avoid putting itself in the crosshairs of established incumbents. Don't target their customers. Instead seek out customers they can't or won't serve. After concerts, more people need cabs than cab companies can handle. Likewise, when major events such as the Democratic National Convention come to town, hotels reach full capacity. Snatching up the excess demand in these instances allowed startups such as Uber and Airbnb to remain "under the radar" of the giants. By the time they had a foothold in the market, the giants had a hard time catching up.

3. **Adopt non-scalable tactics.** Large tech companies tend to obsess over pursuing scalable tactics. If a tactic doesn't work for thousands or millions of customers, these companies perceive it as a poor investment. Experts often recommend that startups behave similarly. Yet startups and large tech companies have different needs. Startups desperately need those first ten customers, while large companies don't care about adding just ten more customers to their already enormous base. By venturing out to people's homes and hiring photographers to take professional pictures for hosts, as Airbnb did, or by sending people to fairs, as Etsy did, startup marketplaces facilitated the onboarding process. To launch a disruptive business, focus on tactics that seem to work and that yield insight into customers and their needs, no matter how small the impact might be at first. Scale becomes a concern later in a company's lifecycle. If you lack customers early on, you have nothing to scale.

4. **Incubate your early customers (and start with the suppliers).** A startup's initial customers help it enormously, and their relationship with the company is extremely fragile. One slip, and customers vanish. If they stay, as happened with Uber, Airbnb, and Etsy, they will help you attract more users, creating a powerful and indirect network effect as an engine for growth. If you are launching a two-sided marketplace, focus on acquiring supply-side customers before going after the demand side. Provide all customers with the best experience, regardless of whether you can do so profitably or in a scalable way. This early investment will yield dividends; as we'll see, your first customers do more than just pay for your business to operate.

5. **Use low-tech, offline tools.** Tech startups tend to dismiss offline customer acquisition tools, such as organizing events, creating on-the-ground operations, or incentivizing users to talk to acquaintances about their services. Yet Airbnb's deployment of such tools fueled its early growth. Only over time, as the company's growth rate stabilized, did it switch to online customer acquisition channels.

6. **Favor operations over technology at first.** Technology can help business processes to scale, but it usually doesn't allow them to get off the ground. For a disruptive business to succeed, it needs to work, plain and simple. Online marketplaces must match supply and demand. Early on, you cannot expect technology alone to accomplish this difficult task. Uber went door-to-door to get its first drivers to sign up. Airbnb did the same for its renters, and when it convinced people to list their homes, its employees went out of their way to find a person to rent each home.[7] A platform manager must take the hand of a buyer and find a supplier so that a transaction can occur. Otherwise, buyers and suppliers might not match up, and they will never return to the platform. Any disruptive business seeking to attract customers must appeal to

them one at a time. Only afterward can technology accelerate the process.

7. **See your business through your customer's eyes.** I've emphasized the importance of viewing disruption through your customer's eyes. This holds doubly true for online marketplaces, with their disparate customer groups. The CEOs of Uber and Airbnb routinely used their services in order to see and experience what their buyers were experiencing.[8] They also made sure they understood the challenges suppliers faced by driving a car or renting out a house. Any new business seeking to attract customers has to inhabit the customer's point of view deeply, making operational adjustments so as to lower the effort, time, and monetary costs that both types of customers pay.

I've derived these principles from a study of two-sided marketplaces I conducted, but I've also spotted them in action while working with dozens of disruptive startups across a number of industries.[9] Rebag, the opening story of this chapter, is a good example. After obtaining seed capital, founder Charles-Albert Gorra didn't focus on building technology infrastructure, or creating a ten-times-better product, or engineering an end-to-end experience. Rather, he tried to understand how to convince women to sell handbags on his website (principle #4: going after supply-side customers first). He came to an important realization: women who owned luxury brands didn't care about the process of selling itself, just the outcome. They wanted a quick and effortless selling process, one that would garner them a significant sum of money. These concerns explained why women weren't selling their used bags on eBay (too difficult) or in consignment stores (took too long, cost too much).

Recognizing that he had to lower the effort, time, and monetary costs for customers, Gorra arrived at a solution: he would offer to buy the product himself. Women would go to Rebag, quickly provide information about their bags' brand and type, and upload a few photos of each bag. The site would inform them within twenty-four hours how much it would offer for their bags. When women accepted, their checks arrived in at most a couple of days. A focus on satisfying the customer's needs, then, drove Rebag's business model. If Gorra had focused on his own needs or his investors' needs, Rebag never would have bought bags and paid for them up front before securing buyers. Instead, Rebag would have operated as an online consignment store, a marketplace, matching sellers with buyers and taking a commission, but never owning the inventory. Gorra chose to reduce the customer's friction costs, even though he would obviously have preferred to lower his working capital and avoid investing in potentially unsaleable inventory (principle #7: seeing things through your customer's eyes).

When I spoke with Gorra during the summer of 2017, the average price of a handbag at Rebag stood at $1,000. The most expensive? A $13,000 used Hermès Birkin Gillies Togo handbag. Used! A new version costs around $21,000. At the time, nobody else was purchasing used high-end bags to resell—neither cash-strapped entrepreneurs in the secondhand markets nor the original makers of these bags. Gorra had found a white space (principle #2: avoid confronting competitors).

In order to acquire these products, Gorra needed to raise more debt and venture capital, convincing investors that he would put their money to good use. In particular, he needed to show that he could buy the right items, those that would not be stuck on the virtual shelf. He also needed to show that he could pay the right price to acquire used bags. If he paid too much, he would forgo a profit; too little, and he would dissuade owners from selling. Finally, he needed to show that he could price bags appropriately for resale. Here is where innovative technology entered into Rebag's business model: the company would develop an algorithm that would dictate what to buy, how much to pay for it, and how much to sell it for.

As a male in his mid-twenties, Gorra knew as much about handbags as you would expect (in other words, not much). He had never worked at designing, producing, or selling women's bags. Yet he had worked as an investment banker at Goldman Sachs and the private equity firm TPG—experience that now came in handy. Gorra took his knowledge of pricing financial instruments and identifying arbitrage opportunities, and in an unprecedented move he applied it to the luxury handbag business. Who would have guessed that exotic financial products and luxury handbags had anything in common? But they did, and Gorra's innovation helped convince venture capitalists to pour in money, first to develop the operation, then to purchase the inventory, and lastly to build out the technology (principle #6: operations before technology). At first, VCs wanted to fund only asset-light online consignment or marketplace businesses. Yet Charles saw a better way for the seller, and he managed to convince prominent investors of the opportunity. As of this writing, Rebag has received $28.3 million in venture funding, with its latest series B round bringing in $15.5 million. Not bad for a three-year-old startup.

When I last spoke with Gorra, he observed that his biggest challenge was "trying to sell a service that most high-income women are not looking for." As he put it, "Very few people are going to Google to search for 'how to sell a bag.'" Consequently, he couldn't use search engine ads to acquire customers. Most online channels such as social media or display ads didn't work, either. As Gorra realized, he needed to educate customers about the idea of selling their handbags. Rebag's most successful marketing campaign to date involved the idea of, as Gorra described it, "teaching people that you can instantly monetize your closet." Rebag built an in-house sales staff that approached influencers, personal shoppers, wardrobe consultants, and salespeople working in high-end stores, asking them to talk to their customers about the option of selling their unwanted handbags on Rebag (principle #1: acquire customers in bulk). If these influencers signed up to become affiliates of Rebag, they would receive a commission on any bag they helped bring in. "This affiliates program has been by far the cheapest channel to acquire customers," Gorra said (principle #5: use offline tools).

After signing up thousands of affiliates, Gorra concluded that this low-cost approach was not scalable (principle #3: do things that don't scale). He could not simply double the investment, hire more internal people, and tap this channel to grow quickly. To fuel his next phase of growth, he had to find and tap alternative channels. One option that worked moderately well was direct response ads in niche cable TV programs. Still, these ads delivered only limited reach. Social media afforded a higher reach, but it was not as effective. As Gorra explored the other available customer acquisition channels, he confronted the inherent trade-off between cost-effectiveness and scalability. No established channel could provide both high reach and high cost-effectiveness. He thus needed to find the cheapest customer acquisition channel(s), which would likely be low scale. Over time, he would have to try to increase scale by forgoing the least amount of cost-effectiveness as possible, closely following the efficient frontier curve (*see Figure* 7.3). By late 2018, Rebag did not employ mass media as a channel to acquire customers. Still, I suspect that the company's steady growth will one day force Gorra to consider it.

As Rebag mastered the seller's side of the secondary market for luxury bags, Gorra shifted his focus to the buyer's side. With some of his venture capital money, he built Trendlee.com, an online retailer of used high-end handbags. In effect, Gorra was building a two-sided retailer, treating buying and selling bags as two distinct businesses. "Rebag has a high-end older customer," he said, "and it promises

FIGURE 7.3 **ILLUSTRATION OF PATH OF CUSTOMER ACQUISITION CHANNELS FOR REBAG**

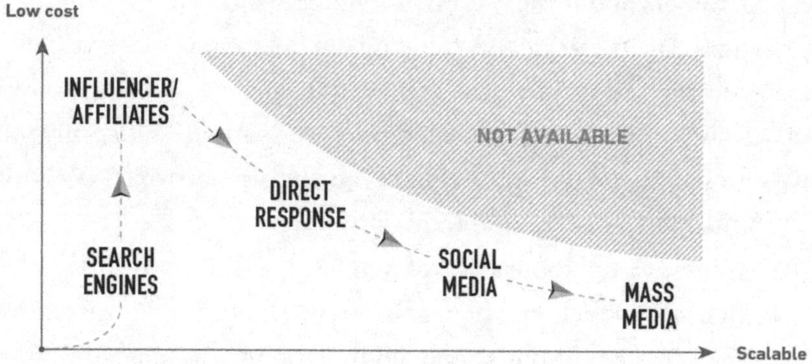

Note: The channels and media in this chart may not apply to all startups.

convenience, whereas Trendlee is an aspirational value play and its customers are younger and less wealthy. There is some overlap, but not much." Gorra plans to join the brands under one name at some point, but only when "both customer segments start to become the same person who buys and then resells used bags."

Is buying and selling secondhand handbags much of an innovation? Is it disruptive to the manufacturers? I taught a workshop on digital disruption to senior executives of luxury brands such as Jaeger-LeCoultre, Chanel, and Hermès, and they are very concerned about secondary online marketplaces. The big question is: does the world need the manufacture of many more luxury bags, or does it just need a more efficient allocation of the bags already in circulation? Gorra seems to think the latter. As I said in Chapter 6, disruption occurs most intensively when some of your customers question the value of your entire industry.

Deliberately or not, Gorra applied all seven principles to acquire his first customers, and he achieved tremendous initial success. Of course, as his business grows and acquires new cohorts of customers, he will have to diverge from these principles. The principles can help you start a disruptive business, but they don't always apply when you're seeking to grow into a mass market—your first million customers, or your first ten million. Instead of focusing on the supply side, on operations building, and on non-scalable offline approaches, Gorra will have to focus more on the demand side, on technology building, and on scalable online tools. Gorra will still have to cater to his customers, but instead of considering the needs of only his early adopters, he'll have to understand and address the needs of a much larger, more diverse population. It's never easy to abandon what has worked in the past, but it's absolutely necessary. In order to keep growing, Rebag will have to grow up.

Customers' Multiple Roles

As I've tried to make clear, decoupling theory prompts us to see customer activity acquisition as *the* central task for any new disruptive business—both startups and new corporate ventures. Rather than overwhelming themselves with a variety of goals and efforts, entrepreneurs and intrapreneurs do better to focus on choosing which customers to service, and then on working their hearts out to acquire them. That is how Charles-Albert Gorra approached it. With every decision he has made, from product development to operations, technology, and hiring, he has sought to acquire good customers at a reasonable cost. Gorra knows that without enough customers, there is no reason to build out anything else.

As a startup, as you acquire customers, make sure you truly deliver value. By centering the business around customer needs and wants, you stand to benefit in ways that go far beyond getting paid. All companies need R&D to build and test new products, marketing to advertise, and operations and quality control to service, troubleshoot, and solve user problems. Startups usually don't have such an extensive workforce early on. Luckily, they don't need to. By choosing their first customers wisely and serving them well, startups can do more with less.

Early Airbnb customers helped the company improve the platform, alerting the founders to what worked well and what didn't. These customers also proved more tolerant of mistakes, and they were willing to wait patiently for improvements because they had a say in the process. Uber and Etsy customers supported these companies by providing free word-of-mouth marketing. Early customers can even provide after-sale support. At one cloud software startup I advise, the CEO decided that he would reroute new user questions and troubleshooting to his oldest and most loyal customers, instead of hiring customer service personnel. Few later customers would provide such support. It turns out that a company's first customers perform many roles often done by employees later in a company's life. Of course, you need to incentivize customers, whether by offering some form of monetary compensation such as discounts or referral fees or providing non-monetary perks such as recognition or VIP status.

Ultimately, two major factors explain startup failure. The first factor, unsurprisingly, is the failure of new businesses to acquire enough customers. This chapter has dealt with that issue. But starting a company also means acquiring enough of the *right* kind of customers, which leads us to the second, less obvious factor, explaining startup failure. Often enough, new ventures create value for their customers but fail to capture a large enough portion of this value to sustain a business. Eliminating some of this leakage of value (as we saw in Chapter 5) is a necessary precondition before moving on to the next phase.

After acquiring their first thousand or so customers, startups must begin a very different process—that of scaling growth. The imperative to grow prompts entrepreneurs to address issues such as what new products or markets to develop, how to build economies of scale and scope, what other activities to steal from incumbents, and how to organize new incoming employees. Entrepreneurs must solve these problems even as they scale up and acquire new customers. It's quite a challenge, and as we'll see in Chapter 8, decoupling offers a fresh and helpful perspective on how to meet it.

8

GOING FROM ONE THOUSAND TO ONE MILLION CUSTOMERS

Once a new venture has proven its business model's merit via the acquisition of its first customers, its next challenge is to grow, and in many cases to transition from a single-product business to a company selling multiple products. What new products or services should the company create and market? Which markets should it enter? An obvious answer might be to choose industries with favorable economics and high growth prospects. As famed investor Warren Buffett once remarked: "When a manager with a reputation for brilliance tackles an industry with a reputation for bad economics, it is the reputation of the industry that often remains intact." Best, then, to avoid weak markets, and plunge into strong, growing ones.

Yet this approach might be less straightforward than it seems. A 1991 Bain & Co. study on growth of companies found that "contrary to conventional wisdom, most profitable corporate growth doesn't come from participating in a 'hot' industry and riding the trends upward. In fact, a large number of companies with sustained profitable growth are in industries that may appear to be mature."[1] The problem is that competitors tend to overcrowd "hot" markets. If many strong competitors flock to a fast-growing market simultaneously, market share and profits become much harder to capture. Bain & Co. found that 80 percent of the time, a company's higher rate of growth owed more to its performance relative to competitors than to the historical growth rate of the market it had chosen to enter.[2] The real estate industry offers a good example. Many cities around the world saw multiyear, double-digit increases in housing prices. This consistent growth has prompted many contractors to invest in building houses. Yet few will reap the benefit of this growth because of overcompetition.

To grow quickly, new businesses must choose their markets with an eye toward achieving a competitive advantage. But how? Back in the early 1990s, C. K. Prahalad and Gary Hamel suggested that companies should enter markets in which they possessed special skills or strengths, or "core competencies," as they called them. Coca-Cola performed marketing and distribution extremely well. Disney excelled at family-friendly character development and storytelling. Fidelity shined at low-cost fund management. These were their core competencies. And experts advised that these companies stick to these competencies when launching new products and entering new markets, as they would retain an advantage over competitors. According to the *Economist*, "The idea spread from core competencies to core everything—core processes, core businesses—everything that constituted the essence of what a company was and did. Management consultants encouraged companies to focus on their core as a source of untapped potential in a time of rapid change and unpredictability." By the early 2000s, Bain consultant Chris Zook and others built on these ideas, arguing that companies should exploit businesses in new markets that lie adjacent to their existing businesses, while investing further to improve their core skills and capabilities.

From the beginning, the notion of "core competency" has always been somewhat vague. Is it a skill? A process? A capability? How do these differ from one another? Zook's answer, in his 2001 book *Profit from the Core* (coauthored with James Allen), was to conceive of core competencies as "strategic assets" and to propose various kinds of adjacent spaces that companies could consider where they might deploy these assets.[3] P&G might deploy its valuable skills in marketing consumer-packaged goods aimed at the middle class to *adjacent customer segments*, selling toiletries, dental hygiene, and hair care products to higher-income families. GE owns assets in industrial manufacturing that it has leveraged in *adjacent industries* such as power, aviation, healthcare equipment, and major appliances. Disney has leveraged its skill at building family brands in the United States into *adjacent geographies* such as Tokyo and Hong Kong. Walmart's skills in securing low-cost sourcing of consumer durables have enabled it to move into *adjacent channels,* such as selling bulk produce in price clubs and groceries in supercenters. Dell has mobilized its assets in direct-to-consumer selling of computers to move into *adjacent activities in the firm's value chain*, such as just-in-time manufacturing and outbound logistics. In all, Zook and Allen proposed six distinct categories of adjacencies. Within each category, executives could choose from among a myriad of options.

The strategy of defining core competencies and growing into adjacent areas is conceptually sound, embodying the notion of synergies derived from scale and scope economies. Most businesses start by leveraging scale economies, making the same product or rendering the same service over and over again and achieving increased market penetration. The efficiencies of production at scale give these businesses an advantage, lowering their unit cost compared to competitors'. When demand dries up, they can shift gears to a diversification strategy, producing products and services in new markets that allow for economies of scope. By producing two or more distinct products requiring similar skills or resources (buses and trucks, for instance), they also lower their unit cost. In both cases, the reduction of the firm's own costs leads to growth in revenues, as the firm either charges customers lower prices or extracts higher profits that it then reinvests.

Uber started by driving people around, and it grew by driving more people in different cities and with different types of cars (first "black cars," then private cars). In 2016, Uber changed its focus from scaling up to scoping outward. It deployed the same mapping and routing algorithms it had developed for its main ride-sharing business to launch other businesses: a food delivery service called UberEats, and a package delivery service called UberRush. For these new businesses, Uber engaged its existing workforce of 40 million active drivers worldwide, making more efficient use of their idle time. In between rides, drivers could earn a few dollars delivering a pizza for Uber. Reportedly, the company created a division called UberEverything, whose purpose was to identify adjacent opportunities around its core competency in the rides business.[4]

It's too early to tell if Uber's approach of building on its core competencies and expanding into adjacent markets will spur rapid growth above and beyond pure scaling. At many companies, this approach has indeed worked. Yet it carries significant downsides. As you enter adjacent businesses, you risk choosing one that your current customers find irrelevant. In that case, you'll shoulder the burden of acquiring a completely new set of customers. In 2006, building on its competency in caffeinated drinks, the Coca-Cola Company released a coffee-flavored soft drink to compete in the fast-growing coffee market. The drink didn't please customers, and Coca-Cola discontinued it just a year later. Likewise, Colgate decided to build on its competency in oral health and chase the fast-growing frozen foods category. In 1982, it launched a line of Colgate-branded frozen entrees. Even Colgate's most loyal customers greeted the novelty with skepticism. Ask your customers. As a brand manager, you may be surprised to learn that they regard your brand as significantly less versatile than you do. What you call closely adjacent, they may regard as far and remote.

A second drawback of the traditional "adjacencies" approach is that most businesses analyzing possible adjacent markets to enter will find numerous candidates—perhaps too many. In expanding beyond its original Windows desktop operating system, Microsoft could have entered the adjacent server operating system market, the adjacent desktop application market, the adjacent desktop hardware market, the adjacent small business services market, or the adjacent consumer entertainment market. It could have plunged into numerous additional markets that were roughly one degree farther away from its original market. Since the 1980s, Microsoft did in fact enter multiple adjacent markets, achieving wild success in some instances (Office and Xbox) and spectacular failures in others (Windows Phone and Zune MP3 player). With so many potential businesses that attempt to build on a company's existing skill set, it's hard to decide which to pursue. Certainly there must be another, more focused way of moving toward rapid growth.

Growing a Business Around CVC Adjacencies

There is another way, and it is rooted in decoupling theory. The vast majority of conventional approaches to growth pertain to possible firm-side synergies: "How can I leverage my powerful brand, vast distribution network, marketing prowess, production skills, or intellectual property to expand into new products or markets?" But we could very well pose similar questions from the customer's perspective: "If customers buy my product in order to perform one of the many activities in their CVC, enjoying reduced monetary, time, and effort costs, then how might we make it worthwhile for them to perform another, neighboring activity in their CVC?" Or, put differently: "What else might we provide to our decoupling customers such that the combination of both activities (and possibly additional ones) reduces their total cost below that of the incumbent, and below the costs they would incur if they used separate vendors?" Proceeding from this vantage point, we can locate possible *customer-side synergies*.

Customer-side synergies: Cost reductions that the customer gains while consuming multiple activities provided by a single firm.*

Once again, it is cost reduction that drives customer behavior. Where can businesses find opportunities to further reduce customer costs? The easiest way of finding them is by assessing the customer's value chain. In particular, customer-side synergy opportunities are most likely to reside in adjacent activities. If your company can deliver these synergies, then a customer that decoupled one activity with you now has an incentive to hire you for additional activities. I call these additional activities *CVC adjacencies*, and they are the next natural steps to pursue in order to grow.

CVC adjacencies: Activities immediately preceding and following those that a customer chose to decouple from an incumbent.

During the early 2000s, when I traveled for work as a consultant, I would often receive an email on my Hotmail account informing me of the company I was visiting, as well as the city in which it was located. I would visit a search engine such as Altavista to obtain the company's street address, and then click on MapQuest to look up the location on a map. I would open another browser window to launch Expedia to purchase my flight, reverting back to Hotmail to check for a confirmation of my ticket. All told, I had to toggle between four websites, each with its own login, copying and pasting information across them and suffering through the occasional "site down for maintenance" issue. In addition, each website tried to upsell me on a paid subscription version of its service, further wasting my time and

* This idea was first presented to me by my colleague Bharat Anand.

trying my patience. Enter Google. When Gmail came out in 2004, it brought search and email together—just one click away. Google Maps, launched in 2005, allowed me to click on an address in Gmail and see its location pop up on a map. A few years later, in 2011, Google Flights allowed me to purchase a ticket, also one click away and with no need to copy or paste information. Google came to fill all the major adjacencies in my work-related travel planning CVC by reducing the effort and time costs I had previously experienced.

Seeking out customer-side synergies confers significant advantages over the traditional, firm-side synergies approach. Whereas many businesses might exist adjacent to your core business, only a few business opportunities lie adjacent to the existing CVC activities you offer your customers. Further, you can identify these adjacencies quite easily. At most, only two adjacent activities exist, one immediately preceding and one immediately following each decoupled activity. Although companies can also sometimes consider non-adjacent activities proximate to the decoupled activity, immediately adjacent activities remain the natural candidates to consider first when trying to grow your business.* Whichever activities you choose to pursue, immediately adjacent or merely proximate, you'll still have to determine how to "steal" these activities from others, whether incumbents or customers performing these activities on their own. Doing so by decoupling requires using the principles discussed in Chapter 3, notably lowering the costs to customers of performing these activities.

GROWTH BY COUPLING

Once your business has succeeded in providing adjacent activities to your early customers, you must ensure that customer-side synergies between the newly provided activities and the original ones

* For instance, "search" and "choose" are adjacent customer value chain activities, as are "pay" and "receive." But "search" and "pay" are not adjacent, nor are "choose" and "dispose."

exist and are strong. Otherwise, you may gain the right to fulfill new activities but lose the ability to provide the original ones. As we saw in Chapter 3, you should reinforce the links between the new set of activities you are providing by attending to what we have called integration costs. Ensure that it costs customers less to perform the new combined set of activities integrally with you, as compared to what it might cost them to perform them elsewhere. If you use Outlook (owned by Microsoft) as your company email provider, you can effortlessly contact each of your business contacts using Skype (bought by Microsoft) from your email account. As you talk to them, you can quickly pull information on them from LinkedIn, another business bought by Microsoft. If you integrate two activities favorably for customers, then you can continue to tack on adjacent activities, moving outward along the CVC, as depicted in *Figure 8.1.* This forms the foundational basis of growth by *coupling*.

Coupling: The act of sequentially adding and strengthening the links between adjacent customer activities captured from an incumbent.

In theory, the process of coupling can continue until the disruptor subsumes all activities from the traditional incumbent and becomes the new incumbent. But of course, you also have to protect yourself from new decouplers. To do that, increase the integration forces that bind the newly coupled activities together. Keep delivering cost synergies for your customers, and they will want to keep their activities coupled with you.

Decoupling theory thus points us toward an alternative way of approaching growth. First, strengthen the core activity (the one your business first used to decouple). Then grow into adjacencies, focusing on one at a time. Strengthen the integration links binding the newly offered adjacent activities before moving outward into additional adjacent activities. Since you're dealing with only two directly adjacent

FIGURE 8.1 **GROWTH PHASES IN ADJACENT COUPLING**

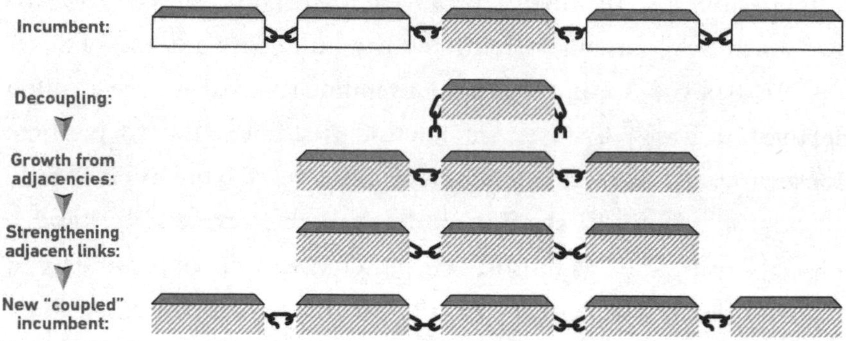

activities (and perhaps a few other close activities) at a time, the path to growth becomes more predictable and easier for your entire organization to visualize. You're starting with your core business activity and venturing outward along a single dimension, using a disciplined approach. Your growth process can become much more methodical and predictable, and consequently more likely to succeed.

Alibaba's Growth Secret

To understand how companies have exploited customer-side synergies in order to grow, consider Alibaba. Founded in 1999 by English teacher Jack Ma, Alibaba by 2019 had become one of the world's largest companies by market capitalization, with more than ten multibillion-dollar businesses in widely ranging sectors such as retailing, e-commerce, online cloud services, mobile phones, logistics, payments, content, and more. Between 2011 and 2016, the company's revenues grew at an average compound annual rate of 87 percent. Profits jumped by 94 percent and cash flow by 120 percent.[5] Such rapid growth was highly unusual for such a large and established digital company. Yet Alibaba continued to grow remarkably fast nearly twenty years after its founding.

So how did Alibaba do it? Founded as an online business-to-business marketplace, the company in 2003 moved into consumer-to-consumer e-commerce and in 2004 acquired both Aliwangwang, a text message service, and Alipay, an online payments service. The next year, it went on to acquire Yahoo China in an effort to provide consumers with content and web services. In 2008, it launched TMall, a business-to-consumer online retailer, followed in 2009 by Alibaba Cloud Computing, a cloud storage company. Other new business launches proceeded in turn: a search engine company named eTao (2010), a startup called Aliyin that created mobile operating systems (2011), and a logistics consortium named Cainiao (2013). In 2015, Alibaba took a majority stake in smartphone maker Meizu. Note how many of these companies operated in non-adjacent industries, in Zook and Allen's sense of the word. The economies of scope between retailing, cloud computing, payments, logistics, and electronics manufacturing are not very clear. Businesses in these industries require different resources and employees with widely varying skill sets in order to compete. So why didn't the company stick with its original, business-to-business online marketplace and focus growth there in order to dominate the market and achieve competitive advantage by traditional economies of scale? Alibaba arguably could have sold more products to more customers in more markets. After all, that's precisely what Walmart did to grow during the second half of the twentieth century.

Alibaba's expansion strategy focused squarely on customer-side synergies and CVC adjacencies. In 2016, around 50 percent of online shopping took place via mobile phones, with the rest occurring on laptops, desktops, and tablets.[6] To shop online, consumers first had to decide which device to use to access the internet and, implicitly, which operating system and browser combination to use. After that, most consumers opened browsers and pointed at websites, accessing their communication services, email, social networks, chat apps, and so on. At some point, they identified a need to make a purchase and performed searches either outside e-commerce websites (for instance, on Google or Baidu) or inside them. From there, consumers arrived at the most appropriate e-commerce sites. In China, business customers went to Alibaba, while consumers went to Taobao to shop for products from other consumers or to Tmall to shop for products from retailers. To obtain more product information or to negotiate prices (a common practice in China), buyers communicated with sellers, usually by chat apps. Consumers then had to pay for their purchase and wait for a logistics operator to deliver it. This represented the extent of the typical online shopper's CVC.

Analyzing this CVC, we spot a clear pattern: in principle, customers could perform each of the relevant activities with one of Alibaba's multiple companies (*see Figure 8.2*). Meizu produced the phone, and Aliyun the operating system. Customers embarking on their purchasing journey could begin using a content site such as Yahoo China, owned by Alibaba, and move into the eTao search engine. Customers could then choose one of Alibaba's online stores—Alibaba itself, Taobao, or Tmall—and communicate with the seller via Aliwangwang. Finally, consumers could pay with Alipay and receive their goods via a Cainiao partner.

FIGURE 8.2 **HOW ALIBABA COVERS THE ENTIRE CVC**

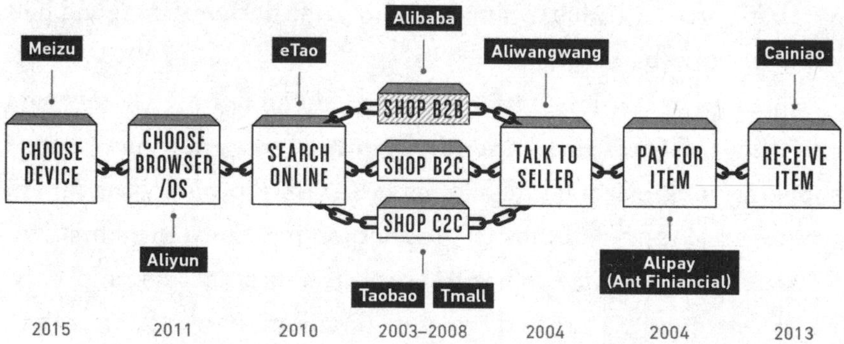

Alibaba began growing by focusing on a single stage of the shopper's CVC with its Alibaba website. It then moved outward to capture other customer activities. Instead of using the traditional industry adjacencies approach (payment, mobile phones, and logistics are not adjacent industries), the company opted to move into adjacent CVC activities. By 2019, the company's businesses were serving most of the CVC activities. Economies of scope might have enabled Alibaba to achieve firm-side synergies to some extent. That's what Walmart had done: it had reduced logistics and real estate costs in the second half of the twentieth century while growing from consumer durables to produce in bulk, and then to perishable groceries and gasoline retailing. But Alibaba didn't immediately pursue firm-side synergies. Its real win lay in achieving customer-side synergies.

Let's say you're a consumer trying to buy a television set from another consumer or from a small retailer. If you can effortlessly search and compare options, talk to the other party online, pay him or her, and receive your product all in the same environment (same site, same login, same checkout), the process becomes simpler and faster for you. Since you're not using different companies as you move along the CVC, you don't need to worry about their varying policies or the different user experiences they offer. It's all one integrated, harmonious process. By growing outward from its original business, aggregating adjacent CVC activities, Alibaba created multiple synergies for the shopper. And that drove more customers to adopt and use more of Alibaba's ever-growing portfolio of services. Serving the interests of customers, Alibaba snatched up a larger share of the customer's spending. The major insight they had? The cost to acquire customers for these new businesses was significantly lower, since Alibaba was already serving them. And with that came nine billion-dollar businesses with tremendous lockstep growth.

Alibaba is hardly the only company to grow opportunistically across the CVC. Airbnb might have chosen to grow around its core competence of matching hosts with renters by, for example, helping customers rent long-term housing, offices, or storage space. Instead,

Airbnb in 2016 launched a program called Trips, offering Airbnb renters a service to upgrade their stay and book local activities, from cooking classes in Florence to violin-making workshops in Paris. The program expanded to include restaurant bookings, with flight and rental car bookings planned for the future.[7] As Airbnb's CEO Brian Chesky explained, "For every dollar you spend in a hotel, you spend a dollar in flight, you spend three dollars in the city. This is called 'daily spend.' Now, historically, it's not been sized to the big market. There's no Hilton of daily spend. There's no Delta of daily spend. But most of travel is daily spend: Where you eat, entertainment, what you do all day. And so we think that's probably, long term, the biggest opportunity."[8] Put differently, Airbnb was also breaking the rules of the traditional adjacency approach. It was following the money across the customer travel CVC, covering the activities of planning and booking, finding a room, and booking local excursions. Airbnb had no special competence in handling restaurant reservations, and the space was highly competitive, dominated by apps such as OpenTable. To compensate, Airbnb partnered with a specialist service provider called Resy. When Airbnb enters the flight reservation business, it will likewise need to develop or secure expertise, and it will compete with giant online travel agents such as Expedia and Priceline.[9] Who will win? It depends on who among them will offer the largest customer-side synergy package possible.

As formidable as such challenges might sound, it might well be worth it for many companies to tackle them head-on. The beauty of leveraging customer-side synergies is that it reduces pressure on companies to try to find new customers for their new offerings. All they have to do is offer them to current customers—a significantly cheaper task to accomplish. In addition, the new offerings need not be best-in-class. Even if Airbnb had introduced a "me-too," undifferentiated product or service, it still could provide value to its original customers. Most business travelers would prefer to fulfill all of their needs using a single app, a single design, a single environment, a single help desk, a single payment processor. It's easier to consolidate and couple providers than to move from TripAdvisor to Hilton to Delta to OpenTable and so on. As long as the service quality and prices remain roughly comparable, Airbnb becomes a more attractive alternative if it can offer an array of adjacent services to its current customers.

Organizing for Growth

If you pursue the path to growth suggested by decoupling theory, you will likely find yourself following in Alibaba's footsteps and entering vastly different businesses. If you're successful, your early customers will benefit tremendously, and they'll reward you with an increasing share of their business. Given the different competencies these businesses require for success, it won't make sense to structure your businesses around identical skills and processes, as Disney and Coca-Cola do. The new businesses might require vastly different functions, so organizing around functional roles the way P&G does won't make sense, either. What makes the most sense is to organize your businesses around customers and the value you provide them. As you expand your business to cover different parts of the customer's value chain, it's natural to organize the company around the CVC as well. Your business units should map one-to-one with major CVC activities. As the old adage goes, structure follows strategy.

There is one caveat. As I discussed in Chapter 3, some CVC activities create value, while others charge for or erode value. It makes little sense to assemble a conglomerate of businesses and position one business unit as the sole value-charging entity, or even worse, to position another as the sole value-eroding unit. Each business unit must continue to function as a business. As such, each should maintain responsibility for at least one value-creating and one value-charging activity, with the head of the unit overseeing it. Within each unit, you might well have a single department that focuses on the value-creating portion (product development, marketing, fulfillment, and so on), the value-charging portion (for instance, monetization or billing), and the value-erosion portion (for instance, compliance). Finally, all of the units should report to a single corporate CEO. As Pandora grew to encompass multiple activities in the listener's CVC, the company could have organized itself into two separate business units, one overseeing the listening portion of the CVC, the other dealing with advertisers. The first unit might have contained divisions responsible for media planning, quality control, and commercial relationships with record labels. The second business unit might have had divisions handling ad sales, ad design, and ad targeting (*see Figure 8.3*). Each of these business units would have combined enough components of the CVC to provide value for their respective customers. The departments within these units would collaborate to produce that value and to extract value from customers in return. The main role of the CEO here is to balance the needs of the listeners against the demands of the advertisers, represented by their respective unit heads.

FIGURE 8.3 **ORGANIZING FOR ADJACENT COUPLING AT PANDORA**

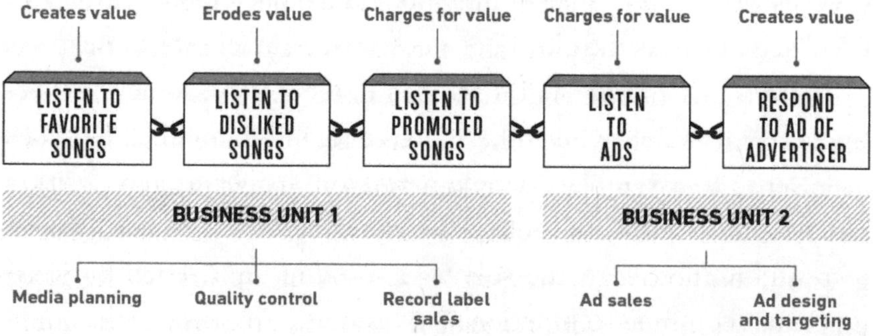

Organizing around customer activities enables the company to integrate multiple products and services in a frictionless way, thereby improving customer experience. Apple has attracted loyal customers across categories by deeply integrating its hardware, software, online, and offline services such as digital content, data cloud, and retail experiences. This closely woven integration characterizes the company's internal organization as well. Consequently, Apple's consumers can perform complex, multi-activity processes such as recording a video on their iPhones, uploading it to iCloud, accessing it on their iMac computers, editing it with their iMovie video editing software, and sharing it with friends and family on any social media app available on the iTunes store, all in a smooth, seamless way. At Apple, one individual, known internally as the DRI (directly responsible individual), bears responsibility for stitching together all relevant functions, products, and groups of people involved in the delivery of any given customer process.

Today, we might take Apple's integrated organizational structure for granted, but at one time it was quite unusual. Steve Jobs approached Apple's business in innovative ways, thinking not in terms of the disparate technology products but in terms of what customers wanted and needed *as human beings.* "It's in Apple's DNA," he remarked in 2011, "that technology alone is not enough. We believe that it's technology married with the humanities that yields us the result that makes our heart sing." In his view, devices in the post-PC world "need[ed] to be even more intuitive and easier to use than a PC, and . . . the software and the hardware and the applications need[ed] to be intertwined in an even more seamless way than they are on a PC. We think we have the right architecture not just in silicon, but in our organization, to build these kinds of products."[10] Jobs repeatedly put his money where his mouth was. A decade earlier, in autumn 2000, he had canceled the launch of the first Apple Store and ordered its complete reconfiguration to conform to customers' natural shopping behaviors. Referring to Apple's head of retail at the time, he explained that "Ron [Johnson] thinks we've got it all wrong. He thinks it should be organized not around products but instead around what people do. And you know, he's right."[11]

The Price of Coupling

As we have seen, a growth-by-coupling strategy affords multiple benefits for companies. First, it constitutes the path of least resistance, marketing-wise. Because you're deliberately exploiting customer-side synergies, customers will more easily embrace your new products and services, as they stand to gain directly from using them. Second, in many cases, a "me-too" offering of comparable or even slightly lesser quality might suffice to convince customers to couple their CVC activities with you. You don't need to be best-in-class in everything you do, nor should you initially aspire to that. Just ensure that your original offering, which won over your customers in the first place, remains better than the rest. Finally, growth via coupling the customer value chain provides a vision for the company's future direction, as well as clear priorities for employees. As Steve Jobs liked to say, "simplicity breeds clarity."

Growth through coupling does have its operational downsides. Employing this strategy may force your company to enter very disparate lines of business, and for this reason your company likely will not succeed in its pursuit unless it acquires new skills. In evaluating where to grow next, think methodically about each activity in the customer's value chain. Map out the CVC activities as seen by the customer. Then switch the focus back to you, determining the skills you would require in order to bring to market an offering that helps customers perform each activity. Compare these skills with those your company currently possesses. If the skills match up well, then you might viably couple that activity. Otherwise, you'll need to fill in skill gaps by building skills internally, borrowing from others via a partnership of some sort, or buying them by acquiring people or businesses. Here's a table I typically provide to companies to help them determine possible growth directions, and to identify and bridge the possible skills gap in order to successfully couple (*Figure 8.4*):

FIGURE 8.4 **EXAMPLE OF TOOL TO DEFINE WHAT TO COUPLE NEXT**

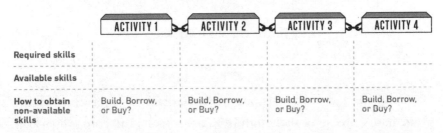

	ACTIVITY 1	ACTIVITY 2	ACTIVITY 3	ACTIVITY 4
Required skills				
Available skills				
How to obtain non-available skills	Build, Borrow, or Buy?	Build, Borrow, or Buy?	Build, Borrow, or Buy?	Build, Borrow, or Buy?

Focusing on your customer's needs doesn't always come cheaply. But if you can pay that price, the upside is substantial. Alibaba and Airbnb both ventured into businesses for which they lacked many of the required skills. Venture capital investors paid for much of the skills acquisition—an investment that paid off handsomely. If your company can afford the requisite skills, and if it mobilizes a coupling strategy successfully, you may see rapid growth. Your business will become more diversified and much more resistant to outside influences such as economic shifts, the emergence of new competitors, and government regulation. Each of these factors might impact a business unit at any given time, but rarely will they impact all units simultaneously. Still, the day will eventually come when your company stops growing or, worse, declines. What do you do then? Chapter 9 offers some answers.

9

RECLAIMING LOST CUSTOMERS

It was 2010, and Comcast, one of the largest U.S. telecom operators, had a problem. Although in many regions the company was a monopoly or duopoly provider of internet service to households and businesses, demand for its cable TV and Xfinity on-demand content services was stalling. The source of the problem, from Comcast's perspective, was Netflix, which had recently begun allowing customers to stream content. Previously, households would sign up for Comcast's internet service connection and Xfinity video on demand. Now Netflix's streaming video offer prompted Comcast customers to make two changes. First, they upgraded their internet speeds so that they could consume data-heavy internet services such as on-demand videos, videogames, and video chats. Second, many stopped using Xfinity, preferring Netflix's "all you can watch for one price" over Xfinity's à la carte movie pricing. In a sense, Netflix decoupled Comcast from the activity of viewing video content, leaving it with only the activity of providing internet connectivity (*see Figure 9.1*).

Netflix's on-demand service in the United States grew so dramatically that by 2015, Netflix accounted for as much as one-third of all internet traffic in Comcast's fiber-optic cables during peak hours.[1] Seeing this extensive use of Comcast's valuable resources, and planning to invest billions of dollars to increase bandwidth to people's

FIGURE 9.1 **COMCAST'S VIEW OF HOW NETFLIX DECOUPLED IT**

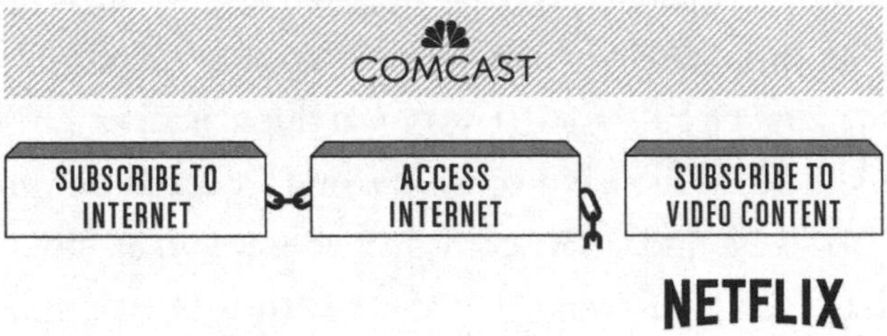

homes, Comcast's CEO, Brian Roberts, demanded that Netflix pay for this benefit. After all, Netflix was exploiting Comcast's infrastructure and had cut the company out of a very lucrative video-streaming business. If Comcast supplied data for Netflix's business, Roberts argued, it was only fair that Netflix pay up. Shouldn't a water park compensate the water company for the water its customers use? Shouldn't a building pay the electric company for energy it uses to air-condition tenants' units? Comcast was supporting Netflix's business with its most valuable resource, so Comcast wanted a cut of the proceeds.

At first, Netflix CEO Reid Hastings declared he would not pay, citing net neutrality rules that at the time forbade internet service providers from discriminating between sources of internet traffic.* In response, Roberts made Netflix's life harder by, in essence, slowing the speed of Netflix traffic for households that reached a certain data limit, a practice known as "throttling." When customers were consuming close to all Comcast's bandwidth in a region, the company needed to prioritize traffic, and it decided to penalize heavy Netflix users at the expense of other sources of internet traffic.

* In December 2017, the Federal Communications Commission in the United States abandoned some of the net neutrality rules put into place during the presidency of Barack Obama that prohibited internet service providers from blocking websites or charging for higher-speed data pass-through. At the time of this writing (May 2018), the U.S. Senate had just approved a resolution to undo those December 2017 changes.

As customers saw the quality of their Netflix video streams decline, they took to the phones to complain. Now, whom do you think people called first, their internet provider, Comcast, or Netflix? I don't know about you, but if I was watching Netflix on my computer and the quality started to erode, and I clicked on other video sites like YouTube and NBC.com and those worked fine, I would call Netflix. Facing an avalanche of calls, threats, and subscription cancellations, Hastings decided to pay Comcast for not throttling its data pass-through. He had no choice: he had to stop the bleeding of customer defection right away.

But Hastings was not defeated. Whether he knew it or not, he likely reasoned that decoupling had not rendered Comcast a mere supplier to Netflix, as Roberts argued. Much the opposite: Netflix now served as Comcast's distribution channel. Comcast sold, among other services, low- and high-speed internet. The former cost around \$30 per month, while the latter cost \$60 to \$100 per month. But both services had similar marginal costs. With the necessary infrastructure in place, it didn't cost Comcast materially more to offer one or the other. The price difference between high- and low-speed internet represented almost pure profit for Comcast. Hastings argued that Comcast's customers were upgrading to high-speed internet for the primary purpose of watching Netflix. Customers had no reason to pay for faster internet if they used it only for email, reading news online, and listening to songs. By decoupling in the middle of the customer's value chain, Netflix effectively became a driver of Comcast's highest-margin service (*see Figure 9.2*). On that basis, *Netflix* wanted a cut of the profits. Hastings demanded publicly that Roberts pay Netflix, instead of the other way around.

After an intense, often public debate that saw Hastings petition the Federal Communications Commission on Netflix's behalf, Roberts called a truce.[2] Neither would pay the other anything.[3] Comcast's attempt to arrest its growth slide by taking on Netflix had failed.

FIGURE 9.2 **NETFLIX'S VIEW OF HOW IT DECOUPLED COMCAST**

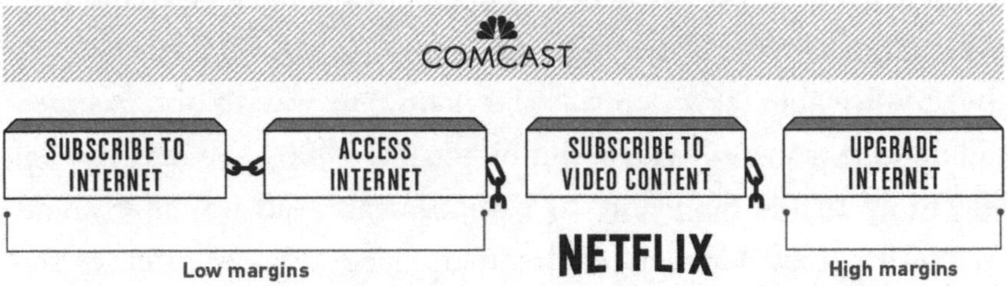

Comcast is hardly the first large incumbent to see its business stop growing and begin moving backward. Other companies include Microsoft in 2008, GE and Motorola in 2009, McDonald's in 2012, IBM in 2014—the list goes on and on. Academics and consultants who have studied these companies have usually attributed their decline to a failure of innovation and adaptation. A study of 410 companies in the Fortune 100 between 1955 and 2006 by my colleague Derek van Bever and his coauthors showed that as many as 350 companies experienced at least one major revenue growth stall, as defined by a multiyear above-average growth rate in revenues followed by a precipitous reduction accompanied by negligible to declining sales growth thereafter.[4] In 87 percent of these cases, the authors contend, the growth stall didn't stem from external factors beyond executives' control. Rather, the top three reasons for growth stalls included shifting customer preferences, lack of innovation, and failure to fully exploit the current business' growth opportunities. The solution, Van Bever and his coauthors suggest, was essentially to innovate faster, smarter, better. They advocate getting executives to ask tougher questions, challenge company assumptions, bring mid-level employees into strategic conversations, and solicit ideas from outsiders. Other experts have offered similar advice. In their view, companies fail to adapt because they fall behind. The solution is to innovate, and then innovate some more.

Comcast's response suggests another, more fundamental factor behind incumbents' stalled growth. During the mid-twentieth century, customers had primarily communicated electronically through landline telephones (which used copper wires) and received in-home entertainment via electromagnetic waves sent through the air. By the 1980s, cable television was the main new way to obtain entertainment, particularly video. But by the late 2000s, the internet was becoming the primary way to communicate and be entertained. As Netflix grew, Comcast's customers needed faster internet service. Instead of treating Netflix as a channel partner, a driver of its most profitable and highest-growth business, broadband internet, Comcast treated Netflix as a competitor to its other decreasing legacy business, cable TV. By reducing the speed at which it provided Netflix data to its own customers, Comcast showed how far it would go to capture value from this "partner" by penalizing its own customers. Netflix was taking advantage of Comcast's valuable resource, so Comcast attacked Netflix, irrespective of the effect on its own customers. The company had lost sight of its customers' ultimate needs for reliable entertainment, communication, and information.

One corollary of decoupling theory is that companies will tend to stall not when they stop innovating per se but when they abandon the laser focus on the customer needs that fueled their early growth to begin with. In modern business parlance, stallers lose their customer-centricity. I'm not implying that companies should deliver on all customer requests and requirements. Customer-centricity means putting a central focus on the customer when making important decisions, rather than focusing on competitors, business partners, employees, leaders, and the company itself. It's a matter of prioritization and purpose, not blind obedience. As they decouple, startups are guided by a deep, intuitive understanding of the importance of customer needs. Large, established companies lose sight of customers, focusing instead on safeguarding the resources they have built or acquired in the act of serving customers. They become attached to those resources, forgetting that customers change, and companies must change with them.

Resources Versus Customers: Who Prioritizes What?

In Chapter 7, we saw that decoupling represents a form of specialization based not on customer type but on the activities of the customer value chain. Decouplers snatch away activities from the established incumbent, which formerly had satisfied all customer value chain activities by itself as part of its mass-market offering. If the incumbent doesn't innovate around its business model, either by recoupling or by decoupling and rebalancing, the incumbent gradually loses some of the most important and profitable CVC activities. This loss of activities by decoupling occurs as part of a broader process of market specialization that squeezes incumbents, pushing them into the market's unprofitable "middle." So why do incumbents allow this process to happen? Why don't they take up extreme positions of their own, akin to their challengers', rather than allow themselves to become trapped in the middle?

As the Comcast story suggests, the answer has to do with how success shapes executives' view of their business. When wealthy incumbents spot a new opportunity or contemplate making changes that impact their current businesses, they first seek to understand how any decision they might make would impact their most valuable resource. They ask: "Do we risk losing this resource?" If so, that's all the more reason not to engage. The resource in question might be cash, but often incumbents possess resources more valuable than cash. Auto manufacturers look to safeguard their factories and close relationships with parts suppliers. Newspapers look to safeguard their printing presses and journalists. Telecom operators look to safeguard their network of copper and fiber-optic cables and antennas. Whatever their resource, incumbents generally follow up by asking: "How can we leverage our most valuable assets to take advantage of the new opportunity?" If the opportunity doesn't mobilize the prized assets, then the incumbent perceives that it holds no advantage relative to others. Why play a game in which you and your penniless opponent stand equal chances of success?

Blockbuster once reigned as the world's largest video rental chain, with sixty thousand employees and nine thousand stores. But in 2003, after five years of nearly 10 percent annual growth under CEO John Antioco, its business came to a shrieking halt, and by 2010, Blockbuster had filed for bankruptcy. Observers have linked Blockbuster's demise to the rise of online services offering DVDs by mail, specifically Netflix. This competing business model eliminated a value-eroding activity: going to a store to rent a movie, TV show, or videogame. The new model was great for the customer. But Antioco never abandoned Blockbuster's model of requiring its own consumers to visit their stores to pick up and return physical media (first videocassettes and then DVDs). Why didn't he spot changes in customers and adapt? Witnessing the rise of Netflix and DVD by mail, Antioco and other Blockbuster executives understood—correctly—that their thousands of stores and employees in no way allowed them a competitive advantage in that new game. So they initially declined to launch a service that required extensive shipping and handling resources rather than stores and consumer-facing employees. From their perspective as a resource-rich incumbent, doing so would confer no great advantage over startups such as Netflix. Their shortsighted decision didn't necessarily stem from faulty analyses on their part but rather came from an underlying incumbent mindset that prioritized what they perceived as their main strength. This caused them to miss an impending, drastically disruptive change in consumer behavior.

I see resource-centric perspectives prevailing among incumbents across a number of industries in which I have worked. Traditional retailers perceive stores as drivers of their revenues. Add more stores, and see revenues grow. Telecom operators perceive homes connected to their network as drivers of revenue. Add more homes, and see revenues grow. Banks perceive their branches in local neighborhoods as drivers of revenues. Add more branches, and see revenues grow. In general, incumbents regard revenue growth as a direct consequence of growth in their most valuable assets. Those resources attract paying customers, which the incumbent milks to exhaustion. That's the incumbent's moneymaking formula, and it's reflected in the key metrics that executives in incumbent businesses use to make decisions: sales per square foot of store space, in the case of retailers; accounts or income per branch, in the case of retail banks; and revenue per mile of fiber optic cable in the case of telecoms.

Because they lack significant resources to attract customers, disruptors approach their business with a different mindset. Uber didn't have cars. Airbnb didn't have hotel rooms. Netflix didn't have stores. For disruptors, revenue growth originates in one place, and one place only: customer acquisition. If such acquisition requires an asset, then the disruptor might want to build, acquire, or borrow that asset from others. But disruptors don't regard the asset as the end game. Regardless of the means to get those resources, startups milk resources to get customers, instead of milking the customers. Their mindset isn't resource-centric but truly customer-centric. Just look at the metrics that startups commonly use: customer lifetime value, average revenue per user, and revenue per active customer.

Resource-centricity: Certain firm-owned resources are your most valuable possessions. All your major business decisions should help you expand and leverage these resources.

Customer-centricity: Your customers are your most valuable possessions. All major business decisions should enhance your ability to increase the number of customers and leverage them.

To understand how a customer-centric perspective might lead a business to take different actions than a resource-centric perspective would, let's go back to Netflix. In 2011, Reid Hastings made one of the bravest strategic decisions I have ever seen the leader of a digital company make. Netflix's original business model of shipping DVDs by mail was growing tremendously, disrupting the industry and hurting Blockbuster. As Netflix's stock price and recurring revenues skyrocketed, the company did something seemingly crazy: it imploded its business model. Netflix had launched a video streaming business a few years earlier, and after some tests, it proclaimed that streaming would become a new, stand-alone service that would eventually dominate the DVD-by-mail service. This decision sparked an uproar among customers, suppliers (the movie studios), and investors, with some calling for Hastings's ouster. Yet Hastings stayed the course, and by 2017, the wisdom of his decision had become obvious. Streaming greatly surpassed the DVD-by-mail business. In the second quarter of 2017, Netflix had more than twelve times the number of streaming subscribers than it did DVD subscribers.[5]

Netflix's decision reflects a deep and abiding customer-centricity on the part of Hastings and other company executives. A traditional incumbent would have focused on its most valuable resources, an inventory of millions of DVDs and multiple shipping and handling facilities around the country. But for a company streaming content online, those assets didn't matter. In fact, they were worthless. The new resource would have to include powerful servers, broadband bandwidth, and licensing agreements with Hollywood studios. The almost total divergence in strategic resources required for the two business models would have impeded the transition, if not for Hastings's prescience and deep customer focus. To execute this courageous business model transformation, he began to use internet service providers' most valuable strategic resources: broadband bandwidth. That in turn brought Netflix face-to-face with Comcast, a company intent on preserving its own valuable resource—set-top boxes and cables—even if, as we have seen, doing so meant penalizing its own customers.

Comcast's disregard for customer welfare in this instance shouldn't surprise us. In a 2007 customer satisfaction survey performed by the American Customer Satisfaction Institute, Comcast was voted the worst company in customer satisfaction of all organizations included, even lower than the IRS. By contrast, Netflix initially paid Comcast to save its own customers. Then, perceiving that the greatest value resided in owning the customer and not the resource, Netflix went back to Comcast to obtain a cut for bringing the telecom more high-value customers. Netflix followed the evolving needs of its customers. Comcast didn't, opting to preserve its resources, and it paid dearly for that mistake. By putting its own customers in harm's way instead of catering to their evolving needs, Comcast responded very poorly to its own growth stall in the cable television division. Incumbents and disrupters often possess fundamentally different views of the same situation. Whereas Comcast saw the depletion of its resource, Netflix saw the upselling of customers.

Innovation Isn't Enough

If incumbents' embrace of a resource-centric perspective constitutes the underlying culprit behind growth stalls, companies can't avoid or mitigate these stalls simply by innovating more, as experts have advised. It's easy enough to convene all of your engineers, scientists, and designers and charge them with creating some great new offering, or to assemble the strategy department and tell them to devise a brilliant new strategy. But if you're Comcast or Blockbuster, that approach alone won't allow you to make the decisions necessary to take on Netflix. Rather, executives at incumbents must set aside their attachment to resources and redirect their company's primary focus back to customers.

At even the most innovative incumbents, resource-centricity tends to dominate, leaving the company vulnerable to growth stalls. Microsoft is an innovation machine, having developed business solutions such as consulting, server products, advertising networks, and consumer products such as phones, Surface tablets, and the Xbox videogame platform. And yet, among all of these product lines, two have long accounted for the lion's share of Microsoft's revenues and profits: Windows and Office. This imbalance affects power relations inside the company. Microsoft's most senior, highly paid, and powerful bosses have risen through the ranks managing Windows or Office software products. They generate most of the company's cash flow, so they get to make decisions on almost everything important, including innovation. As a result, when a young software engineer dreams up a new search engine algorithm, or a hardware engineer has an innovative idea for a smartphone, one of the Windows or Office bosses often gets to sign off on whether to develop the idea, and then how to commercialize it. If the senior executive finds that the search engine or phone could help the company sell more Windows operating systems or Office productivity suites, the idea stands a better chance of receiving funding. If not, the idea might well fizzle, no matter how innovative or promising it may have been. Executives running Windows and Office don't decide the future of everything at the company, but they do wield considerable clout and often enjoy an unspoken right of first refusal over new ideas and innovations.

It gets worse. If an idea bears no apparent complementarity to Windows or Office but is too good to pass up (say, a new virtual reality headset or a next-generation social network), senior Windows or Office bosses usurp the idea from lower-level or less powerful managers. Although they might intend to develop and market the idea, they often wind up sitting on the innovation and, in the process, precluding others from working on it. This tendency was so pervasive that employees outside the Windows and Office twin towers have a name for it: "licking the cookie." Think back to grade school, when you ate meals with other kids. To establish their dominance, the bully types would steal cookies from other kids and eat them. When the bullies became too stuffed to eat any more, they would grab cookies from the table, lick them, and put them back—just so the smaller kids couldn't eat them, either.

Robbie Bach, former president of Microsoft's Entertainment and Devices Division, oversaw the company's gaming, music, video, phone, and retail sales businesses for two decades. In an interview with me, he recalled an instance when he had his cookie licked. "My group wanted to design a better media player," he said, "but the Windows team wanted its own media player. And so they got to design it. Do I think people were devious about it? No. People would let their ego get in the way of it. In that case, both groups lost. None was successful. This was all very detrimental to our customer. What happened? Apple won."[6] At some point, Microsoft's executives stopped making product launch decisions that were in customers' best interest, and instead made decisions that benefited *themselves*. The company possessed a powerful innovation engine, but other forces within the company still derailed innovative products, killing many promising and even game-changing opportunities.[7] Decision-makers didn't want to invest time, money, and reputation on highly uncertain and unproven ideas when deploying resources toward the big moneymakers afforded a more certain payback.

We shouldn't single out Microsoft. Under new leadership by Satya Nadella, the company has begun to redirect its gaze back to customers. And innovation inside most other successful companies proves equally challenging. Take the high-end shopping mall developer Westfield Corporation. In 2012, Westfield tried to innovate by creating a new digital unit, Westfield Retail Solutions, charged with devising innovative solutions for its retail partners.[8] While senior executives understood the new unit's importance, the project suffered from lack of support and collaboration at the middle management level. Joelle Kaufman, former executive vice president of strategy, remembered that there was "tremendous excitement about what we were doing [at Westfield Retail Solutions]. But when push comes to shove, it did not change anything. They [the managers of the traditional part of the business] were focused on their day-to-day." And because they didn't see digital affecting their day-to-day financial targets, they didn't support it. It was in their self-interest to pursue other priorities.

At most large, prestigious firms, we find similar dynamics at work. Lack of innovation is a customer-centricity problem, *not* an R&D problem. Therefore, asking your product developers inside the company to "just innovate" will rarely head off a growth stall. To innovate, you first need to eliminate impediments to customer-centricity among both leaders and managers. This challenge brings you face-to-face with human nature. The reality is that companies are not customer-centric; people are. So let's spend a moment examining what individuals within companies need in order to put customers first.

Companies Are Not Customer-Centric; People Are

As scholars in the discipline of motivational psychology have found, people will freely perform a desired task only if two conditions are satisfied. First, they must possess the basic skills and resources to perform the task. Lacking the ability to perform the task, they might attempt it, but they certainly won't succeed. Second, even if people can perform the task, they must *want* to do it. It follows that to motivate employees to focus on customers' needs, companies must equip them to do so, and provide the proper incentives.

To equip employees to favor the customer's evolving needs and wants, companies must put a great deal at employees' disposal, including opportunities to observe or connect with customers, intellectual approaches for understanding customers and responding to their demands, internal processes that employees can deploy inside a company to work on behalf of customers, and finally, actual experience in dealing with customers. Most large firms have set up processes for delivering these opportunities and tools, although employees may not take full advantage of them.

What about the second part, incentives to drive customer-centricity? This represents the main obstacle for companies, and it's what some at Microsoft, Westfield, Blockbuster, and Comcast lacked. As Westfield's, Kaufman observed, resource-centric managers in Westfield's traditional (and declining) part of the business might have appreciated the virtues of innovation rooted in customer-centricity, but they didn't feel rewarded for pursuing it. Their careers benefited mainly from growth in the traditional, resource-rich part of the business. Thus, when asked to help incoming, resource-poor managers working on new initiatives, they tacitly declined. "There is this subtle resentment," Kaufman said, paraphrasing the thinking of old-guard managers as follows: "We deliver 99 percent of the revenues. Digital gets most of the investment but we bear most of the costs. Executives spend so much time with them. I want to be in the sexy new business, too. We are asked to incur costs to fund these new initiatives, but then we don't reach our profit goals and it impacts our bonuses." Kaufman argues that unless organizations can make customer-centric innovation "a win for everyone in the organization," they will all lose.[9] In the language of this chapter, resource-centricity will prevail.[10]

To tackle this issue of lack of incentives, CEOs, managing directors, board members, and other business heads must accept that only two approaches exist for realigning employees' priorities to customers' needs. First, they can change how employees earn financial recognition (salaries, bonuses) and promotions, providing other kinds of incentives as well. That's a tall order in many large organizations, as quite often no single executive fully controls compensation and promotion decisions. It requires a collective effort at the leadership level. Second, leaders can change the people, bringing in executives and managers who already are properly incentivized to put customers first. In sum, either change the incentives for the same people, or change the people. As the following examples suggest, both options can work.

INCENTIVIZING CUSTOMER-CENTRIC INNOVATION AT INTUIT

Software maker Intuit has sustained a strong record of customer-centric innovation by carefully tailoring incentives. Founded in 1983, Intuit develops and sells financial, accounting, and tax preparation software such as TurboTax and QuickBooks. In 2017, its revenues, mostly generated in the United States, stood at $5.2 billion, and Q4 sales and annual operating income were both growing at 12 percent per year. Also in 2017, a consultancy ranked Intuit's financial performance in the 99th percentile of public companies, and its main product, QuickBooks, claimed a market share of 80 percent.[11] Intuit represented the fairly unique case of a mature incumbent growing at near late-stage startup rates.

Notwithstanding its financial and market success, in 2018 Intuit was in the midst of disrupting itself. To maintain its growth and industry leadership, the company had already undergone several successful waves of self-inflicted disruption. Now it sought to innovate its business model, shifting from a closed, centrally managed software company into an open platform. By presenting itself as a platform, Intuit would spur independent developers to create mobile and desktop apps that could plug into its products, benefiting customers, developers, and the company.[12] Or so Intuit's leadership team hoped. Throughout Intuit's existence, cofounder and current board chairman Scott Cook had sought to imbue the company with a culture that was both uniquely innovative and focused on customers. As Cook defined it, innovation meant "novelty and significance." That is, new initiatives had to offer meaningful improvement for the customer—novelty alone wasn't enough. To help nurture such innovation, Cook ensured that the company handsomely funded innovation. Intuit's R&D spending as a percentage of revenues towered at 19 percent, higher than Google, Microsoft, Amazon, and Apple, which ranged from 4.7 percent (Apple) to 15.5 percent (Google).[13] Yet, as Cook knew, funding alone wasn't enough to overcome the silent, organizational change-killers that lurked inside large companies. Noted Cook: "Employees have ideas and they are excited about them. The problem is the company gets in the way. All the meetings, all the [executive] suits, the approvals, all the PowerPoints needed. We, as senior managers, need to remove the barriers that get in the way of innovation."

To counter these barriers, Intuit institutionalized an approach called Customer Driven Innovation. As Cook explained: "The solution we have found to work is to not allow managers to 'play Caesar' [voting on projects with a thumbs-up or thumbs-down] and substitute their approval for the results of customer-driven tests and experiments. Consumers drive what we develop further. So, the company knows we make decisions based on test results. We should honor the consumer test result, not the manager's opinions."

As part of Customer Driven Innovation, Intuit instituted several key processes and types of incentives. Many people associate the word "incentive" with monetary rewards, but other kinds of rewards can also prompt people to pursue customer-focused innovation. Just as lowering the money, time, and effort costs motivated customers to decouple, so, too, providing employees with more time to innovate on behalf of customers and making it easier for them to do so will incentivize them to engage in this activity.

Intuit made it easier for employees to pursue customer-focused innovation by enabling employees to stay in close contact with customers. The company regularly arranged for a small group of employees to experience "follow-me-homes"—visits to customers' homes or workplaces, during which employees could observe customers opening up the software product, installing it, and using it. In 2011, a follow-me-home prompted software developer Hugh Molotsi to lead a small, internal, startup-like team to create Merchant Services, a credit card payment processor tool for small businesses to use with QuickBooks.[14] By 2017, employees were conducting about ten thousand hours of follow-me-homes each year. As Brad Henske, the company's former CFO, remarked, "I read the other day that Microsoft hired anthropologists to study how people work. We have those people here—we call them employees."[15]

Intuit also instituted financial incentives to reduce internal resistance to customer-focused innovation. "As a manager," Cook explained, "your bonus is a function of revenue and profit delivery. Any idea that is truly big will hurt your bonus during the two to three years that you are in that job. Given the way middle and senior managers are financially incentivized under pay-for-performance, it is quite rational for them to not allow new innovations. We are changing that." By incorporating financial incentives and also making decisions based on results of customer testing instead of managerial judgment, Cook eliminated two major barriers that prevented thousands of junior-level employees at Intuit from coming up with new ideas.

In changing the incentives for Intuit employees in order to encourage customer-centric innovation, Cook didn't put a blanket system in place, but rather tailored incentives in response to employees' varying needs and desires. While monetary incentives worked for top and midlevel decision-makers, research showed that some Intuit managers didn't respond well to money as an incentive. "A survey was conducted among past innovation award winners," Cook said. "Our theory going in was that what they wanted was money. They said what they really wanted was time. It was much more important than money. So let's give them a relief from their day-to-day obligations. And we gave 3 months off full-time or 6 months half-time." In large incumbents especially, blanket incentive systems will likely fail. When employees value money, companies should provide it. But when employees value time, companies should provide that, too. And so on. "To each according to his need," as Karl Marx once said.

As the Intuit example illustrates, incentives remain the best instrument for spurring customer-centric innovation. They're the tool most likely to work consistently over time and across the entire workforce. Without proper incentives, all you can do is pray for innovation to happen, and hope for the best.

DRIVING CUSTOMER-FOCUSED INNOVATION THROUGH TALENT ACQUISITION: THE CASE OF AXEL SPRINGER

In fostering customer-centric innovation, Intuit declined to alter its employee profile significantly.[16] But sometimes new employees are precisely what a company needs. In 2019, Axel Springer was Europe's largest print media company, ranking among the world's top twenty-five media conglomerates by revenues, and owning and operating multiple newspaper and magazine businesses.[17] In 2002, sensing the need to modernize and change, the company's board of directors brought in Mathias Döpfner, formerly editor in chief of a print newspaper, to serve as CEO. Hoping to help Axel Springer become the world's leading digital publisher, Döpfner in 2006 began a full-blown transformation, digitizing the media company's three core businesses: journalism (content), advertising, and classifieds. Döpfner's challenge was daunting indeed: at the time, less than 1 percent of the company's revenue came from digital products.[18]

When I interviewed Axel Springer's president of paid models and board member Jan Bayer, he revealed just how focused the company's leadership was on its new direction. Axel Springer's board didn't do much to defend against the decline in revenues of legacy businesses such as magazines and newspapers. In board meetings, Bayer said, "we didn't discuss the decline of newspaper circulations. We thought this was natural. Our CEO, Mathias Döpfner, was only looking ahead." When I asked Bayer what, if anything, had surprised him in this transition, he noted that he had "underestimated the speed and acceleration of the decline [of our legacy businesses]." Given this steep decline, and with so many old-media professionals inside the company, the company had no choice but to bring in new blood—adjusting the incentives wouldn't suffice to promote such drastic innovation as quickly as needed. Specifically, the company needed people who not merely knew digital technology and business models but loved working in those areas and had "diverse and entrepreneurial personalities."[19]

Döpfner decided to introduce such talent by acquiring tech and digital startups. Between 2007 and 2017, he and the board acquired about 150 startups from around the world, including the U.S. properties Business Insider, eMarketer, and Thrillist.com. Döpfner and the board also made minority investments in non-media businesses such as Airbnb and Uber. Their approach, in essence, was to mimic the activity of a venture capital firm. They attempted to keep startup founders at all costs, allowed them to operate independently from the rest of the company, and maintained the same basic incentive structures the smaller businesses had had in place prior to their acquisition. Founders retained ownership of a portion of their businesses, and they received payouts if they increased their profitability. According to one founder whose company was acquired by Axel Springer, the biggest incentive the company put in place was "allowing our brands the opportunity to remain independent and build our own future."[20]

Döpfner's drastic change initiative worked. By 2017, according to Bayer, a full 75 percent of Axel Springer's revenues originated in digital products and businesses. Not surprisingly, perhaps, this momentous change caused some pain to the company's established businesses. A cultural clash erupted between the old guard (newspaper and magazine publishers) and the new guard (digital entrepreneurs). As Döpfner explained in a Stanford case study, "The problem at the beginning was that the structure of the organization was around 90 percent losers (i.e., print) and around ten percent winners (i.e., digital). Thus the losers were positioned to reject and overpower the transformation simply because there were more of them. So I said: 'We have to create joint responsibilities to induce buy-in from the print side.'"[21]

How would Axel Springer create such "joint responsibilities"? The answer was to force newly acquired digital startups and existing businesses in the same space to become dependent on one another. For instance, the company prompted its major tabloid newspaper, *Bild*, to integrate its operations with its online equivalent, Bild.de. Axel Springer's offline classifieds business had to pair up with its online classifieds business, and so on. Each publication had to become a thriving business, which meant that tenured employees and members of the new guard had to get along. It fell on the general managers of these businesses to see to content production, design, marketing, and profit-and-loss across both digital and print.

In the end, Döpfner adjusted the composition of Axel-Springer's workforce in order to foster change and innovation that benefited its customers. He didn't engage in mass firing, opting instead to keep the "old" people in the declining existing businesses. In effect, he let employees choose their own destinies. Either they could remain where they were and gradually phase out as that part of the business shrank, or they could learn, adapt, and switch to the new and growing businesses. Those who adapted would join up with the outsiders, digital or tech entrepreneurs who had already proven that they possessed the skills and intrinsic motivation to launch and grow digital media businesses. Opportunity as defined by each individual employee served as the real incentive for helping to move the company forward. Collectively, employees had to learn to cater to two groups of customers at once: older, loyal audiences and younger, more fickle readers. It wasn't easy for the old guard and new-media personnel to find the proper balance together, but under Döpfner's leadership, they did.

Reorienting Around Customers

Many established companies experience a period of fast growth, interrupted by a precipitous break in growth and a subsequent period of flat or declining sales. The right intervention, as I've argued, isn't to attempt to innovate your way out of a growth stall, but rather to first reorient the organization around customers. Fast-growing new entrants are, by design, focused on the customer rather than on the hard assets or other resources they possess. That's *why* they experience such rapid growth. Over time, as firms grow and become established, they try to maintain, grow, and leverage their most valuable resources at all costs, an approach that leaves them vulnerable to new entrants. Incumbents can avoid a stall, but that means taking steps to avoid and address impediments to a customer-first orientation. As I've suggested, it means paying attention to individuals and their professional priorities.

At the corporate level, leaders must move managers away from resource-centric thinking and prompt them to recover their lost focus on customers. Leaders might consider implementing penalties for managers who try to leverage the company's major assets for new projects. Blockbuster, for instance, might have charged a high "rent" for any manager proposing to utilize store space or store employees for a new line of business. Microsoft could have done the opposite of what was customary and charged Windows or Office bosses a premium to their budgets for taking possession of a new idea or innovation in the company's R&D labs. They would have to pay a holding fee to lick and not eat any cookie. But leaders must also encourage the development and use of other assets, particularly those that might help the company cater to changing customers. Leaders can do this by introducing internal rebates that managers might receive for investing in these new assets. Just as California offers a tax rebate for people buying electric cars, so, too, management might provide funds for employees to build or acquire new resources for the purpose of serving customers' changing needs. Obviously, leaders should expect that these new resources will deliver real, enhanced value for customers in one of three forms: more value-creating activities, reduced value-charging activities, or the elimination of value-eroding activities.

CEOs should also put appropriate incentives in place at all levels of the organization to ensure that executives and managers benefit when they make decisions that further customers' interests. Take a deep and comprehensive look at the incentive structure throughout your company. Somehow, somewhere, some way, people lost interest in customers. They're spending all their time thinking about competitors, collaborators, or their own career prospects. Make it worth their while to start thinking about customers again. When old-guard managers at Westfield failed to share resources with peers in the company's newer, potentially disruptive businesses, it was because these managers had no incentive to do so; their career progression and remuneration depended on old business metrics. Are your managers similarly adversely incentivized?

If so, one option to fix this might be to tie a portion of your old-guard managers' bonus structure to new areas and initiatives that they helped develop using their own budgets. Such a move would prompt employees who aren't directly tasked with leading new innovations to place bets on new initiatives in the company. With their own resources in the game, managers would feel more committed to the new initiatives, and more inclined to support them. One thing is certain: the usual tactics companies deploy to spark innovation—including motivational pep talks by the CEO, articulation of a beautiful vision, and allocation of resources to innovation—will all fail if the right incentives don't exist to propel collaboration among executives and managers on the customer's behalf.

Discuss how to adjust incentives—whether by changing the incentives for the same people or by changing the people themselves. After all, management bears the primary responsibility for sustaining growth. The drive to recover a customer-centric orientation must originate at the highest level of an organization, and senior leaders—up to and including the board of directors—must personally oversee the shift. Further, these leaders should take into account the firm's total customer base, putting it ahead of the welfare of any particular business unit. When Comcast's cable TV business suffered a growth stall, its CEO went after the channel partner of one of Comcast's thriving business units, internet services. To ensure that other CEOs don't make this mistake, boards of directors should create metrics that pertain to the health of firms' customers and their value chain, not the financial health of each business unit in isolation. Such a move, along with an abandonment of a resource-centric mindset, would have clarified to Comcast's CEO his primary responsibilities toward his customers.

Ultimately, a customer-centric company has a governing body and an executive team that not only understands digital disruption in general, and decoupling in particular, but also appreciates the force animating all healthy companies from their earliest days: a drive to better fulfill the customer's needs. Customer-centric companies also have leaders who understand the importance of rapid and decisive action. In the field of medicine, research has shown that stroke and heart attack victims fare much better if they receive interventions quickly. Something similar holds true for companies. Management should treat a growth stall as a matter of grave concern, or the company might never fully recover.

10

SPOTTING THE NEXT WAVE OF DISRUPTION

This book has examined an ongoing wave of market disruption—decoupling. This wave is growing fast but one day it will subside, as previous waves have. Afterward, how can we spot the next wave? Where will disruption appear next, and what new opportunities and threats will it portend?

Although companies typically address such concerns by crafting detailed scenarios of possible futures, lately such an approach has come into question. Take the well-established and mature oil industry. "What is a challenge at the moment," Shell CEO Ben van Beurden said in 2018, "is that we don't know anymore where the future will go."[1] Shell's Guy Outen, executive vice president for strategy and the person responsible for scenario analysis, explained that the long-stable energy industry has shifted in recent years from "complicated to complex."[2] In this context, planning for the future has become extremely difficult, and even somewhat futile—as it now is in many industries. For that reason, long-term planning approaches that require a firm's executives to first look into the future, decide what position they want their company to occupy, and then work backward in time to determine the strategic assets needed in order to achieve said position rarely work. Either the future is too uncertain for management to agree upon, or not enough details of that future are visible to allow for precise strategic planning. In the case of the world's future sources of energy, for instance, the highly uncertain question is not whether renewable sources of energy will grow relative to fossil fuels but what percentage of the overall market they will represent. Will it be 30 percent, 50 percent, 70 percent? And by when? By 2020? By 2050? By 2100? For companies such as Shell, GM, Boeing, Tesla, and many others, any of these scenarios would represent drastically different planning routes to take today. But, as the Danes say, it is difficult to make predictions, especially about the future.[3]

In an effort to make forecast-based planning easier, entrepreneurs and managers have quite understandably sought to simplify their analyses, focusing only on their own markets or industries. Annual surveys by IBM have shown that less than a quarter of CEOs sought innovative ideas outside of their own company, suppliers, or consumers.[4] Similarly, when queried by PwC about potential partners or allies, half of CEOs didn't mention a single firm or entity from outside of their own industry.[5] Executives read their own market reports, talk to their own suppliers, attend their own industry conferences, and survey consumers of their own products and services. For them, the prospect of looking elsewhere is too much to handle in an increasingly uncertain, rapidly changing world.

Decoupling theory points us toward another way of preparing for the future, one that doesn't require us to narrow our view and also doesn't force us to make firm predictions about distant future scenarios. As we've seen, the theory regards disruption as a customer-driven phenomenon. Customer needs change, and with that comes new customer behavior, paving the way for companies new and old to offer products better tailored to these evolving needs. The theory also prompts us to pay attention to the big, pervasive changes that affect customers, not small shifts that only affect one market or industry. As I've discussed, changes in how customers procure products and services must span multiple markets in order to have true disruptive effects. Otherwise, they are simply passing fads.

The focus on customer-driven trends that are pervasive and

enduring frees us to a large extent from having to predict distant future events. The big changes that will surely figure prominently many years from now are already upon us, if you know where to look. We can prepare for the future by studying the present—what is called "present-casting." This is a much simpler and more accurate proposition than forecasting, and in fact it already has a number of fans in the marketing world. In 2009, Google's chief economist Hal Varian published a controversial paper entitled "Predicting the Present with Google Trends" in which he showed how to use historical data (for instance, about popular Google search terms) to learn about a nascent trend. Since then, many researchers have used historical and present-day data to show present-casting's merits in domains of consumer activity such as travel, real estate, health, and transportation. Collectively, these researchers have shown that capturing present trends is more accurate when data are bountiful, and it serves businesses better than inaccurately trying to predict future changes not already present. As the sixth-century-BC Chinese poet Lao Tzu once wrote, "Those who have knowledge, don't predict. Those who predict, don't have knowledge."[6]

The question then becomes: how can we best track present-day customer trends? Focusing on a single industry comes up short, not least because shifts in customer behavior are notoriously difficult to observe. Individual consumers don't always choose rationally, prone as they are to biases that make them less consistent and thus less predictable.[7] Further, when confronted by too many options, consumers become fatigued and make suboptimal choices.[8] Asking customers about their behaviors and preferences doesn't shed much light, as customers remember their choices selectively, and they value short-term gains over long-term ones despite their professed desire for the latter. On a collective level, our behavior creates statistical noise that makes it harder for trend-spotters to identify enduring changes. To take a small example, many of us have on occasion departed from our routine preferences and purchased that exotic fruit juice or that unusual special dish at a restaurant only to never do it again. Markets likewise often exhibit irregular spontaneous movements with no identifiable cause.[9] Pet rocks and mood rings, short-lived fads in the 1970s, still baffle many sociologists today. Sometimes these shifts lead to strong, patterned waves of new behavior that amount to a major change, but most of the time we see a series of back-and-forth movements with neither rhyme nor reason. In recent decades, milk consumption has risen, only to decline again. Bell-bottom jeans were once in, then out, then in again. In many ways we, the customers, are like storm fronts that suddenly and unexpectedly change direction, speed up, or strengthen.

Such interpretive difficulties mean that you likely won't spot the next wave of disruption quickly enough if you focus exclusively on your own market. At the same time, venturing beyond our industries confronts us once again with the problem of complexity. There are just too many industries to cover. According to one classification, the Global Industry Classification Standard (developed by MSCI and Standard & Poor's Financial Services), there are eleven macro sectors, twenty-four industry groups, sixty-eight industries, and 157 sub-industries.[10] Probing each of these markets for new waves that might migrate into our own markets would require a herculean effort. So, how else might we proceed?

The Big Seven

It turns out that we can spot global waves of disruption by considering a small, manageable list of industries that are routinely monitored by market and research analysts globally. The typical household purchases thousands of goods and services throughout the year in hundreds of categories, but the overwhelming majority of that spending—94 percent in 2016 in the United States[11]—occurred in just seven categories, what I call the Big Seven. The Big Seven categories correspond to a series of consumption choices that people must make in the course of their daily lives: where to live (housing, home goods, and maintenance), how to move (air and land transportation), what to eat (food, drinks, and their preparation), what to wear (fashion, cosmetics, and personal grooming), how to learn (formal and informal education), how to entertain (media, electronics, and sports), and how to heal ourselves (healthcare, physical and mental treatments). If you want to understand potential shifts in your industry, you should look to these categories for early signs. That's because the Big Seven allow you to identify the major changes in needs, wants, preferences, and behaviors incubating in households that may extend into other categories and industries, including your own.

Mapping Change Across Industries

Changes in the Big Seven travel far. In fact, the Big Seven are known to influence or "contaminate" one another as well as other, seemingly unrelated industries when it comes to customer needs and behavior. Once people decide to choose a more convenient provider of food, for instance, they tend to pursue convenience in how they dress, live, move, learn, heal, and entertain themselves as well. These decisions are rarely made in isolation, on a market-by-market basis. Take shared on-demand services such as Uber Pool and Airbnb. A Pew Research Center study found that about 20 percent of Americans routinely incorporated four or more of these services into their daily lives. This same group of consumers then moved on to adopt similar convenience-seeking services across other industries.[12] The same goes for the need for variety (what marketers call variety-seeking behavior), need for uniqueness, need for value-for-money, and need for sustainability. Once consumers gain a taste for any of these particular needs in one category of Big Seven goods, many quickly seek it in the other categories where purchases are frequently made.

I noticed an interesting example of this "contagion effect" across the Big Seven in 2010, when I presented my research at Facebook's headquarters and first saw Mark Zuckerberg in person. As great a leader as Zuckerberg was, one element of his persona didn't impress: his mode of dress. Zuckerberg wore a gray crewneck T-shirt, jeans, and Nike footwear. As I have since learned, Zuckerberg wears the same outfit to work each and every day, adopting it as his "uniform." An ethic of simplicity seems to lie behind this practice. As Zuckerberg has said, "I really want to clear my life to make it so that I have to make as few decisions as possible about anything except how to best serve [Facebook]."[13] Adopting a standard, go-to option when getting dressed each morning means that Zuckerberg has one less personal decision to make each day.

Initially, I wrote off Zuckerberg's practice as a minor eccentricity. But as more young people I met started adopting their own standard work uniform, I realized that his behavior evinced a broader trend, what I called "set it and forget it" (SIAFI). Zuckerberg and his peers were simplifying their lives, making a set of initial decisions about what to wear, and then sticking with those decisions for an extended period. Others, including Elon Musk and Barack Obama after the presidency, were following suit (no pun intended) as well.[14] Meanwhile, new business models were cropping up to satisfy this new customer need for simplicity and ease in fashion. For men, Trunk Club sold entire work outfits, carefully curated combinations of shirts, sweaters, pants, belts, and shoes, saving consumers the trouble of building outfits themselves. Subscription services such as Stance, ArmourBox, and Scentbird cropped up to offer consumers easy ways of purchasing items they routinely wear—underwear and socks, gym clothes, and perfume, respectively. Set it up and forget about it!

Subscription services offer a great means of satisfying the set-it-and-forget-it mentality. Take the food category. In recent years, meal subscription services such as Plated, Blue Apron, Chef'd, and hundreds of others have allowed individuals and families to set up a food delivery regime, specifying the types of cuisine, ingredients, portion sizes, and frequency of delivery they desire up front. Consumers can then press a button and forget about it—ingredients and the recipes arrive at their doorstep. Incumbents in the grocery industry, including supermarkets such as Walmart and Kroger, missed this wave by many years, focused as they were on their own industry exclusively. Kroger introduced its first meal subscription service only in mid-2017, Walmart six months after that—a full five years after the founding of market leader Blue Apron.[15]

Meal service subscriptions aren't the only way consumers today can set it and forget it when purchasing food. Amazon Fresh frees consumers of the need to draft a shopping list each week and go to the supermarket. Instead, they review their shopping list just once, specifying how frequently they want Amazon to deliver certain items at their doorstep. Milk once a week? Check. Toothpaste once every couple of months? Check. The online service makes standard recurring purchases seamless, with very simple browsing and order history features.

If you worry about potential price changes for your favorite foods, there's a hack for that, too. Brandless is an online grocery store that simplifies the act of comparison shopping. The average U.S. supermarket carries around forty-five thousand different items, and consumers often spend precious time sorting through the different types, sizes, brands, and prices of grocery items to purchase.[16] Brandless standardizes everything. First, there are no brands to choose from. All products are called "Brandless" and are the online equivalent of a generic store brand. There are also no size options—Brandless offers only the most popular size. Finally, everything Brandless sells in all categories costs $3 per item (for items generally cheaper than $3, say vegetable broth, that's three for $3). With decisions about brands, sizes, and prices all off the table, the act of shopping becomes much simpler, and consumers know well in advance how much they will pay for their basket. Twenty items per week? Do the math.

Thanks to their promise of long-term time and effort savings, subscriptions coupled with automated lists are taking over various categories of consumer purchases, not just food. Some services require more up-front effort: consumers must investigate the service and decide which purchases to automate. Yet the reduced effort afterward more than makes up for it (granted, as consumers learn more about their tastes, they do make some tweaks to their subscriptions).

Instead of purchasing songs individually, Generation Z consumers tend to prefer subscribing to music streaming services such as Spotify—a prime example of SIAFI in entertainment. These consumers take time initially to create playlists and share them with their friends. When they wish to listen, all they do is choose from among a handful of playlists. Spotify features around two billion playlists composed by users, aspiring DJs, and the company itself. By mid-2017, Spotify had seventy million music streaming subscribers, compared to Apple's thirty million, and fewer than twenty million in the case of Amazon.[17] Yet services such as Spotify are hardly the only examples of SIAFI in entertainment. Amazon offers a STEM Club toy subscription focusing on playthings that encourage learning in the fields of science, technology, engineering, and math. Just choose the age of your child and frequency of delivery, and the company picks from the highest-rated educational toys that it sells and sends them periodically to your house. Parents can SIAFI, too!

Once consumers acquire an initial taste for the savings in time and effort that subscribing to products allows, they look to subscribe in other parts of their consumption lives, including housing. Acquiring a home and maintaining it is one of the most expensive and time-consuming processes consumers undertake. Digital startups such as Thumbtack, TaskRabbit, and Hello Alfred facilitate household repairs and chores, allowing consumers to find the best people for the job and put those providers on a regimented schedule. Set it and forget it! While consumers must still provide directions and monitor performance, the potential time savings they reap are enormous.

If you don't own a home, co-living startups such as Roam allow you an intriguing way to set it and forget it. You can rent a very small (micro) apartment in a city center, maintenance free. Whenever you feel like it, you can pick up and move to another apartment in another city without having to sign a new contract. Roam and other startups like it serve the needs of engineers, designers, writers, consultants, and other independent professionals who seek adventure and can work remotely from anywhere in the world. According to Roam founder Bruno Haid, "Just managing my stuff and going back and forth between Airbnbs and housesitting became more cumbersome over time." Using Roam, you pay around $1,800 a month and can choose to live six months in London, another three months in Bali, and then the last few months of the year in Miami, all by signing up just once and preselecting your sequence of locations and durations for the upcoming year. Roam will even ship your furniture and possessions from place to place if you desire.

Across industries, smarter businesses have begun to catch up to younger generations' desire for set-it-and-forget-it services that simplify their lives. After launching Uber for custom trips and Uber Pool for sharing rides with strangers, the ride-hailing company is piloting Uber Commute in the Washington, D.C., area to help standardize how we move from home to work and back. Even players in the health industry are embracing the SIAFI approach. In the United States, 20 percent of the population takes more than three pills per day.[18] For these patients, getting prescriptions, buying them, and tracking which pills to take, when, and in what combination constitutes a major chore. The startup PillPack simplifies all of this through a subscription product. You sign up and provide the doctor's prescriptions for pills you need to take. PillPack purchases them and repackages them in sequential plastic sleeves stored in a dispenser-type box. An app alerts you when to take the next sleeve of pills. Just rip off the sleeve from the dispenser and swallow the pills. Each sleeve comes imprinted with the date and time when the pills need to be taken. No more buying medications individually, fumbling through containers, and running out of a certain pill while having too many of another. Set it and forget it.

I have yet to find a good example of SIAFI services or subscriptions in one of the Big Seven: how we learn. Informal short-term education is flooded with subscription services, but not long-term formal education such as undergraduate and postgraduate or professional degree programs. Most colleges have four-year programs, while postgraduate degrees other than the JD or MD tend to require two years to complete. These offerings assume that young people receive an education, absorb as much knowledge as possible, and then deploy their knowledge in the workforce. While teaching undergraduates, graduate students in business, and senior executives, I have noticed two trends. First, undergrads and some graduate students are growing impatient with the sequential, multiyear education they require in order to earn a degree. If they could, they would rather take a few courses and then enter the job market. There they could practice what they have learned, and also understand better what kind of knowledge they require going forward. I've also noticed that many senior executives want to return to school more frequently. The old model of "first learn, then practice" is becoming outdated. People are taking to heart the common expression that "education is a lifelong goal," one that we cannot compartmentalize temporally.

This need for ongoing learning beckons for a subscription service model, one in which students would set up a structure for receiving education and then forget about it. No longer would they need to take tests, apply, interview, and perform other tasks required to go back to school. Once they have a subscription, they could just decide when to return to the classroom and what courses to take next. People should be able to jump in and out of formal education, taking classes along their professional journeys as they see fit. While new and innovative educational models have cropped up in recent years (for instance, Minerva, Singularity University, and Udacity), by 2019 only one major, reputable university was offering education on a subscription model, to my knowledge. The Ross School of Business had launched a lifetime program with access to courses, content, and professional development services for alumni of the University of Michigan. My employer, Harvard University, might soon need to evolve its nearly four-century-old business model or risk disruption by simplicity-seeking customers. Harvard's management would benefit by looking closely at current trends in how we eat, live, dress, move, entertain, and heal ourselves.

In looking to the Big Seven in order to spot new waves of disruption, companies should bear in mind one particular tenet of decoupling theory: attending to the demand side (i.e., studying customer behaviors and underlying motivations) rather than the supply side (i.e., studying companies and their offerings). The rising desire for SIAFI represents a growing wave of consumer behavior, and as I have suggested, businesses have responded to it with distinct and specialized products and services, including subscriptions, product-as-a-service (PaaS), and playlists (in the case of content). It's not the rise of subscriptions, say, that is disruptive—this is merely one type of response. The underlying driver is customers' emerging need to secure providers and provisions up front, thereby incurring a setup cost, so as to receive a constant flow of value in the foreseeable future. Across industries, supply-side developments represent a delayed reaction to changing demand-side needs. Looking at the demand-side opportunity as opposed to the supply-side response of businesses thus allows you to stay a big step ahead of your competitors.

It's also quite risky to jump on a supply-side bandwagon. If you see that businesses in various industries are rolling out subscription services, you might feel tempted to create a subscription service yourself. But did you really spot a new wave? No. As many companies have failed with subscription services as have succeeded. Subscriptions for snacks? A startup called Munchpak tried it—and failed.

Subscriptions for craft-making products? A startup called Adults & Crafts tried it—and failed. Subscriptions for artisanal beer? Craft Beer Club tried it—and failed. The truth is that most people lack a strong motivation to SIAFI when it comes to snacks, crafts, and alcohol. They like variety and the process of looking for novelty, and they don't seek to standardize up front in order to mitigate a large, perceived cost carried into the future. More generally, offerings in different categories don't allow us to understand the root cause or primary drivers of demand. And it's precisely these drivers that you must tap into if you wish to identify and ride a consumer-driven disruptive wave.

By the way, a similar argument applies when it comes to spotting disruptive opportunities and addressing them with new technologies. Avoid looking only at the rise of drones, virtual reality, artificial intelligence, digital currencies, and other supply-side technological offerings. They are not necessarily waves of disruption. Ask yourself: What are these technologies fundamentally delivering to a broad spectrum of customers in various markets? Why are people embracing them, and why now? What underlying change in consumer needs and preferences is responsible for these technologies becoming perceived as valuable offerings?

Where Is the Potential for Disruption Increasing?

With an understanding of the Big Seven in place, let's now explore how to go about detecting where the greatest opportunities for disruption lie. The method I propose is simple: by identifying sizable increases in costs to consumers across the Big Seven, we can detect where consumers might soon switch to a new disruptive product or service provider. Significant cost increases over a long and sustained period usually prompt consumers to make major changes in where and how they procure products and services. In these situations, an opportunity exists for disruptors to deliver significant cost reductions via new business models (e.g., decoupling).

In the United States, the Bureau of Labor Statistics (BLS) has compiled data on the costs of many consumer products and services for the past few decades.[19] Based on that research, I was able to estimate the rise (or fall) in costs for the Big Seven over the past twenty years. Let's review these cost trends in each of the seven categories.

Consumer learning (including college tuition, primary education, and childcare) has seen the fastest cost increases of any of the Big Seven: a 144 percent rise over two decades, in real terms, after controlling for inflation (*see Figure 10.1*).[20] For this reason, education represents, in my view, the biggest opportunity for disruptive change. While the data do not correct for improvements in the quality of these goods and services, we can certainly question whether that quality has kept up with cost across the board. Some argue that cost-adjusted quality has actually decreased in recent decades.[21] The opportunity for disruptive businesses or startups to reduce this quickly escalating monetary cost for consumers is huge, as long as they can do it without compromising on quality.

The next consumer market most prone to disruption, as measured by rapid cost increases, is *consumer healing*, which includes healthcare and well-being products and services. The real cost of healing Americans has increased by 100 percent in real terms, on average, and is expected to rise even faster in developed countries grappling with aging populations.[22] Thousands of new startups have cropped up in this space. Collectively, they will reshape how much we pay for healthcare in the years to come, and they will also lead to a new emphasis on preventing diseases, not merely treating them.

The third biggest opportunity for disruption lies in *consumer living* (including housing, maintenance, and the cost of heating and cooling our homes), where prices have increased by 63 percent in real terms. As countries experience housing market bubbles, costs have risen even more, creating pent-up demand for alternative approaches to both housing construction (with disruptors such as WeLive and Common) and housing purchases and sales (with disruptors such as Redfin). Changes here will likely impact the size, location, and very definition of our private living spaces, affecting in turn the furniture, kitchenware, and other goods we purchase for our homes.[23]

The fourth biggest opportunity for disruption lies in *consumer eating*. Average real prices for food have risen by 56 percent since 1997.[24] Over the past few years, the sector has seen many new entrants in food production, distribution, and retailing, with consumers opting for more natural, organic, local, healthful, and functional foods. Although such trends are not new in this industry, they have recently gone mainstream, threatening large food manufacturers such as Nestlé, Kraft, and Hormel. Multi-category mass-production food manufacturers, once thought of as powerful corporations, will soon see their ubiquitous global brands become liabilities, as opposed to the assets that they once represented.

The fifth largest opportunity for disruption lies in *consumer moving*, including private vehicles, car manufacturing, air travel, and public transportation. Vastly different on the surface, these industries have seen real cost increases of about 24 percent for typical U.S. consumers.[25] Since the average price of a new car is around $36,000 and the average price for a round-trip flight in the United States goes for about $350, transportation accounts for a significant amount of annual consumer spending in absolute terms.[26] I have discussed disruption in private car transportation in previous chapters. In the years to come, we'll likely see considerable disruption in public transportation and parcel transportation.

Two of the Big Seven have actually seen real cost *decreases* over the past twenty years. Costs to the consumer in *consumer dressing* (e.g., apparel and shoes) have declined around 4 percent, aided in part by the rise of vertically integrated makers and Asian manufacturers.[27] Last, costs in *consumer entertaining* (including televisions, toys, videogames, and sports) have fallen about 77 percent, mostly because of the lower cost of consumer electronics and computers.[28] Declining costs don't necessarily dissipate the possibility of disruption in these domains. We have mentioned a number of disruptive startups in these industries, including Birchbox, Rebag, Twitch, and Netflix. The startups driving most of the recent disruption in these areas, however, tend to offer more convenient and time-saving products and services, or better quality altogether, as opposed to better pricing.

FIGURE 10.1 **THE EVOLVING MONETARY COSTS OF THE BIG SEVEN (RELATIVE TO 1997)**

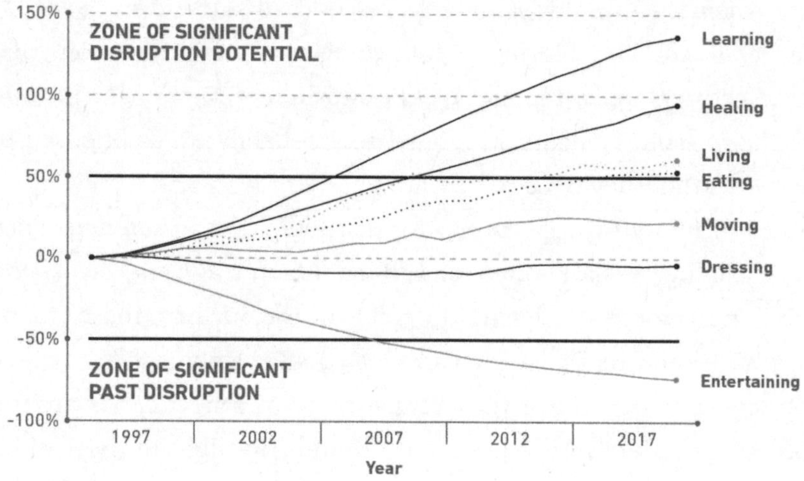

Source: Adapted from U.S. Bureau of Labor Statistics.

As *Figure 10.1* shows, the rise in monetary costs in the United States over the past two decades in the areas of learning, healing, living, and eating all top 50 percent, suggesting that these categories show strong potential for future disruption, whether via decoupling or some other means. Startups or new corporate ventures that can offer comparable quality of goods at lower prices will likely disrupt these markets. In how we move, dress, and entertain ourselves, we might see sizable disruption, but that will probably come through a reduction in the time and effort it costs consumers to acquire, use, or dispose of (when appropriate) goods and services. Monetary cost disruption will likely not be the primary driver of disruption, particularly in the entertainment sector, where consumers have already seen significant cost reductions.

I've described cost-related trends in the Big Seven in the U.S. market only. What about global markets? It is remarkable how important spending in the Big Seven is across markets. It represents 91 percent of spending in Mexico, 87 percent in Germany, and 86 percent in Japan. Wherever you look, the Big Seven's share of household budgets accounts for around 86 to 94 percent of every peso, euro, yen, or dollar spent (*see last row of Table 10.1*).

TABLE 10.1 **CONSUMER HOUSEHOLD EXPENDITURE BY DOMAIN AND COUNTRY IN 2016**

CATEGORY	AUSTRALIA	CZECH REPUBLIC	GERMANY	IRELAND	JAPAN	MEXICO	SWEDEN	UK	USA	MEDIAN
Eating	16.6%	24.4%	13.8%	14.7%	25.4%	28.6%	15.9%	11.7%	14.0%	15.9%
Dressing	2.6%	3.6%	4.5%	3.9%	3.9%	3.2%	4.8%	5.5%	3.1%	3.9%
Living	36.4%	31.1%	30.7%	27.6%	29.5%	24.6%	31.4%	31.8%	33.0%	31.1%
Healing	4.9%	2.4%	5.3%	5.1%	3.7%	3.9%	3.5%	1.8%	20.0%	3.9%
Moving	14.9%	12.5%	17.3%	16.1%	13.6%	23.0%	15.7%	15.4%	15.8%	15.7%
Entertaining	10.1%	17.4%	14.5%	22.2%	8.0%	6.6%	17.4%	19.0%	5.1%	14.5%
Learning	2.6%	0.5%	0.9%	2.7%	2.0%	1.5%	0.3%	1.8%	2.5%	1.8%
% of Total Spending	88.1%	91.9%	87.0%	92.3%	86.1%	91.3%	89.0%	87.0%	93.5%	89.0%

Source: Adapted from Australian Bureau of Statistics, Eurostat, OECD, U.S. Bureau of Labor Statistics.

In most developed countries for which I compiled Big Seven data, people devote most of their spending to two categories, living and eating. Collectively, these two categories represent 42 percent of spending in Ireland and nearly 56 percent in the Czech Republic. But I found some notable differences. For instance, Australians spend considerably more on living than other countries, since housing costs run exceptionally high there.[29] In Germany, where the government has expanded and improved public transportation and levied high taxes on vehicles and fuel to discourage car ownership, people spend considerably more of their income—17 percent—on moving around.[30] Irish, Swedes, and Brits spend considerably more, relatively speaking, on entertainment—up to 22 percent of their income. As one researcher explained, "There is a limit to the amount of stuff people can accumulate. People are spending money on experiences—holidays, seeing new exotic places, going to music festivals . . . rather than accumulating more things."[31] Mexicans spend considerably more on eating—nearly 29 percent of their income. International data on food expenditures show that families in poorer countries usually spend higher fractions of their income on food, although in absolute numbers average Mexicans spend half of what Americans do, and a third of what Hong Kong residents pay.[32] Finally, Americans spend considerably more on healing themselves, about 20 percent of their income—ten times greater as a percentage than what Britons spend, and four times greater than what Germans spend.[33]

Given that consumers in different countries spend different amounts on different categories of goods and services, the locus of opportunity for disruption is very much country-specific. And since the *degree* of price increase is one indicator of an opportunity for cost-reducing disruption (assuming similar quality), we should pay attention to the rise in real prices within each country and Big Seven domain, in conjunction with the amount of relative spending in the category. We might regard learning, living, healing, and eating as holding great potential for disruption in the United States, but we cannot say the same for other countries. Looking at the rise in real prices in the Big Seven in Germany, we find that over the past twenty years, none of the Big Seven costs, maybe with the exception of learning, has risen more than 50 percent in real terms (*see Figure 10.2*). This might owe to the high-quality public universities and hospitals that exist in Germany, all state-funded and nearly free to consumers. Private alternatives do exist, but they are less popular, lack as much power to raise prices, and usually specialize in niches underserved by the public sector. Monetary-value-based disruption opportunities thus seem less plentiful in Germany than in the United States. As a general rule, a disruptor in Germany would have to settle for exploiting a lesser opportunity, or seek out effort- or time-reduction disruption offerings in that country.

FIGURE 10.2 **THE EVOLVING MONETARY COSTS OF THE BIG SEVEN IN GERMANY (RELATIVE TO 1997)**

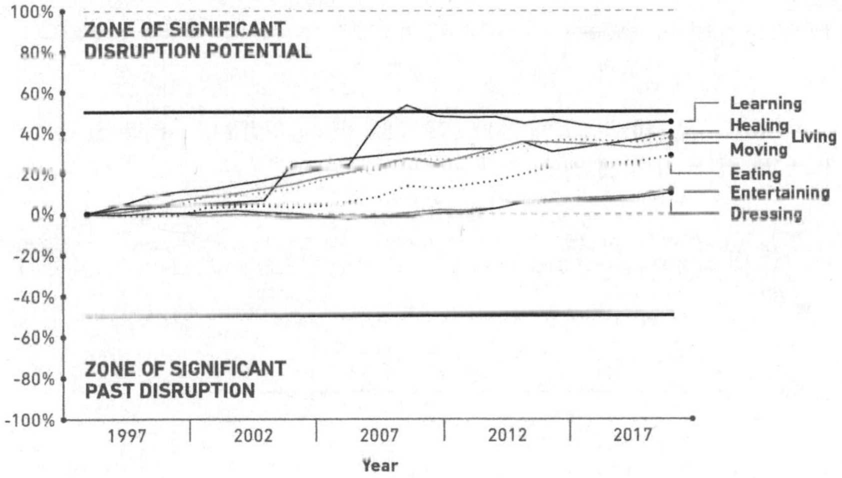

Source: Eurostat.

Whereas in Germany only one of the Big Seven domains of consumer spending (learning) has entered the zone of significant potential disruption, four domains in the United Kingdom have: moving, healing, living, and learning. The real prices of learning have grown as much there as in the United States, since the private sector plays a bigger role in education there than in other European countries and has exerted considerable pressure on prices. The cost of living has also grown, on average, by 75 percent in real terms due to the high demand for and low supply of housing. Healing and moving have seen price increases of more than 50 percent, with eating not far behind. Only dressing has seen a substantial reduction in real prices over the past decade. In sum, the United Kingdom is a land of opportunity for monetary-cost-based disruption (*see Figure 10.3*). More generally, though, a disruptive opportunity in one country might not constitute much of one in another. At least where monetary costs are concerned, the overall disruption potential is greater and broader in some countries than in others. Entrepreneurs and investors who see a successful business model in one country and seek to apply it in another should note these structural differences.

FIGURE 10.3 **THE EVOLVING MONETARY COSTS OF THE BIG SEVEN IN THE UNITED KINGDOM (RELATIVE TO 1997)**

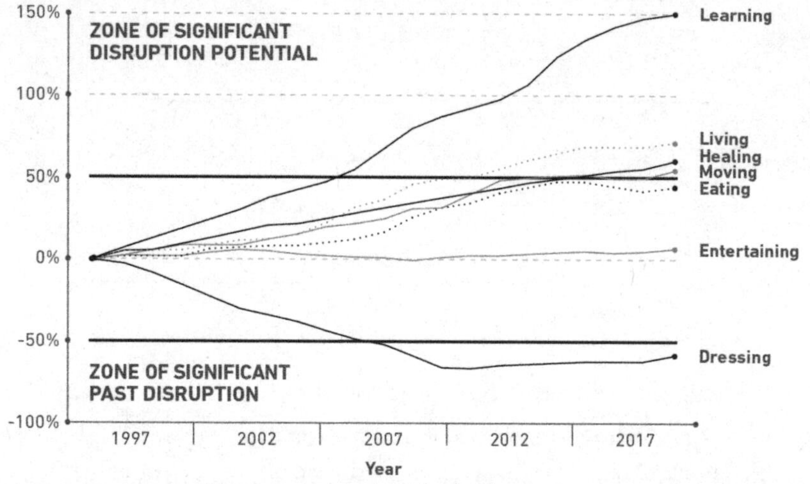

Source: Eurostat.

Charting the Potential for Effort- and Time-Related Disruption

We've examined disruption potential related to monetary costs, but what about the potential related to time and effort costs? Compiling accurate data on the effort that consumers incur in order to acquire and use goods pertaining to the Big Seven is significantly harder, if not impossible, to do at the country level. In the United States, however, we can use high-quality data from the Bureau of Labor Statistics to understand where consumers use most of their time. Since January 2003, the BLS has been collecting data for the American Time Use Survey on a monthly basis. In 2016, the bureau interviewed 10,500 individuals, asking them to keep a log of the activities they performed between 4:00 a.m. on the day before the interview until 4:00 a.m. on the day of the interview. The bureau's researchers then coded these descriptions into one of 399 routine activities, such as sleeping, working, watching television and movies, eating and drinking, and interior cleaning.[34] In my own research, I dove deep into the data to further map people's activities onto the Big Seven consumption categories and then to evaluate whether each activity created or eroded value from the consumer's perspective. For example, spending time eating at a restaurant would constitute a value-creating activity, but the time taken to drive to the restaurant would constitute a value-eroding activity. My research yielded an analysis of how much effort Americans expend on average each week to obtain desired benefits across the Big Seven domains. These efforts represent costs as well—we just pay them with our time and energy, not our money.

Excluding time spent working and sleeping, Americans spend most of their leisure time (twenty-eight hours, or 39 percent of the time spent with all the Big Seven consumption domains) entertaining themselves. After that comes eating (including grocery shopping, pantry organizing, food preparation, serving, and kitchen cleanup, not just eating per se), accounting for an average of fourteen hours per week, or about 19 percent of the time we spend on the Big Seven. The third most common way we spend our time is participating in home living activities such as cleaning, shopping for home furnishings and goods, landscaping, organizing, performing home repairs, and communicating with family members living at our home. We spend an average of nine hours per week on these activities, or 12 percent of time spent with the Big Seven. Moving, including commuting and other automobile transportation, occupies 8.1 hours per week; dressing, 7.8 hours; learning, 3.6 hours; and healing, 1.9 hours per week, respectively (*see Figure 10.4*).

FIGURE 10.4 **THE RELATIVE TIME AND EFFORT COST GAP**

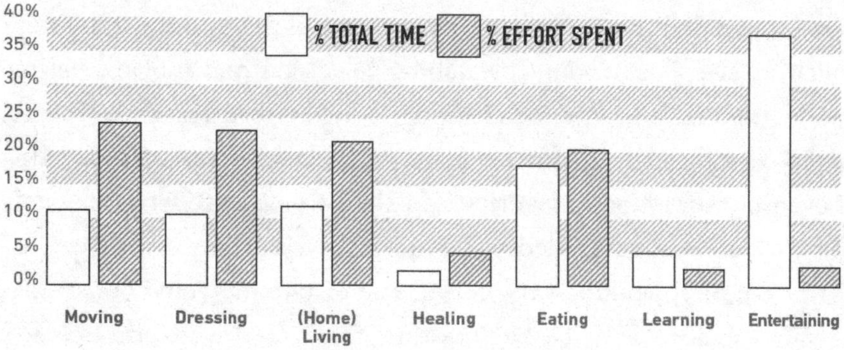

Note: % effort spent sums to 100 percent and % total time sums to 100 percent. Source: Adapted from U.S. Bureau of Labor Statistics.

In performing these activities, we shouldn't conflate the total time we spend on them with the time we actually spend to obtain benefits. For instance, the effort we spend procuring entertainment content actually represents only 2 percent of the overall effort we spend in all the Big Seven. This is unproductive time. But the time we spend entertaining ourselves represents 39 percent of the total time we spend on the Big Seven. The reason is that it's easy to entertain ourselves now that we do most of our video viewing and socializing quickly and effortlessly at home or online. As with entertainment, the time we spend learning (which includes reading; work performed for a class, degree, certification, or licensure; and the actual time spent in class) is largely productive. U.S. households spend 5 percent of their total time learning, but they spend only 2 percent of their total effort on procuring sources for learning. Eating offers us a more balanced picture. We spend 19 percent of our time on this Big Seven domain, and expend 20 percent of our total effort procuring food, preparing it, and cleaning up. While healing doesn't account for much of our time spent on the Big Seven domains, it requires more effort in relative terms. U.S. households expend 5 percent of their effort but only 3 percent of total time taking care of their health. Health-related services that save time in and outside the home could bridge this small gap.

Three of the Big Seven domains force U.S. households to expend significantly larger amounts of effort relative to total time spent. Moving is one such case, representing 25 percent of our total effort with the Big Seven but only 11 percent of our total time. Similarly, dressing and home living take up much more effort than time spent, relatively speaking. Since we arguably can choose how much time to spend with these activities, but not how much effort we need to expend in order to gain the desired benefit, these three domains—moving, dressing, and living—represent the largest time cost-to-benefit consumption domains among the Big Seven. Any business that can create products and services to reduce this unproductive time spent procuring and extracting the benefits in these domains, without reducing the actual benefit delivered, will likely attract the attention of U.S. households and perhaps prove highly disruptive.

In the moving domain, we have discussed at length how ride-hailing services have enabled consumers to enjoy a potentially better experience than they would when traveling by taxi. But it is in substituting for personal driving—thereby converting driving time (and effort) into a productive use of time—that ride-hailing might drastically disrupt how we get around. For those interested in owning cars, autonomous driving technologies can also help to free up unproductive time (if those technologies fulfill their promise). When it comes to dressing ourselves, most of the unproductive time arises during the tasks of washing, dressing, and grooming oneself, as well as doing laundry. Startups such as Rent the Runway have launched unlimited dress rental services that allow people to rent, use, and return major portions of their wardrobe, as opposed to owning all the pieces and going to the trouble of cleaning them. Likewise, the home living services I've mentioned—Thumbtack, Hello Alfred, and TaskRabbit—help address the time required to clean and maintain your own home. But if you really want to minimize the work required in this domain, forgoing home ownership entirely and using a flexible rental service for co-living such as Roam, Common, or WeLive can free up large chunks of unproductive time.

When it comes to disruption, not all markets are created equal, and not all decoupling tools apply equally in each market. The potential for monetary-cost-based disruption looms large in education and healthcare. Since the prices charged to consumers in these industries have risen dramatically over the past two decades, companies that provide cheaper alternatives will feed consumer-driven disruption. As for transportation, fashion, and housing, the companies that will best foster disruption aren't those that manage to reduce financial cost, but rather those that reduce the time consumers spend gleaning the benefits of consumption. Am I suggesting that eating and entertaining offer little opportunity for disruption? Absolutely not. But relative to the other elements of the Big Seven, and when it comes to these types of consumer costs, the opportunities in eating and entertaining are much more difficult to spot at the country level. You will need to probe deeper and study the costs accrued by subsets of the population.

ADOPTING THE BIG SEVEN

By allowing us to track how people allocate the lion's share of their money and time, the Big Seven can help us spot change early, before it trickles down to hundreds of other markets and sectors. Study the Big Seven, and you'll be more adept at spotting nascent waves of disruption, no matter what industry you're in. I myself have found the Big Seven extremely helpful. As I explained in Chapter 1, I was looking across a number of markets when I spotted startups breaking apart existing business models (decoupling), then reconfiguring those pieces (coupling). In most cases, incumbents were responding by trying to glue the decoupled pieces back together themselves (recoupling). I wasn't deliberately looking at hundreds of industries to uncover these patterns. I was unconsciously attending to seven domains of consumption in particular. *Unlocking the Customer Value Chain* is the fruit of tracking the Big Seven. Generalizing across consumption domains should allow you, too, to spot the next wave of disruption.

As you work with the Big Seven, focus on the present, where the data are available, rather than on the future. Present-casting, for the purpose of uncovering nascent waves of disruption, essentially boils down to three steps: *broaden your view* in a manageable way by tracking the Big Seven, *determine where the costs are exceedingly high*, and then *translate trends* across domains so as to discern large changes that are enduring and will likely affect your own industry. As we've seen, significantly higher monetary costs exist in some of the Big Seven domains than in others, while some domains carry a larger gap between effort time and total time spent on a given activity. Both of these factors create significant pent-up demand for new business models and innovations. That latent demand in turn has the potential to disrupt markets—including your own.

Broaden Your Span of View + Determine Where Costs Are Exceedingly High + Translate Trends Across Domains

If you work for an established business, incorporate present-casting into your job description. And don't relegate to top management the task of alerting others to incoming storms. If you or someone else in the organization senses that a meaningful group of consumers is changing its behavior, whether in an adjacent category or in a more distant one, take it seriously. Give yourself more time to collect data and determine patterns of common behavior that might eventually reach your shores. If you're looking only at your market or an adjacent one, you might not have enough time to understand consumers' shifting needs and craft an appropriate response.

Since consumer behavior never stops changing, make wave-spotting a routine process within your organization. Conduct a Big Seven present-casting exercise once every year or two. Doing so at six-month intervals or less is overkill, as it will possibly only allow you to pick up minor and ephemeral shifts. Conversely, conducting present-casting too infrequently—once every three years or more—might lead you to detect major shifts too late. Of course, tailor your present-casting process to the demands of your industry. If you cater to markets in which quick-changing customer tastes prevail (for instance, pop music or youth clothing), perform wave-spotting more frequently. If you serve elderly customers or the government, lowering the frequency should mitigate the odds that present-casting exercises will turn up the same trends over and over again.

Whatever frequency you choose, be sure to include both industry insiders as well as outsiders in the process. Outsiders who don't possess the views and biases that prevail in your industry will help you broaden your scope of view (action #1). Insiders, meanwhile, will generally do a better job identifying where costs are exceedingly high for customers in their industry (action #2). Working together, insiders and outsiders do a better job than either group alone of translating trends between other markets and the insider's market (action #3). The combination of the outsider's breadth and the insider's depth will give you the greatest chance of spotting the next wave of disruption before others.

Think of wave-spotting as your company's own "radar system," akin to what government and others use to spot shifting weather patterns. A wave-spotting exercise is not unlike a storm path prediction model (*see Figure 10.5*). Instead of geographical areas, wave-spotting looks at markets or industries. And instead of day-by-day changes in weather, wave-spotting picks up changes that unfold over long periods. Still, both systems give users three insights. They allow you to identify the source of a disruption (in the case of wave-spotting, the intrinsic consumer behaviors fueling change), the rate or intensity of its growth, and the path it seems to be taking (in the case of wave-spotting, any new markets the wave hits beyond the one in which it originally appeared).

As the results of wave-spotting exercises come in, be sure to present them to both top executives and board members. Given their diversity, board members should be able to assess an incoming storm's importance, deciding whether management should address it energetically and identifying the appropriate level of resources management should deploy when mounting a response. Given these basic parameters, the CEO and their team bear responsibility for proposing specific responses and action plans.

If everyone performs their role, and if informative wave-spotting analyses continue to flow in, your company should avert unexpected

FIGURE 10.5 **DEPICTION OF A STORM'S PATH AND INTENSITY**

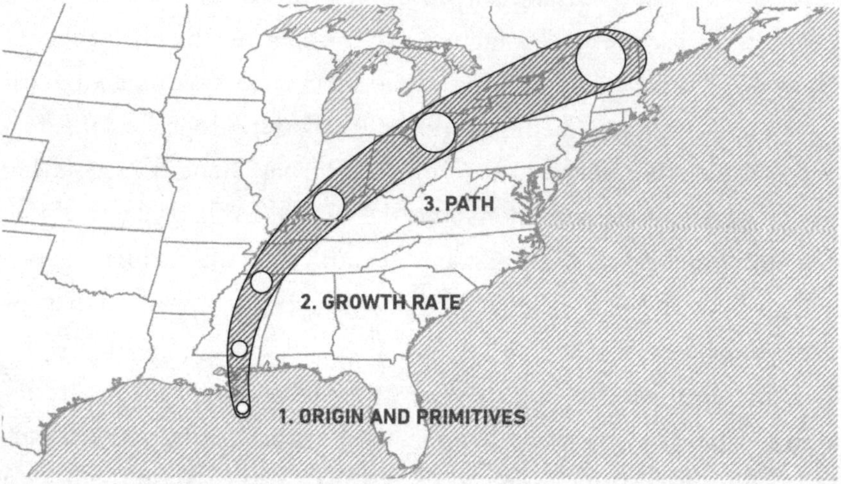

surprises and catastrophes. You'll have to adapt to changes, but you'll be able to do so in a much calmer and more informed way. The next wave of disruption won't be quite so disruptive after all.

EPILOGUE

Unlocking the Customer Value Chain presents a new approach to digital disruption, one rooted not in a study of technology or business strategy generally, but in the disciplines of marketing and consumer behavior. As we've seen, analyzing disruption from the customer's perspective rather than that of the firm and its competitors allows for a new interpretation, as well as new tools for mastering both disruption and an incumbent's response to it. Yet the theory of decoupling carries even broader implications for how we think about business.

So many of us today become distracted by technology and innovation in ways that aren't helpful. When I read about Steve Jobs, Jeff Bezos, Elon Musk, and other brilliant tech entrepreneurs, I often fall into self-doubt. These figures are the heroes of our times. How can other entrepreneurs possibly measure up? Many executives I know feel similarly insecure, confiding to me that they could never replicate the accomplishments of a Jobs or a Bezos. Trade conferences only compound these feelings, where we encounter self-proclaimed experts trumpeting the latest tech trends: 3-D printers, wearables, drones, virtual reality, robots, bots, blockchain, machine learning, and artificial intelligence. For many of us, it's overwhelming. The world seems to be changing faster than ever, and becoming ever more complex. Unless we and our companies keep up, none of us will survive. Academics and consultants too often suggest complex frameworks for reinventing businesses using various kinds of technology. The more you see these overloaded frameworks, the more you may feel clueless about where to start.

As scientific research has shown, our fears paralyze us when they become too overwhelming. So, too, do complexity and uncertainty. Many business leaders today experience such decision paralysis. The solution is to put aside the noise of cutting-edge technology, groundbreaking innovation, and visionary entrepreneurs and go back to the fundamentals of business. It might seem counterintuitive to do this, but it's the only way to move ahead fearlessly. In writing this book, one of my personal goals has been to demystify disruption by simplifying and clarifying the phenomenon. My other goal has been to redirect the attention of executives and managers, thus spurring them to take action. Just as technology has led businesspeople to lose sight of the basics of business, so all the attention paid to the builders of technology, the tech startups, and the tech giants has led businesspeople to focus excessively on competing with these supposed "weapons of disruption" at the expense of the customer. Go back to what you know, to what really matters—business and customers.

Doing so requires that we make another shift. We must learn to "cool ourselves down," parting with the aggressive stance toward competition that many companies take. As the conventional thinking goes, business is war. Uber, Facebook, Google, and many more large companies around the world all have war rooms.* They aim to take territory. To fight back. To vanquish the competition. And to accomplish these goals, they mobilize various "strategic weapons" at their disposal. Indeed, the link between the worlds of war and business is invariably strategy. Business leaders think of themselves as generals, scanning the battleground, poring over their plans, and

* Uber's war room, used to combat archrival Lyft and camouflage its operations from the eyes of transportation regulators, was recently renamed the "peace room" in response to multiple internal scandals that have since become public knowledge.

eventually leading the charge. Is it any accident that so many business leaders have sought strategic inspiration in Sun Tzu's classic fifth-century-BC manual on waging war, or that they've read other recent books with titles like *Business War Games*, *Asymmetric Warfare for Entrepreneurs*, and *The CEO's Secret Weapon*?

The metaphor of warfare does have its practical uses. When Alfred Sloan built GM, he explicitly based the company's organization on military hierarchy. Generals (top managers) determined the strategies, and soldiers (middle management) followed their orders. Many other business executives have since embraced the war analogy to varying degrees, perceiving it as a clear way of articulating roles and responsibilities, and also of motivating people. Confronted with the threat posed by an external enemy, many people inside organizations are more inclined to set aside their personal needs and commit time, energy, and money to a common worthy cause.

I wonder, though, whether we've pushed the war analogy too far. Some of the similarities that formerly seemed to hold between war strategy and business strategy clearly no longer do. In traditional warfare, a relatively small number of antagonists fought one another, vying for a fixed amount of territory under conditions of engagement that were fairly well understood. If you won ground, your opponent ceded it, and vice versa. If you took a particular action, your enemy would likely respond in one of just a few predictable ways. A few decades ago, most industries operated this way. Just a few very large players competed with one another in a single, well-defined market. Coca-Cola fought Pepsi. Sony fought Panasonic. Mercedes fought BMW and Audi. GE fought Siemens. Competition was fairly predictable due to the size and number of players, and everyone competed for the same, fixed spoils.

Today, many industries and markets operate differently. The internet provides a cheap and accessible channel for distribution, marketing, and commerce, drastically lowering the cost of starting businesses. As a result, digital startups have flooded markets in consumer goods, electronics, transportation, industrials, and telecoms, to name a few. The large incumbents in these industries no longer face one or a few large "enemies," but dozens or hundreds of small and unpredictable ones. The tasks of planning, strategizing, and executing no longer proceed in a top-down, hierarchical, deliberate, and predictable fashion. Rather, employees at all levels have to plan and execute continuously and iteratively to keep pace with the changes taking place around them. In this context, the war metaphor no longer offers such a useful way of conceptualizing options, decisions, and actions.

The war metaphor also leads us to shift our gaze away from customers. When firms and their leaders perceive that they are at war and need to mobilize weapons to "kill off" the enemy, they regard customers as merely a trophy they receive for winning the battle, or as a loss they experience in the course of vanquishing their competitors. Customers fall away to the margins, and executives focus the preponderance of their attention on their competition, taking overly aggressive actions that usually prove counterproductive and sometimes even scandalous.

One important strand of psychological research has shown that when people in various capacities exhibit more aggressive behavior, they tend to perceive the world differently than they would in a less aggressive state. When we are driving in heavy traffic, become irritated, and behave aggressively, we lose focus on our "customer": the safety of our passengers and ourselves.[1] Similarly, aggressive behavior in the workplace reduces our focus on our actual customers and their needs. From the 2016 Volkswagen diesel engine emissions cheating scandals to the 2017 scandal centering around Wells Fargo's practice of opening fake accounts for oblivious customers and Uber's controversial efforts to combat archrival Lyft and camouflage its operations from the eyes of transportation regulators, a take-no-prisoners attitude on the part of executives has led to an erosion or outright violation of customer-centricity, which in turn hurts businesses and society. At the extreme, scholars such as Eugene Soltes, who has studied white-collar crimes, have revealed links between highly aggressive behavior and corporate malfeasance.[2]

But the harm done by adhering to a war metaphor is even worse. When executives and managers treat competitors aggressively, their aggressive thinking becomes reinforcing, profoundly influencing workplace cultures. The language colleagues use with one another becomes harsher, more antagonistic, less civil.[3] Us-versus-them thinking and a generalized fear of loss prevail. Over time, companies hire more-aggressive people and fire less-aggressive ones, coarsening the culture even more. Gender diversity suffers, as women on average tend to behave less aggressively than men. If you want to understand why so many workplaces have failed to retain female leaders and foster a cordial workspace, you can't ignore the profoundly aggressive mindset (a warlike mentality being only one manifestation) that is ingrained in business thinking and practice at certain large companies around the world.

I believe it is time to deescalate and pacify the practice of business. This statement doesn't just reflect a value judgment on my part, although I would like to see more women in management and leadership positions at the best companies. Rather, it is a matter of practicality. Pacifying the corporate world will, I believe, lead to fewer scandals, less toxic work environments, less gender imbalance, and, ultimately, a much greater focus on satisfying the needs and desires of customers.

I'm not suggesting that companies should become less competitive. On the contrary, businesses must remain highly competitive—but without aggressively seeking their competitors' demise. In sports, successful athletes such as Tom Brady, Lindsey Vonn, LeBron James, the Williams sisters, and Roger Federer treat competitors with dignity, perceiving them as sources of learning and inspiration, and even as possible collaborators. Doing so will yield *better* competition, not less of it. Ultimately, it will lead to better business for all.

Digital disruption might pose a dire challenge at first, but it also affords us an opportunity to evolve our mindsets, and our businesses, in powerful ways. Coupling, decoupling, and recoupling comprise a powerful tool—a trident that allows you to hook many customers. Let's grasp this opportunity—for our customers' sake, and ultimately for our own. I wish you the best of luck!

Thales S. Teixeira
Boston, 2019

NOTE ON TERMINOLOGY

Three terms appear prominently in this book: "disruption," "decoupling," and "customer value chain." Since my usage of these terms either is novel or departs from that of previous authors, it's worth a few words noting the differences.

Disruption

Unlocking the Customer Value Chain deals with the phenomenon of decoupling, a type of business model innovation that can prove highly disruptive to certain markets. In 1995, Clayton Christensen published his now famous *Harvard Business Review* article defining and explaining "disruptive technologies."[1] This article used the term "disruptive technology/product" to refer to a special class of technologies that would eventually form the basis of his theory of disruptive innovation.* In his 1997 bestselling book *The Innovator's Dilemma,* Christensen introduced the term "disruptive innovation," which was subsequently elaborated on in numerous books and articles by Christensen and his colleagues.[2] The present book stays true to Christensen's theory in its use of his term "disruptive innovation."

Lately, a related term, "disruption," has taken on a life of its own.

* There is only one mention of "disruptive innovation" in the article.

According to *Webster's*, "disruption" means "to interrupt the normal course or unity of something, to break apart, rupture."[3] In most of his recent articles, Christensen seems to imply that "disruption" should refer only to his theory of disruptive innovation.* In a 2015 article, "What Is Disruptive Innovation?," Christensen and colleagues use "[theory of] disruptive innovation" and "disruption" interchangeably. I respectfully disagree with the conflation of these terms. "Disruptive innovation" is a very specific, well-defined term associated with a theory proposed by Christensen in his 1997 book. "Disruption" is a noun of general usage. Anyone can speak of disruption, disruptors, and attempts to disrupt without connoting anything related to Christensen's specific theory.

"Disruption" didn't appear at all in the original 1995 article, only appearing in more recent publications by Christensen and colleagues.[4] In *The Innovator's Solution*, Christensen's second book, he attached the adjective "disruptive" to various nouns, among them "innovation," "strategy," "business model," "company," and "theory." In effect, Christensen moved from narrowly defining disruptive technologies, a type of product or process, to talking about disruptive approaches, strategy types, and finally an outcome, market disruption. Therein lies the conceptual problem. We shouldn't associate products, approaches, and outcomes with one another on a one-to-one basis. This creates many problems, one of which is circular reasoning: Christensen defines "a disruptive innovation" (a choice) as causing "disruption" (an outcome). In other words, a technology is disruptive if it disrupts. Christensen's use of these terms conflates a cause (or process) with an effect (or outcome).†

* Here I disagree with Christensen when he writes, "Disruption is a theory" (Clayton M. Christensen and Michael E. Raynor, *The Innovator's Solution: Creating and Sustaining Successful Growth* [Boston: Harvard Business School Press, 2003], 25). His theory is narrower, one of disruptive innovation, and it's just one theory about how disruption occurs.

† Another problem that arises, and a general criticism of the theory of disruptive innovation, is that, as the authors state, "the term 'disruptive innovation' is misleading when it is used to refer to a product or service at one fixed point, rather than to the evolution

In this book, I will respect the dictionary definition and use "disruption" colloquially to denote an attempt to interrupt the normal course of an industry (as in "disrupt industry X") or to interrupt the normal course of an incumbent company (as in "disrupt company Y"). In other words, I refer to "disruption" as an outcome, and I speak of companies "disrupting" others as a process intended to force the occurrence of such an outcome.

Further, in keeping with popular usage, I regard the primary signs that disruption is occurring as the transfer of a material amount of market share from one business or businesses to the disruptor in a relatively short period of time. We can debate the precise definition of the words "material" and "short." For my purposes, it's important to note that to an outside observer, the transfer is relatively fast and sizable. In other words, "disruption" is an abrupt discontinuity that interrupts the normal course of gaining and keeping share for the original participants in a defined market. In that sense, the statement that "startup A is disrupting the retail market" should convey that startup A is attempting to interrupt, or is in the process of interrupting, that industry's historical market share holdings. It would be more precise, albeit more cumbersome, to refer to startup A as a "would-be disruptor," capturing merely its intention to disrupt. On the other hand, claiming that "startup B disrupted the taxi industry in San Francisco" implies that the transfer of market share actually took place. This is factually the case for Uber in some but not all cities around the world where it has entered. So, contrary to what

---

of that product or service over time" (Clayton M. Christensen, Michael E. Raynor, and Rory McDonald, "What Is Disruptive Innovation?," *Harvard Business Review,* December 2015). The authors then go on to claim that disruptive innovations are thus classified based upon "the path they followed from the fringe to the mainstream." Therefore, one can only determine if a new technology or business model is a disruptive innovation after the fact, after observing its trajectory. The classification of an innovation is determined by where it leads to, its path, not by what intrinsic features the innovation has. Even so, "some disruptive innovations succeed; some don't." This definition leads it to become a descriptive theory, a very useful one by the way, but one without a tight ex ante forecasting power.

Christensen and colleagues have written more recently, I do believe it is accurate to say that Uber disrupted the taxi industry.*

Decoupling

I define "decoupling" as the rupturing of the links between adjacent consumption activities that have traditionally been provided to customers by an incumbent. As a class of business model innovation implemented by companies, decoupling is analogous to Christensen's disruptive innovation, but distinct in its causal mechanism. Disruption is an outcome produced by various mechanisms, including disruptive innovations, deregulation, the appearance of a new business model, or decoupling, to name a few.† In some cases, decoupling can lead to disruption—the fast and sizable transfer of market share from incumbent (decoupled) to entrant (decoupler). But any decoupling-based business model can only be judged to be disruptive, or not, relative to a well-defined market or incumbent. For more on this topic, please refer to "Note on Differences Between Decoupling and Disruptive Innovation."

Decoupling is one among many theories of disruption, and one with particular application in digital disruption. As I elaborate in this book, decoupling doesn't address competition due to drastically different end-quality products for consumers. Building a superior product or better service does not by itself constitute decoupling. And unlike other forms of business model innovation, such as un-

* Christensen, Raynor, and McDonald, in "What Is Disruptive Innovation?," claim that Uber is not disrupting the taxi industry. I disagree, and the data show a rapid change in market shares from taxi operators to Uber in many cities around the world. That is enough to claim disruption at some level. Is it a disruptive innovation? Christensen, who coined the term, is best suited to answer that question. He and colleagues argue it is not.

† Here Christensen and I agree with each other. Not only technologies but also business models can be disruptive, in some cases even more so than new technologies. Yet, due to our difference in defining the term "disruptive," he means business models can be classified as disruptive innovations, whereas I mean they can disrupt markets.

bundling, decoupling takes place at the level of the customer's value chain, not at the product level.

Customer Value Chain (CVC)

So what is a value chain? Michael Porter defined this term in his 1985 book *Competitive Advantage,* presenting it as the discrete and interrelated activities that a firm performs that create value.[5] A value chain is composed of primary activities, such as operations and marketing, and support activities, such as HR management and procurement. In order to understand disruption, I consider *activities* as the unit of analysis. However, instead of Porter's firm-centric view, I take a customer-centric view and define the customer's value chain as *the discrete activities that customers perform in order to accomplish their consumption needs and wants.* We can group these activities generically into broader stages that we commonly refer to as the act of searching for, evaluating, purchasing, using, and disposing of goods and services. All customer activities generate either value or cost for customers. An activity can, but need not, create value, and such activities often generate a cost for the customer. For instance, trialing products at a store creates value for customers, but it also requires time and effort. The activity of physically going to the store, on the other hand, only generates costs.

The customer value chain bears similarity with other concepts commonly used in marketing, such as the "customer funnel," the "customer journey," McKinsey's "Customer Decision Journey," and Harvard Business School's "decision-making process."*[6] Like these constructs, the customer value chain comprises a series of discrete

* In the past, I would refer to the CVC as the decision-making process, as we teach MBA students at Harvard. But so many of my students, clients, and audience members have come to refer to it as the "customer value chain" that I have decided to join the crowd myself.

activities, often sequentially performed by the customer. One aspect that sets the customer value chain (CVC) apart is that it encompasses the entire, end-to-end consumption experience; the other terms mostly refer to the purchasing part of the process. When necessary and informative, the CVC also incorporates the use and disposal of products (e.g., returning, reselling, or throwing away). The other unique aspect of the CVC is that different types of value (created, charged, eroded) are associated with each activity. As I show, the CVC can serve as a useful unit of analysis for decoupling, helping us understand how the process works and what executives can do to respond to it.

NOTE ON DIFFERENCES BETWEEN DECOUPLING AND DISRUPTIVE INNOVATION

In my past presentations to company executives and general audiences, audience members have sometimes asked me how decoupling compares to Clayton Christensen's theory of disruptive innovation. Theories are hard to compare when they speak to different phenomena and approach them from different angles. Nevertheless, in this section I will try my best to compare and contrast some overlapping aspects of my theory and Christensen's, with the caveat that Christensen has updated and evolved the basic tenets of his theory over the years in response to new observations and past criticisms.

Christensen's original theory of disruptive innovation describes a dynamic whereby an entrant, usually a small or newly formed company, manages to overtake established incumbents using what he initially termed "a disruptive technology" and eventually broadened to include "a disruptive innovation."[1] Christensen's theory starts by assuming that incumbents focus on improving their products for their most profitable customers. While doing so, incumbents overdeliver on the needs of some customer segments and ignore the needs of others. This creates an opportunity for challengers to enter at the lower end of the market (e.g., lower-performance products at lower prices, represented by parallel arrows at the bottom of *Figure A.1*) and target those overlooked customers. Incumbents, chasing higher profitability, tend to focus on the higher end of the market (represented by parallel arrows at the top of *Figure A.1*) and initially disregard low-end challengers. Entrants eventually move upmarket as their ability to offer higher-performance products increases (represented by the curved arrow in *Figure A.1*). They begin competing with the incumbent in the higher end of the market while still reigning as the undisputed leader in the lower end of the market. Eventually, mainstream customers migrate to the entrant en masse, and the incumbent, who has nowhere to go, loses significant market share to the disruptor (*see Figure A.1*). This phenomenon occurs only if the challenger uses a disruptive technology (or innovation) that the incumbent disregards at some point. An often-cited example is the disruption of mainframe and minicomputer manufacturers in the 1970s and 1980s by personal computer makers.

FIGURE A.1 **DEPICTION OF CHRISTENSEN'S THEORY OF DISRUPTIVE INNOVATION**

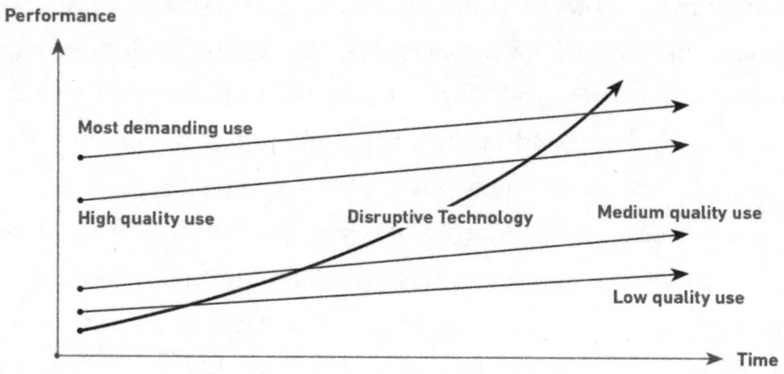

Source: Based on Christensen's presentations.

Christensen's theory of disruptive innovation has three key features worth noting. First, it clearly defines where in the product performance dimension the challenger enters: at the bottom of a key performance dimension, below the incumbent (*time point A in Figure A.2*). As such, Tesla, with its high-end electric cars, would not be a disruptive innovator.[2] Second, Christensen's theory specifies the trajectory of the challenger with respect to this primary dimension.

The challenger's product performance improvement starts off slow and picks up (*time point B in Figure A.2*). Accordingly, Uber would not be considered disruptive, as Christensen himself has argued.[3] Last, the theory specifies the incumbent's response. Its product performance improves, but not as quickly as that of the challenger due to different underlying technology choices. Eventually, the challenger's product performance surpasses the incumbent's, allowing the challenger to overtake the incumbent and resulting in disruption of market shares (*time point C in Figure A.2*). Over the years, Christensen has provided more details around where, how, and why this dynamic occurs. I won't elaborate on these contingencies here. Nonetheless, his theory can be described, for the most part, by his explanation of where the challenger enters, what the challenger's trajectory is relative to the incumbent, and what the incumbent's response is.

FIGURE A.2 **DEPICTION OF THREE MAIN ELEMENTS OF CHRISTENSEN'S THEORY OF DISRUPTIVE INNOVATION**

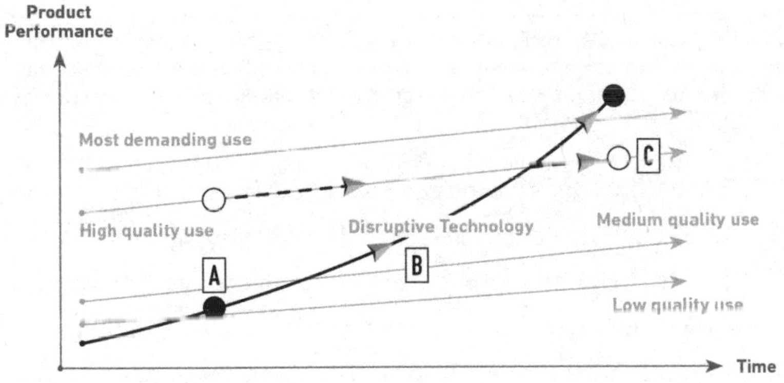

The black circle represents the challenger's relative position, while the white circle represents the incumbent's relative position during two time periods. The solid arrow represents the challenger's trajectory, whereas the dashed arrow represents the incumbent's trajectory.

Decoupling theory also rests on a number of important assumptions. First and foremost, it assumes that digital disruption occurs thanks to the customer's decisions. For this reason, the dynamics of players, challengers, and incumbents play out (and should be seen) at the level of the customer's value chain. These dynamics could originate in product performance differences, as in Christensen's theory, but they don't need to. Business model differences between incumbent and challenger might also result in differences in how value is created for customers, how value is charged, and how value is eroded. This issue aside, if we were to reframe the theory of decoupling in light of the three elements that describe Christensen's theory of disruptive innovation, then the answers provided by decoupling theory would be as follows (*Figure A.3*):

FIGURE A.3 **DEPICTION OF THREE MAIN ELEMENTS OF DECOUPLING THEORY**

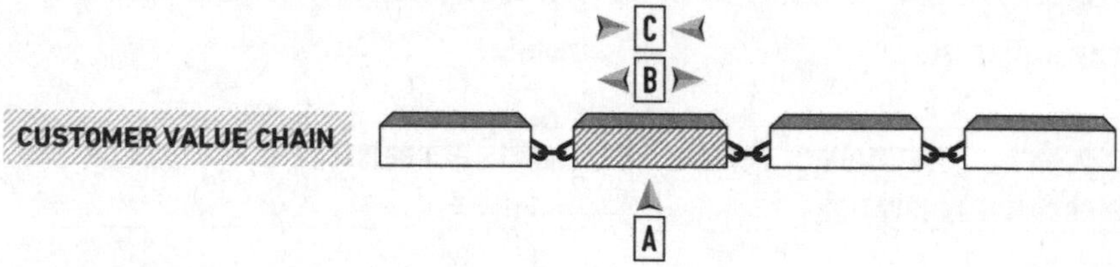

The shadowed rectangle represents activity provided by the challenger, and the white rectangles represent activity provided by incumbent. The B arrows represent the challenger's trajectory, whereas the C arrows represent the incumbent's trajectory.

1. **Where does the challenger enter?** Answer: It enters at one of the customer value chain activities (by *decoupling*).
2. **What is the challenger's eventual trajectory?** Answer: It captures adjacent customer value chain activities (by *coupling* them).
3. **What is the incumbent's most common response?** Answer: It often attempts to regain lost activities (by *recoupling*).

While the answers to these three questions are not, in my opinion, the most noteworthy elements of decoupling theory, they should allow readers to compare and contrast decoupling to disruptive innovation theory. In the examples of Tesla and Uber, only the latter is disrupting the transportation market. It does so by decoupling consumers' search for private modes of transportation, providing only the actual rides. Tesla competes with other car manufacturers on design, performance of its technology, and brand attributes, but it doesn't do so via decoupling. As the following table illustrates, we might regard some highly successful companies or technologies (in 2018) as exemplifying Christensen's disruptive innovation but not decoupling theory, and vice versa. Note that market success does not in and of itself mean that a company is disruptive according to either of these two theories. Finally, we can identify individual companies that illustrate both theories. According to Christensen, Netflix used streaming as a technology to disrupt the video rental market. But before its video-on-demand phase, Netflix decoupled the act of renting a DVD movie from going to the store.

EXAMPLES	DISRUPTIVE ACCORDING TO DISRUPTIVE INNOVATION THEORY?	DISRUPTIVE ACCORDING TO DECOUPLING THEORY?
Tesla	No	No
Uber	No	Yes
PCs	Yes	No
Netflix	Yes	Yes

What, then, is the key difference between decoupling and all other theories of disruption, including Christensen's? In other theories, disrupted incumbents lose *customers* to challengers due to greater performance by their *products* (in Christensen's case, using disruptive innovations). In decoupling, disrupted incumbents lose *customer activities* to challengers, primarily because challengers lower the *costs* of those activities to customers. On a more practical matter, many theories focus executives' attention on technology as a driver for disruption, and encourage them to track developments of all proven and unproven technologies. The challenge is to evaluate, before the fact, which technologies may one day become "disruptive." The theory of decoupling focuses attention on customers and their process of making choices. The challenge here is to judge which activities fail to satisfy customers due to excessive monetary, effort, or time costs. Those weak links create opportunities for would-be disruptors to attack.

NOTE ON CALCULATING MaR^{TM} AND $TMaR^{TM}$

Market at Risk (MaR^{TM})

Start by assessing whether the customer sees a lower (negative) or higher (positive) total cost of decoupling using the following formula:

$$Cost_{decoupling} = Cost_{decoupler}(Money, Time, Effort) - Cost_{incumbent}(Money, Time, Effort)$$

Next, determine your target customers' implicit sensitivities to these three costs. You can usually do this with a survey or via conjoint analysis. Now multiply the two factors to calculate the decoupler's potential to steal customers away from a given incumbent:

$$\text{Potential of Decoupler} = Cost_{decoupling} \times Sensitivity_{costs}{}^{*}$$

Finally, to arrive at the market at risk of any given incumbent, multiply the potential of the decoupler by the market share of the incumbent. Mathematically, we have:

* To be precise, the required mathematical operation is to integrate the cost of decoupling over the sensitivity distribution in the interval from 0 to the cost difference points. As a result, Potential of Decoupler becomes a number between 0 and 1.

$$\text{Market at Risk} = \text{Potential of Decoupler} \times \text{Market Share}_{\text{incumbent}}$$

MaR is the *maximum potential losses*, assuming that all customers in the market were aware of and compared the incumbent's offering to that of the disruptor's on the basis of monetary, time, and effort cost alone, without factoring in other dimensions of choice. MaR also doesn't consider executional factors such as marketing spending, channels of distribution, and availability of funds. In a sense, MaR represents the potential disruptive value of the disruptor's business model, not the value of a disruptive business per se.

Total Market at Risk (TMaR™)

Somewhat analogously, we can perform the same MaR calculation for a disruptor vis-à-vis all industry incumbents one at a time, summing them up to determine the total industry's market at risk, TMaR, or conversely, the decoupler's maximum potential for disruption, as such:

$$\text{Total Market at Risk} = \Sigma_{\text{incumbents}} \text{Potential of Decoupler} \times \text{Market Share}_{\text{incumbent}}{}^{*}$$

* The symbol Σ denotes summation, e.g., $\Sigma_i x_i = x_1 + x_2 + x_3 + x_4 + \ldots$

ACKNOWLEDGMENTS

I owe deep thanks to many people for their help and encouragement during the writing of this book. Clay Christensen was among the first to see the early ideas around decoupling and encouraged me to, in his words, "find other very different examples [of the theory in action] to establish its validity." For reading and commenting on early drafts of this book: David Bell, Pete Caban, Jim Collins, Janika Dillon, Tom Eisenmann, Dan Gruber, Linda Hill, Mark Hill, Joelle Kaufman, Walter Kiechel III, Ryan Newton, Kash Rangan, Camille Tang, Ken Wilbur, and Krystal Zell. Eugene Soltes and Iva Teixeira were exceedingly gracious with their time, reviewing many chapters and providing detailed comments on each one. To all of you, words can't describe my gratitude. At Harvard, for their general support of my work, and for helpful conversations along the way: Bharat Anand, Lynda Applegate, Frank Cespedes, Ben Edelman, Willis Emmons, Ben Esty, Kathy Giusti, Shane Greenstein, Richard Hamermesh, Linda Hill, Felix Oberholzer-Gee, John Quelch Jr., Ryan Raffaelli, Eugene Soltes, and Feng Zhu. In particular, I'd like to thank Dean Nitin Noria and my former research director, Teresa Amabile, for opening up seemingly closed doors. In my academic home, the Marketing Unit, I'd like to thank each and every one of my colleagues, particularly David Bell, Doug Chung, John Deighton, Rohit Deshpande, Sunil Gupta, Rajiv Lal, Donald Ngwe, and Kash

Rangan. I've had two assistants, Ciara Dugan and Barbara Trissel, whose office support has made my life and work considerably easier.

This book would have been impossible without the support of business leaders who graciously invited me into their companies and allowed me to explore. I'd like to thank senior executives at my past client companies: Active International, Banco Pan, Bayer, BMW, Coty, The Grommet, Mediabong, Microsoft, Nike, Roland Berger, Siemens, Technos, Thales Group (unrelated to me), TV Globo, Unilever, and YouTube. I'd also like to thank my hosts at companies where I presented my early work—Coca-Cola, DFJ Ventures, Disney, Facebook, Google, Grupo Padrão, Netflix, Norwest Venture Partners, Paramount Pictures, Progress Partners, Sephora, and Warner Brothers—as well as the trade organizations that have invited me to present my research: ABF, Abinee, Amcham Campinas, ARF, Cannes Lions, Ibvar, Inma, NEFMA, and NENPA.

Thanks as well go to the following CEOs, former CEOs, or chairpeople who graciously gave me their valuable time: Katia Beauchamp (Birchbox), Darrell Cavens (zulily), Andre Clark (Siemens Brazil), Scott Cook (Intuit), Charles Gorra (Rebag), Jason Harris (Mekanism), Ron Johnson (Enjoy), Hubert Joly (Best Buy), Yan Liu (TVision), Thiago Picolo (Technos), Jules Pieri (The Grommet), Niraj Shah (Wayfair), Maria Thomas (Etsy), and Sarah Wood (Unruly). Special thanks go to Anthony Broadbent from Bright Bridge Ventures and Asesh Sarkar from Salary Finance, both of whom provided data for the analyses presented in Chapter 6. Finally, I'd like to thank all other business leaders that I interviewed for this book, and whose wise words I've documented and referenced through the book. Your contributions are greatly appreciated.

I'd like to thank participants in my workshop on responding to digital disruption, from whom I learned so much. These include mid- and senior-level executives at AON, Avon, BNP Paribas, Chanel, Christian Dior, Deutsche Bank, Dynamo, Estee Lauder, Hermès, Jaeger-LeCoultre/Richemont, JGP, Kraft Heinz, L'Oreal, Mercaux,

Microsoft, Munich Re, Pearson, Renault, Technos, Unilever, Vizient, and countless others. Thank you as well to former HBS students who took my courses on digital marketing strategy, e-commerce, Introduction to Marketing, and PhD seminars in quantitative marketing methods.

I also wish to acknowledge the wonderful coauthors I've had over the past decade: David Bell, Morgan Brown, Alison Caverly, Ruth Costas, Rohit Deshpande, Leandro Guissoni, Sunil Gupta, Peter Jamieson, Rana el Kaliouby, Akiko Kanno, Leora Kornfeld, Jura Liaukonyte, Alex Liu, David Lopez-Lengowski, Sarah McAra, Donald Ngwe, Rosalind Picard, Rik Pieters, Matthew Preble, Kash Rangan, Nobuo Sato, Savannah (Wei) Shi, Horst Stipp, Elizabeth Watkins, Michel Wedel, Kenneth Wilbur, and Priscilla Zogbi. All of you have helped me develop my own thinking on a variety of topics. Thank you!

Then there is my rock star literary team, which proved so instrumental in this book's conceptualization and crafting. To my editor Seth Schulman—you are the *kwan*, the best in class. I also could not have hoped for better collaborators in my former student and coauthor, Greg Piechota, a tremendous thought partner, and in my agent, Lorin Rees, who came into my office one day as a total stranger and proclaimed, "You *have* to write this book." Thank you, Lorin, Greg, and Seth, for your trust in this project, your hard work, and your dedication from day one. I feel so blessed to have been part of this team. Thank you, too, to my editor Roger Scholl and his staff at Crown. You believed enough in this book to back it up financially, and you invested countless hours polishing it, improving the language, and sharpening the thinking.

On a personal note, I'd like to thank my parents, Joao Batista and Assunta Teixeira. You have been eternal sources of patience ever since your highly disruptive son was born. I might not always say it, but I feel a deep sense of gratitude. To my own children: Kalina, I am so proud of you, and I have been ever since you said your first word, "justchoo" (meaning "this") while pointing to objects in the room, and later your first complete sentence, "Chicken has, has Boston" (Boston has chickens, I think). Your mere presence brightens my day. Marley, you are the most loving and caring little boy I have met. One day you will stand on the shoulder of giants, just as you have physically stood on my below-average-height shoulders. Thank you so much for being you. Finally, I'd like to thank my wife, Iva, who is the whole package: fearless, powerful, smart, beautiful, a true partner in life. I am immensely grateful for your full support of my work. For all I have, I am, no doubt, *the* chosen one. I love you very much.

Greg Piechota would like to thank the following individuals: first and foremost, his wife, Magdalena Królak-Piechota, without whose support he'd never have reached this point; and second, Ann Marie Lipinski, a curator at the Nieman Foundation for Journalism at Harvard. Without her, Greg and I would never have met and had the opportunity to work together.

Our passion for powerful new ideas unites us all!

NOTES

Introduction

1. Paula Gardner, "Borders CEO Recalls 'Painful Time' 5 Years After Book Seller's Bankruptcy Filing," MLive, February 16, 2016.
2. Rahul Gupta, "Nokia CEO Ended His Speech Saying This 'We Didn't Do Anything Wrong, but Somehow, We Lost,'" LinkedIn, May 8, 2016.
3. Khadeeja Safdar, "J. Crew's Mickey Drexler Confesses: I Underestimated How Tech Would Upend Retail," *Wall Street Journal*, May 24, 2017.
4. Clayton M. Christensen, Michael Raynor, and Rory McDonald, "What Is Disruptive Innovation?," *Harvard Business Review* 93, no. 12 (December 2015): 44–53.
5. Motoko Rich, "For the Future of Borders, a Focus on Innovation," *New York Times*, July 19, 2006.

Chapter 1

1. Emily Jane Fox, "Best Buy: Earnings 'Clearly Unsatisfactory,'" CNN, November 20, 2012, http://money.cnn.com/2012/11/20/news/companies/best-buy-earnings/, accessed May 7, 2014.
2. Andrea Chang, "Retail Groups Lash Out After Amazon Announces Price Check App Promotion," *Los Angeles Times*, December 7, 2011.
3. Google Shopper Marketing Agency Council, "Mobile In-Store Research, How In-Store Shoppers Are Using Mobile Devices," April 2013, 26, http://ssl.gstatic.com/think/docs/mobile-in-store_research-studies.pdf.

4. Nick Wingfield, "More Retailers at Risk of Amazon 'Showrooming,'" *New York Times*, February 27, 2013.
5. Miguel Bustillo, "Phone-Wielding Shoppers Strike Fear into Retailers," *Wall Street Journal*, December 15, 2010.
6. Christopher Matthews, "Are We Witnessing the Death of the Big-Box Store?," *Time*, May 24, 2012.
7. Miguel Bustillo, "Best Buy CEO Resigns," *Wall Street Journal*, April 11, 2012.
8. Thomas Lee, "Best Buy's New Chief Is Selling from Day 1," *Star Tribune*, September 9, 2012.
9. Maxwell Wessel, "Best Buy Can't Match Amazon's Prices, and Shouldn't Try," *Harvard Business Review*, December 10, 2012.
10. "Continuing Operations Store Count and Retail Square Footage 2005–2011," Investor Relations site at Bestbuy.com, http://s2.q4cdn.com/785564492/files/doc_financials/2017/q3/Store-Count-and-Square-Footage-Q3FY17.pdf, accessed March 17, 2017.
11. Lee, "Best Buy's New Chief Is Selling from Day 1."
12. Stephanie Clifford, "Mobile Deals Set to Lure Shoppers Stuck in Line," *New York Times*, November 19, 2011; Matt Schifrin, "How Best Buy Can Beat Showrooming," *Forbes*, July 5, 2012; "Turning the Retail 'Showrooming Effect' into a Value-Add," Wharton Business School, University of Pennsylvania, September 26, 2012, http://knowledge.wharton.upenn.edu/article/turning-the-retail-showrooming-effect-into-a-value-add.
13. Larry Downes, "Why Best Buy Is Going out of Business . . . Gradually," *Forbes*, January 2, 2012.
14. Drew Fitzgerald, "Fear of Showrooming Fades," *Wall Street Journal*, November 4, 2013.
15. Wessel, "Best Buy Can't Match Amazon's Prices."
16. "Evolution of International Fixed Voice Revenue for Select European Countries, 2000 to 2013," in "The Impact of VoIP and Instant Messaging on Traditional Communication Services in Europe," IDATE, September 2015.
17. "A Year of Birchbox: A Full Review of the Subscription Service," *Beauty by Arielle* blog, July 1, 2013, http://www.beautybyarielle.com/2013/01/a-year-of-birchbox-full-review-of.html.

18. This has since changed. By 2017, Birchbox offered full-sized items for sale.
19. "Interview: Philippe Pinatel, SVP and GM of Sephora Canada, Talks Beauty E-Commerce," *Cosmetics Magazine*, August 2015.
20. Lauren Keating, "Report Finds That Only 1.9 Percent of Mobile Gamers Make In-App Purchases," *Tech Times*, March 25, 2016.
21. Unfortunately, Aereo did not last long, as the United States Justice Department later ruled its business model illegal and ordered it to shut down.
22. Company website: https://www.motifinvesting.com/benefits/what-we-offer.
23. "American Time Use Survey Summary—2015 Results," U.S. Bureau of Labor Statistics, June 24, 2016.
24. Matt Phillips, "No One Cooks Anymore," *Quartz*, June 14, 2016.
25. Chef Steve's personal website: https://www.mygourmetguru.com, accessed March 17, 2017.
26. Natt Garun, "7 Bizarre Airbnb Rentals That Are Almost Too Weird to Believe," *Digital Trends*, May 6, 2013, http://www.digitaltrends.com/web/7-bizarre-airbnb-rentals-that-are-almost-too-weird-to-believe, accessed March 25, 2017; offer for 2017 Maserati Ghibli at Turo.com: https://turo.com/rentals/cars/nj/fort-lee/maserati-ghibli/230992, accessed on March 25, 2017.
27. Catherine Shu, "Spoiler Alert App Makes Donating Food as Easy as Tossing It in a Dump," TechCrunch, July 6, 2015.
28. Jen Wieczner, "Meet the Women Who Saved Best Buy," *Fortune*, October 25, 2015.
29. Miriam Gottfried, "How to Fight Amazon.com, Best Buy–style," *Wall Street Journal*, November 20, 2016.
30. Wieczner, "Meet the Women Who Saved Best Buy."

Chapter 2

1. Alejo Nicolás Larocca, *My Pan-Am Story: Forty Years as a Stewardess with the "World's Most Experienced Airline"* (Buenos Aires: Editorial Dunken, 2015), 75–76.
2. William Stadiem, *Jet Set: The People, the Planes, the Glamour, and the Romance in Aviation's Glory Years* (New York: Ballantine Books, 2014).

3. Sophie-Claire Hoeller, "Vintage Photos from the Glory Days of Aviation," Business Insider, July 15, 2015.
4. Christopher Muther, "What Happened to the Glamour of Air Travel?," *Boston Globe*, September 6, 2014; Mark Thomas, "Air Transport: Market Rules," Fact Sheets on the European Union, European Parliament, March 2017, http://www.europarl.europa.eu/atyourservice/en/displayFtu.html?ftuId=FTU_5.6.7.html.
5. Patricia O'Connell, "Full-Service Airlines Are 'Basket Cases,'" *BusinessWeek*, September 12, 2002.
6. Siobhan Creaton, *Ryanair: How a Small Irish Airline Conquered Europe* (London: Aurum Press, 2005).
7. "Ryanair: The Godfather of Ancillary Revenue," report by Idea Works Company, November 19, 2008.
8. "Ryanair: Annual Report for the Year Ended March 31, 2016," Ryanair Investor Relations website, https://investor.ryanair.com/wp-content/uploads/2016/07/Ryanair-Annual-Report-FY16.pdf.
9. "Leading Airline Groups Worldwide in 2015, Based on Net Profit (in Billion U.S. dollars)," Statista.com. One other possible explanation for Ryanair's profitability is lower overhead costs, including pilots' salaries, as described in Liz Alderman and Amie Tsang, "Jet Pilot Might Not Seem like a 'Gig,' but at Ryanair, It Is," *New York Times*, November 16, 2017.
10. In order to analyze whether the accumulation of patents leads tech startups to grow revenues, I collected historical data about patents granted by the U.S. Patent Office to the most innovative companies in 2015 (those that were granted forty or more patents that year). From this sample, I selected for further analysis the digital technology companies that were startups on or after 1995, the beginning period covered by the data set. I matched this data to the annual revenues from the companies that had become public or published their annual revenues up until 2015. Twenty companies had enough data for a regression analysis to be done, among them Google, Amazon, Facebook, Yahoo, Salesforce.com, eBay, LinkedIn, Zynga, PayPal, Rakuten, and ten others. For each firm, a pair of regressions was estimated to compare whether revenues drove patents or the other way around. The better-fitting model would provide the answer. I found that the average explanatory power of a model that assumed cumulative revenues explained patents granted, year by year, was

84 percent (known as R-square), while the R-square for the models that assumed the inverse relationship, that it was the cumulative number of patents that explained revenue growth year over year, was on average only 42 percent. A follow-up company-by-company analysis further showed that for seventeen out of the twenty companies, the best explanation was that the number of patents granted was a consequence of revenues, not the cause. So while some big tech companies might have a few individual patents that allow them to grow sales from proprietary tech innovations, in general this is not supported for the digital technology startups I analyzed. This finding does not apply to established tech firms in 1995 such as Microsoft or Intel.

11. Dan Milmo, "Ryanair Plan for Standing-Only Plane Tickets Foiled by Regulator," *Guardian*, February 28, 2012. O'Leary has consistently looked for new ways that Ryanair could offer a service more akin to a bus experience. He has made headlines by proposing ideas for further cost-cutting measures, such as charging passengers for using toilets while flying, or introducing standing-only tickets. According to British newspapers, he has proposed that passengers who purchase the airline's cheapest tickets to London—selling for as little as one euro—fly in standing berths, "same as on the London Underground, handrails and straps." At an airline industry conference in London in late 2016, O'Leary raised eyebrows among competitors by laying out a new vision for how Ryannair could make flying free within the next five to ten years. Instead of making money with tickets, he explained, he would profit by striking deals with airports to receive a cut of the cash spent in restaurants, bars, and shops. In such a scenario, he argued, the flights could be free and would always be full. For more, see Chris Leadbeater, "Ryanair CEO: 'How I Plan to Make Air Travel Free Within 10 Years,'" *Daily Telegraph*, November 23, 2016.
12. Ramon Casadesus-Masanell, agreeing that "there is no generally accepted definition" of a business model, opts to focus on large established business. He sees companies as being like machines: you need to understand how they are assembled and how they work. The parts of a company are the choices managers make, whereas the way it works are consequences of these choices. Among the many choices of a business model, Casadesus-Masanell highlights three: what the company prioritizes, what it owns of

value, and how its people are organized. This is what he means by policies, assets, and governance. To him, this definition of a business model is a useful way for large company executives to identify how the entirety of their business works.

For entrepreneurs starting their own business, Casadesus-Masanell's definition is not a particularly useful one. For them, Alexander Osterwalder, author of the Business Model Canvas, has a readily applicable definition of a business model. He sees business models as interdependent construction bricks. As you would build a building, you start off with the economic base of your business: where money comes from (revenues) and where it goes (costs). Then you build it upward. On the revenue side, you have to determine who will pay (customer segment), what they will get (value proposition), how to reach them (channel), and how this will evolve (relationships). On the cost side, you determine the partners, activities, and resources needed to provide your customers value. This definition of a business model works well for builders. But what if your business needs only partial fixing?

Clayton Christensen, the father of the theory of disruptive innovation, perceiving the complexity of the task of defining a business model that can be broadly applicable, proposes only four building blocks. Two concern priorities: the value to the customers and the profit for the business. The other two are execution-related: the resources available and the processes necessary to deliver on the priorities. Christensen does a nice job of simplifying the components into a theoretical portion, of what value will be created for the customers and how the firm will make money, and an executional portion.

Ultimately, the most appropriate definition depends on what you plan to do with it. If you plan to conduct an exhaustive reevaluation of your key operating assumptions with senior management in a large company, Casadesus-Masanell's definition could be the most appropriate definition of a business model to use. On the other hand, if you are in the early stages of starting a small business, then Osterwalder's definition may be more appropriate. And if you already think of execution, then Christensen's definition readily allows for that.

Due to its simplicity and broad applicability, in this book I choose to use, with minor adaptations, the definition by Allan Afuah of the University of Michigan in his book *Business Model Innovation: Concepts, Analysis, and Cases* (New York: Routledge, 2014).

13. Charles Baden-Fuller and Mary S. Morgan, "Business Models as Models," *Long Range Planning* 43, no. 2 (2010): 156–171.
14. "Join Costco," Costco website, https://www.costco.com/join-costco.html.
15. "Costco Wholesale, Annual Report 2016," report for the fiscal year ended August 28, 2016, http://phx.corporate-ir.net/phoenix.zhtml?c=83830&p=irol-reportsannual.
16. "The First 'Fare Wars,'" in "America by Air," Smithsonian National Air and Space Museum, https://airandspace.si.edu/exhibitions/america-by-air/online/heyday/heyday03.cfm, accessed May 2017.
17. David J. Teece, "Business Models, Business Strategy and Innovation," *Long Range Planning* 43, no. 2 (2010): 172–194.
18. Feng Li, "Digital Technologies and the Changing Business Models in Creative Industries," paper presented at the 48th Hawaii International Conference on System Sciences, 2015.
19. "Now or Never: 2016 Global CEO Outlook," KPMG International, June 2016, https://home.kpmg.com/content/dam/kpmg/pdf/2016/06/2016-global-ceo-outlook.pdf.
20. Ramon Casadesus-Masanell and Feng Zhu, "Business Model Innovation and Competitive Imitation: The Case of Sponsor-Based Business Models," *Strategic Management Journal* 34, no. 4 (2013): 464–482.
21. Geoffrey A. Fowler, "There's an Uber for Everything Now," *Wall Street Journal*, May 5, 2015.
22. David Harrison, "Complementarity and the Copenhagen Interpretation of Quantum Mechanics," UPSCALE, Department of Physics, University of Toronto, 2002, https://faraday.physics.utoronto.ca/PVB/Harrison/Complementarity/CompCopen.html.
23. "There are only two ways I know of to make money: bundling and unbundling," said Jim Barksdale in London in 1995, promoting the internet browser company Netscape to investors. It became one of the most famous quotes of the digital age, as it reflected a key observation that it was much easier to bundle and unbundle digital products than it previously had been to do with hard products. See also Justin Fox, "How to Succeed in Business by Bundling—and Unbundling," *Harvard Business Review*, June 24, 2014.

24. Lucy Küng, Robert Picard, and Ruth Towse, *The Internet and the Mass Media* (Los Angeles: Sage, 2008), 143–144.
25. Alex Pham, "EMI Group Sold as Two Separate Pieces to Universal Music and Sony," *Los Angeles Times*, November 12, 2011. EMI Group Limited no longer exists as an independent company as of 2016.
26. Anita Elberse, "Bye Bye Bundles: The Unbundling of Music in Digital Channels," *Journal of Marketing* 74, no. 3 (2010).
27. "Unbundle Products and Services: Giving You Just What You Want, Nothing More," part of the series "Patterns of Disruption," Deloitte University Press, 2015, https://dupress.deloitte.com/content/dam/dup-us-en/articles/disruptive-strategy-unbundling-strategy-stand-alone-products/DUP_3033_Unbundle-products_v2.pdf.
28. "1999 Form 10-K," New York Times Company, March 14, 2017, and "2016 Form 10-K," New York Times Company, February 2, 2017, http://investors.nytco.com/investors/financials/quarterly-earnings/default.aspx.
29. "EMI's Southgate Expresses Confidence in Global Music Market," *Billboard*, March 8, 1997, 1; Ben Sisario, "EMI Is Sold for $4.1 Billion in Combined Deals, Consolidating the Music Industry," *New York Times*, November 11, 2011.
30. "Investor Factbook 2009/2010," McGraw-Hill Companies Investor Relations website, http://media.corporate-ir.net/media_files/IROL/96/96562/reports/MHP09Book/corporate-segment-information/eleven-year-revenue.html; "Annual Report as of December 31, 2016," McGraw-Hill Education Inc., http://investors.mheducation.com/financial-information/annual-reports/default.aspx.
31. Robert Gellman, "Disintermediation and the Internet," *Government Information Quarterly* 13, no. 1 (1996): 1–8.
32. David Oliver, Celia Romm Livermore, and Fay Sudweeks, *Self-Service in the Internet Age: Expectations and Experiences* (London: Springer Science & Business Media, 2009), 100–101.
33. Justin Walton, "Top 5 Apps for Stock Traders," Investopedia, November 13, 2015, http://www.investopedia.com/articles/active-trading/111315/top-5-apps-stock-traders.asp.
34. Decoupling isn't a completely new phenomenon. In a 2003 *Harvard Business Review* article entitled "The Customer Has Escaped," Joseph Nunes and Frank Cespedes alluded to some non-digital examples of "unbundling

offerings," as they called it. Yet as Google Ventures (GV) general partner Tyson Clark explained to me in personal correspondence, "It strikes me that 'decoupling' and 'unbundling' were being used synonymously (incorrectly) at GV as we looked at companies that were actually trying to separate, as you [Thales Teixeira] put it, the value-creating activities from the value destroying activities. It's a powerful distinction."

35. Thales Teixeira, Nobuo Sato, and Akiko Kanno, "Managing Consumer Touchpoints at Nissan Japan," Harvard Business School Case 516-035, September 2015.
36. Teixeira, Sato, and Kanno, "Managing Consumer Touchpoints at Nissan Japan."
37. Christina Rogers, Erik Holm, and Chelsey Dulaney, "Warren Buffett Buys New-Car Retail Chain," *Wall Street Journal*, October 2, 2014.
38. Turo, company website, https://turo.com/how-turo-works, accessed March 2017.
39. BlaBlaCar, company website, https://www.blablacar.co.uk, accessed August 2016.
40. Mike Spector, Jeff Bennet, and John D. Stoll, "U.S. Car Sales Set Record in 2015," *Wall Street Journal*, January 5, 2016.
41. According to Allan Afuah in *Business Model Innovation*, Google did not invent search engines or sponsored ads, but it was better at business model innovation, monetizing search engines via auctions.
42. Trov, company website, http://trov.com, accessed March 2017.
43. "Trov, Total Equity Funding," company profile at Crunchbase, https://www.crunchbase.com/organization/trov#/entity, accessed March 2017.
44. "37 Cart Abandonment Rate Statistics," Baymard Institute, https://baymard.com/lists/cart-abandonment-rate, accessed March 2017.
45. "Klarna: No Sale Left Behind," CNBC, June 7, 2016, http://www.cnbc.com/2016/06/07/klarna-2016-disruptor-50.html.
46. Parmy Olson, "How Klarna Plans to Replace Your Credit Card," *Forbes*, November 7, 2016.
47. Jim Collins, *Good to Great: Why Some Companies Make the Leap and Others Don't* (New York: HarperBusiness, 2001).
48. Teece, "Business Models, Business Strategy and Innovation."
49. See interview at https://youtu.be/20d-6nXK3q0.
50. As research has shown, executives also react to disruption by blaming

it on regulatory changes and consumer behavior. See Economist Intelligence Unit, "Thriving Through Disruption," September–October 2016, http://eydisrupters.films.economist.com/thriving.

51. Afuah, *Business Model Innovation*.

Chapter 3

1. Airbnb, company website, https://www.airbnb.com/about/about-us, accessed July 2018.
2. Marriott International, company website, https://hotel-development.marriott.com, accessed March 2017.
3. Greg Bensinger, "New Funding Round Pushes Airbnb's Value to $31 Billion," *Wall Street Journal*, March 9, 2017.
4. Griselda Murray Brown, "How Demand Is Rising Among Wealthy Buyers for 'Hotel-Serviced Living,'" *Financial Times,* October 25, 2013.
5. 2014 Annual Member Survey of the United States Tour Operators Association, cited in "The Rise of Experiential Travel," report by Skift, 2014.
6. "Unbundling the Hotel: The 62 Startups Marriott and Hilton Should Be Watching," CB Insights, June 16, 2016, https://www.cbinsights.com/blog/unbundling-the-hotel.
7. Peter F. Drucker, *Management*, rev. ed. (New York: Collins, 2008), 98. On page 61 of that seminal work, Drucker explained: "It is the customer who determines what a business is. It is the customer alone whose willingness to pay for a good or for a service converts economic resources into wealth, things into goods. What the customer buys and considers value is never a product. It is always utility, that is, what a product or a service does for him. Because its purpose is to create a customer, the business enterprise has two—and only these two—basic functions: *marketing* and *innovation*."
8. Adam Lashinsky, "Amazon's Jeff Bezos: The Ultimate Disrupter," *Fortune*, November 16, 2012.
9. iHeartCommunications Inc., Form 10-K, March 10, 2017, https://www.sec.gov/Archives/edgar/data/739708/000073970817000005/ihcomm201610-k.htm; iHeartMedia Inc., company website, http://iheartmedia.com/Corporate/Pages/About.aspx, accessed March 2017. iHeartMedia, owner of iHeart Radio, filed for bankruptcy in early 2018.

10. Pandora Media Inc., "About Pandora Media," https://www.pandora.com/about, accessed August 2016.
11. Pandora Media Inc., 4th Quarter and Full Year 2016 Financial Results, p. 1, http://investor.pandora.com/interactive/newlookandfeel/4247784/Pandora_Q4_Financial_Results_Press_Release.pdf.
12. Twitch, company website, http://twitchadvertising.tv/audience/, accessed July 2018.
13. Steam, company website, http://store.steampowered.com/, accessed August 2016.
14. Ben Gilbert, "Meet Gabe Newell, the Richest Man in the Video Game Business," Business Insider, January 18, 2017. Steam is owned by the privately owned Valve Corporation, which doesn't release any financial numbers. Sergey Galyonkin, a gaming industry analyst and expert, estimated the value of games sold on Steam in 2016 at $3.5 billion. As Steam's average cut was 30 percent, its annual revenue might be around $1.05 billion. In recent M&A transactions in the video gaming industry, companies such as Mojang, PopCap, Playdom, and SuperCell sold at a revenue multiple of 7.4 to 9.4. This would make Steam's business alone worth $7.8–9.9 billion.
15. Juro Osawa and Sarah E. Needleman, "Tencent Seals Deal to Buy 'Clash of Clans' Developer Supercell for $8.6 Billion," *Wall Street Journal,* June 21, 2016.
16. Waze, company website, https://data-waze.com/2016/09/13/waze-releases-2nd-annual-driver-satisfaction-index, accessed March 2017.
17. Dara Kerr, "Google Reveals It Spent $966 Million in Waze Acquisition," CNET, July 25, 2013.
18. Dollar Shave Club, company website, https://www.dollarshaveclub.com, accessed March 2017.
19. According to one source, "EIPs are simple cognitive operations such as reading a value, comparing two values or adding them into a person's memory, and are used in science research to measure cost of effort, for instance when scanning or reading a data chart, [or] comparing or adding numbers. EIPs are particularly useful for measuring consumer behavior effort in restricted contexts such as computer interfaces or Web pages." Antonio Hyder, Enrique Bigné, and José Martí, "Human-Computer Interaction," in

The Routledge Companion to the Future of Marketing, edited by Luiz Mountinho, Enrique Bigné, and Ajay K. Manri (London: Routledge, 2014), 302.
20. Beth Kowitt, "Special Report: The War on Big Food," *Fortune*, May 21, 2015.
21. Aaron Smith, "Shared, Collaborative and On Demand: The New Digital Economy," *Pew Research Center*, May 19, 2016.

Chapter 4

1. Stewart Alsop, "A Tale of Four Founders—and Four Companies," *Alsop Louie Partners*, blog, September 2012, http://www.alsop-louie.com/a-tale-of-four-founders-and-four-companies.
2. Eric Johnson, "How Twitch's Founders Turned an Aimless Reality Show into a Video Juggernaut," *Recode*, July 5, 2014.
3. Alsop, "A Tale of Four Founders."
4. Jessica Guynn, "It's Justin, Live! All Day, All Night!," *San Francisco Chronicle*, March 30, 2007.
5. Guynn, "It's Justin, Live! All Day, All Night!"
6. Jesse Holland, "Courts Find Justin.TV Not Guilty of 'Stealing Cable' in Lawsuit Filed by UFC," SB Nation/MMA Mania, March 22, 2012.
7. Andrew Rice, "The Many Pivots of Justin.TV: How a Livecam Show Became Home to Video Gaming Superstars," *Fast Company*, June 15, 2012.
8. Oscar Williams, "Twitch's Co-founder on the Curious Appeal of Watching Gamers Game," *Guardian*, March 17, 2015.
9. Lisa Chow, "Gaming the System (Season 3, Episode 2)," Gimlet Media podcast, April 22, 2016.
10. Drew FitzGerald and Daisuke Wakabayashi, "Apple Quietly Builds New Networks," *Wall Street Journal*, February 3, 2014.
11. Bree Brouwer, "Twitch Claims 43% of Revenue from $3.8 Billion Gaming Content Industry," TubeFilter, July 10, 2015.
12. Chris Welch, "Amazon, Not Google, Is Buying Twitch for $970 Million," *The Verge*, August 25, 2014.
13. Erin Griffith, "Driven in the Valley: The Startup Founders Fueling GM's Future," *Fortune*, September 22, 2016.
14. Unfortunately, this was not enough, and in 2016 Washio went out of business after only three years in service and spending $17 million from inves-

tors. Meanwhile, TaskRabbit said it was profitable in 2016 in all nineteen cities where the service operated. According to Bloomberg, it took the company eight years to reach a revenue of $25 million. Since its launch, TaskRabbit raised $50 million in venture capital. On September 2017, it was acquired by IKEA.

15. Claire Suddath, "The Butler Didn't Do It: Hello Alfred and the On-Demand Economy's Limits," *Bloomberg BusinessWeek*, January 21, 2016.
16. Matt Greco, "Watch Me Play Video Games! Amazon's Twitch Platform Draws Users and Dollars," CNBC, May 14, 2016.
17. Arthur Gies, "Here Are the Winners of Valve's $20+ Million 2016 International Dota 2 Championships," *Polygon*, August 13, 2016.
18. In June 2016, Prologis managed 1,959 logistics real estate facilities with a combined space of 676 million square feet in eighteen countries: https://www.prologis.com/node/4436, accessed June 2016.
19. Shelfmint, company website, http://www.shelfmint.com, accessed June 2016.
20. In 2016, San Francisco–based Storefront merged with a French startup, Oui Open, in order to speed up their global expansion. A similar business model applied to the groceries sector was adopted by Shelfmint, a New York–based startup founded in 2014.
21. Keaton Row closed in March 2017.
22. Founded in 2009, Trunk Club raised $12.44 million in venture capital before being acquired by fashion retailer Nordstrom in 2014 for $350 million. Keaton Row raised $17.3 million from investors between its launch in 2011 and 2015. In 2016, the company changed its business model. Instead of serving as a platform for third-party stylists around the United States, it employed a few in-house experts in its New York office and used them to provide all stylist services to consumers.
23. To find how investors value startups disrupting markets with different types of decoupling, we analyzed a sample of 325 U.S.-based companies that had the last round of financing in 2016 and were valued at $10 million or more, according to CB Insights. We identified fifty-five startups offering business-to-consumer products or services that used decoupling for early market entry. We then analyzed the startups' influence on the typical consumer value chain to classify them according to the type of activities being decoupled by looking at their main value proposition. We found

twelve startups decoupling value-creating activities, twenty-nine startups decoupling value-eroding activities, and fourteen startups decoupling value-charging activities. The startups not part of the analysis were either not decouplers, more than one type of decoupler, or unable to be classified based on the website's stated value proposition to the consumer. Average valuation numbers were calculated using CB Insights' data on the last round of funding or acquisition prices. Since then, some startups have gone public. These market valuations were not considered.

24. Peter Bright, "Microsoft Buys Skype for $8.5 Billion. Why, Exactly?," *Wired*, May 10, 2011; Catherine Shu, "Japanese Internet Giant Rakuten Acquires Viber for $900M," TechCrunch, February 13, 2014; Matt Weinberger, "Amazon's $970 Million Purchase of Twitch Makes So Much Sense Now: It's All About the Cloud," Business Insider, March 16, 2016.
25. Douglas MacMillan, "Dropbox Raises About $250 Million at $10 Billion Valuation," *Wall Street Journal*, January 17, 2014; Ingrid Lunden, "Spotify Is Raising Another $500M in Convertible Notes with Discounts on IPO Shares," TechCrunch, January 27, 2016 (by 2018, Spotify had gone public and was valued at nearly $30 billion); NASDAQ, "Zynga Inc. Class A Common Stock Quote and Summary Data," June 24, 2016; Lora Kolodny, "Jay-Z Backed JetSmarter Raises $105 Million to Become Uber for Private Jets," TechCrunch, December 12, 2016; Erin Griffith, "Exclusive: Birchbox Banks $60 Million," *Forbes*, April 21, 2014.
26. Thales S. Teixeira and Peter Jamieson, "The Decoupling Effect of Digital Disruptors," Harvard Business School Working Paper no. 15-031, October 28, 2014, 8; Claire O'Connor, "Rent the Runway to Hit $100M Revenues in 2016 Thanks to Unlimited Service," *Forbes*, June 15, 2016.
27. Overview of FreshDirect, Crunchbase, https://www.crunchbase.com/organization/fresh-direct#/entity, accessed July 2016.
28. Dan Primack, "Unilever Buys Dollar Shave Club for $1 Billion," *Fortune*, July 19, 2016.

Chapter 5

1. William Lidwell and Gerry Manacsa, *Deconstructing Product Design: Exploring the Form, Function, Usability, Sustainability, and Commercial Success of 100 Amazing Products* (Beverly, MA: Rockport, 2011), 166–167.

2. Jeremy Coller and Christine Chamberlain, *Splendidly Unreasonable Inventors* (Oxford: Infinite Ideas, 2009), 3–4.
3. Randal C. Picker, "The Razors-and-Blades Myth(s)," John M. Olin Law and Economics Working Paper no. 532, University of Chicago Law School, September 2010.
4. Jack Neff, "Gillette Shaves Prices As It's Nicked by Rivals Both New and Old," *Advertising Age*, April 9, 2012; Emily Glazer, "A David and Gillette Story," *Wall Street Journal*, April 12, 2012.
5. Henry Chesbrough and Richard S. Rosenbloom, "The Role of the Business Model in Capturing Value from Innovation: Evidence from Xerox Corporation's Technology Spin-off Companies," *Industrial and Corporate Change* 11, no. 3 (2002): 529–555.
6. Market data according to research firm Slice Intelligence, cited in Jaclyn Trop, "How Dollar Shave Club's Founder Built a $1 Billion Company That Changed the Industry," *Entrepreneur*, March 28, 2017.
7. Korea-based Dorco is a supplier for most of Dollar Shave's blades. Ben Popken, "Does Dollar Shave Really Shave?," *Market Watch*, April 20, 2012.
8. "DollarShaveClub.com—Our Blades Are F***ing Great," YouTube, March 6, 2012, https://www.youtube.com/watch?v=ZUG9qYTJMsI.
9. Dollar Shave Club's website lists the following perks: no hidden costs, cancel anytime, and 100 percent money-back guarantee: https://www.dollarshaveclub.com/blades, accessed July 2017.
10. "Management's Discussion and Analysis of Financial Condition and Results of Operations," in "Effects of Merger Proposed Between the Gillette Company and the Procter & Gamble Company," Gillette, 2004, https://www.sec.gov/Archives/edgar/data/41499/000114544305000507/d16016_ex13.htm. P&G does not break down profits at the level of the Gillette unit. Its entire grooming business, which includes Braun electric shavers and shaving-related cosmetics, reported a 22 percent net profit margin in 2016. "Annual Report 2016," Procter & Gamble's corporate website, http://www.pginvestor.com/Cache/1500090608.PDF?O=PDF&T=&Y=&D=&FID=1500090608&iid=4004124.
11. U.S. Patent and Trademark Office, http://www.patentview.org.
12. Jessica Wohl, "P&G Buys High-End Brand the Art of Shaving," Reuters, June 3, 2009.

13. Anthony Ha, "Dollar Shave Club Launches Razor Subscription Service, Raises $1M from Kleiner (and Others)," TechCrunch, March 6, 2012.
14. By 2016, Gillette's share of the U.S. market had shrunk by one-third, to 54 percent, and Dollar Shave Club was acquired by P&G's archrival Unilever for $1 billion. For details, refer to Mike Isaac and Michael J. de la Merced, "Dollar Shave Club Sells to Unilever for $1 Billion," *New York Times*, July 20, 2016.
15. "Give Commercials the Finger: TiVo Introduces TiVo BOLT," press release, TiVo, September 30, 2015, http://ir.tivo.com/Cache/1001214134.PDF?O=PDF&T=&Y=&D=&FID=1001214134&iid=4206196.
16. Amanda Kooser, "Store Charges $5 'Showrooming' Fee to Looky-Loos," CNET, March 26, 2013; Thales S. Teixeira and Peter Jamieson, "The Decoupling Effect of Digital Disruptors," Harvard Business School Working Paper no. 15-031, October 28, 2014, 9.
17. Matthew Inman, "Why I Believe Printers Were Sent from Hell," The Oatmeal, http://theoatmeal.com/comics/printers, accessed January 4, 2018.
18. Jeff J. Roberts, "What Today's Supreme Court Printer Case Means for Business," *Fortune*, March 21, 2017.
19. Kyle Wiens, "The Supreme Court Just Bolstered Your Right to Repair Stuff," *Wired*, June 1, 2017.
20. On November 29, 2016, Lexmark International Inc. was acquired by a consortium of investors composed of Apex, PAG Asia Capital, and Legend Holdings and taken private.
21. I first heard about the idea of rebalancing from Eduardo Navarro when he was the chief strategy officer of Telefonica. They applied it to a rather narrow telephony pricing decision. Here I propose the concept broadly as value rebalancing.
22. Mitchell Smith, "Shop Owner Shrugs Off Criticism of $5 Browsing Fee," *Brisbane Times*, March 27, 2013.
23. According to their website, "Celiac Supplies operates as an educational centre for individuals, school groups and the hospitality industry. Celiac Supplies no longer sells gluten free products. It is now an advisory service for gluten free diets and people having trouble combining more than one allergy in their diet. Fees apply for consultancy service." http://www.celiacsupplies.com.au/, accessed October 10, 2017.

Chapter 6

1. Noel Randewich, "Tesla Becomes Most Valuable U.S. Car Maker, Edges Out GM," Reuters, April 10, 2017.
2. Jeff Dunn, "Tesla Is Valued as High as Ford and GM—but That Has Nothing to Do with What It's Done So Far," Business Insider, April 11, 2017.
3. Julia C. Wong, "Tesla Factory Workers Reveal Pain, Injury and Stress: 'Everything Feels like the Future but Us,'" *Guardian*, May 18, 2017.
4. Tom Krisher and Dee-Ann Durbin, "Investors Pick Tesla's Potential Instead of GM's Steady Sales," *Toronto Star*, June 1, 2017. The article quotes one analyst who says: "The financial markets are much more interested in investing in the potential of what might be huge than in the reality of what's already profitable and likely to remain so for years to come."
5. Brooke Crothers, "GM, Worried About Market Disruption, Has an Eye on Tesla," CNET, July 18, 2013. Ironically, catching up with Tesla meant looking toward GM's past. GM had pioneered electrification, launching the first mass-produced all-electric EV1 in 1996 as a means of responding to California's greenhouse gas emission regulations. The product was unprofitable, so when the state eased its regulations, GM recalled the cars, took them out to the Arizona desert, and crushed them. Twenty years later, GM was back in the game with the Chevrolet Bolt.
6. Tom Krisher, "GM Starts Producing 200-Mile Electric Chevrolet Bolt," Associated Press, November 4, 2016; Sarah Shelton, "1 Million Annual US Plug-in Sales Expected by 2024," HybridCars.com, June 11, 2015.
7. "Driving Forward: The Future of Urban Mobility," Report published in Knowledge@Wharton Series, University of Pennsylvania, February 2017, 1–2.
8. Jim Edwards, "Uber's Leaked Finances Show the Company Might—Just Might—Be Able to Turn a Profit," Business Insider, February 27, 2017.
9. Rachel Holt, Andrew Macdonald, and Pierre-Dimitri Gore-Coty, "5 Billion Trips," Uber Newsroom, June 29, 2017.
10. "Summary of Travel Trends," in *2009 National Household Travel Survey*, U.S. Department of Transportation, June 2011, 31–34.
11. "Form 10-K (Annual Report) for Period Ending 12/31/2016," Avis Budget Group, February 21, 2017, 18; Catherine D. Wood, "Disruptive

Innovation. New Markets, New Metrics," ARK Investment Management, November 2016, 6–7.

12. Johannes Reichmuth, "Analyses of the European Air Transport Market: Airline Business Models," Deutsches Zentrum fur Luft- un Raumfahrt e.V., December 17, 2008, 9.
13. Shaun Kelley and Dany Asad, "Airbnb: Digging In with More Data from AirDNA," industry overview report by Bank of America Merrill Lynch, October 27, 2015, 6.
14. Zach Barasz and Brook Porter, "Are We Experiencing Transportation's Instagram Moment?," TechCrunch, April 26, 2016.
15. Caitlin Huston, "Watch Uber's Self-Driving Cars Hit the Road in Pittsburgh," *Market Watch*, September 15, 2016.
16. Adam Millard-Ball, Gail Murrary, Jessica ter Schure, Christine Fox, and Jon Burkhardt, "Car-Sharing: Where and How It Succeeds," U.S. Transportation Research Board, Washington, DC, 2005, 4–11; Pierre Goudin, "The Cost of Non-Europe in the Sharing Economy," European Parliamentary Research Service, January 2016, 86.
17. David Kiley, "Why GM Wants to Take Over Lyft and Why Lyft Is Saying No," *Forbes*, August 16, 2016.
18. Carol Cain, "Why Maven Is Such a Good Bet for GM," *Detroit Free Press*, June 17, 2017.
19. Actually, General Motors paid founders of Cruise Automation almost $600 million in cash and GM stock, and the rest in deferred payments and employee compensation under the condition the founders stay with the company for a certain period of time. Bill Vlasic, "G.M. Wants to Drive the Future of Cars That Drive Themselves," *New York Times,* June 4, 2017.
20. Cruise Automation, company profile, Crunchbase, https://www.crunchbase.com/organization/cruise/investors, accessed May 2017; Alan Ohnsman, "Cruise's Kyle Vogt: GM Will Deploy Automated Rideshare Cars 'Very Quickly,'" *Forbes*, March 13, 2017.
21. Cadie Thompson, "Your Car Will Become a Second Office in 5 Years or Less, General Motors CEO Predicts," Business Insider, December 12, 2016.
22. *Tesla Motors vs. Anderson, Urmson and Aurora Innovation*, case 17CV305646, filed with Superior Court of California in Santa Clara,

January 25, 2017, https://www.scribd.com/document/337645529/Tesla-Sterling-Anderson-lawsuit.

23. John Howard and Jagdish Sheth, "A Theory of Buyer Behavior," *Journal of the American Statistical Association*, January 1969, 467–487; George Day, Allan Shocker, and Rajendra Srivastava, "Customer-Oriented Approaches to Identifying Product Markets," *Journal of Marketing* 43, no. 4 (1979): 8–19.
24. John Hauser and Birger Wernerfelt, "An Evaluation Cost Model of Consideration Sets," *Journal of Consumer Research* 16 (March 1990): 393–408.
25. Joseph Alba and Amitava Chattopadhyay, "Effects of Context and Part-Category Cues on Recall of Competing Brands," *Journal of Marketing Research* 22, no. 3 (1985): 340–349.
26. John R. Hauser and Birger Wernerfelt, "An Evaluation Cost Model of Consideration Sets," *Journal of Consumer Research* 16, no. 4 (1990): 393–408.
27. John Dawes, Kerry Mundt, and Byron Sharp, "Consideration Sets for Financial Services Brands," *Journal of Financial Services Marketing* 14, no. 3 (2009): 190–202.
28. Clayton M. Christensen, Michael Raynor, and Rory McDonald, "What Is Disruptive Innovation?," *Harvard Business Review* 93, no. 12 (December 2015): 44–53.
29. Clayton M. Christensen, *The Innovator's Dilemma* (Boston: Harvard Business Review Press, 1997), 28–30.
30. Zheng Zhou and Kent Nakamoto, "Price Perceptions: A Cross-National Study Between American and Chinese Young Consumers," *Advances in Consumer Research* 28 (2001): 161–168; Eugene Jones, Wen Chern, and Barry Mustiful, "Are Lower-Income Shoppers as Price Sensitive as Higher-Income Ones? A Look at Breakfast Cereals," *Journal of Food Distribution Research*, February 1994, 82–92.
31. Theo Verhallen and Fred van Raaij, "How Consumers Trade Off Behavioural Costs and Benefits," *European Journal of Marketing* 20, nos. 3–4 (1986): 19–34; Carter Mandrik, "Consumer Heuristics: The Tradeoff Between Processing Effort and Value in Brand Choice," *Advances in Consumer Research* 23 (1996): 301–307.
32. Donald Ngwe and Thales S. Teixeira, "Improving Online Retail Margins by Increasing Search Frictions," working paper, July 2018.

33. The top three banks in terms of the value (in millions of GBP) of their consumer loan portfolios (at the end of their respective 2016 fiscal years) given here were identified using Capital IQ Inc., a division of Standard & Poor's, and by screening for companies in that database that were incorporated in the United Kingdom and whose total loan portfolios at the end of their respective 2016 fiscal years were greater than zero. After excluding institutions that either did not have consumer loan portfolios or did not report numbers for their consumer loan portfolios in the Capital IQ database, the top three banks were HSBC Bank, Barclays Bank, and Lloyds Bank. The author used the consumer loan data, as presented in Capital IQ, for these specific banking entities rather than those of their parent or holding companies (HSBC Holdings, Barclays, and Lloyds Banking Group, respectively). While these three banks were all incorporated in the United Kingdom, it was not clear how much of their consumer loan portfolio were loans issued to consumers within the United Kingdom and how much might have been issued to consumers outside of the United Kingdom. Capital IQ defined consumer loans as "loans given to individuals for the purchase of domestic and household durable goods on hypothecation. It includes all forms of installment credit other than Home Mortgage Loans and Open-End Credits." Source: Capital IQ Company Screening Report, "Consumer Loans [FY 2016] (£GBPmm, Historical Rate)," Capital IQ Inc., accessed July 19, 2017.
34. The author calculated the total consumer credit market (and individual bank and collective credit card market shares) for the purpose of this MaR analysis as follows. First, the author took the total values, in millions of GBP, of eight major U.K.-incorporated banks' consumer loan portfolios at the end of their respective 2016 fiscal years—HSBC Bank (£114,314), Barclays Bank (£56,729), Lloyds Bank (£20,761), Royal Bank of Scotland (£13,780), Bank of Scotland (£10,667), National Westminster Bank (£10,273), Santander UK (£6,165), and Nationwide Building Society (£3,869)—and added them together to arrive at a combined market of approximately £236.6 billion in consumer loans. For the purpose of this analysis, the author defines the total consumer loan market as the cumulative consumer loans of just these eight banks (i.e., a £236.6 billion market). This figure does not incorporate consumer loans issued by other banks or financial institutions, and may include loans issued to consumers outside

of the United Kingdom. The author then calculated each of these eight banks' individual shares of the £236.6 billion market. Next, the author incorporated credit card data. The Bank of England reported the total amount (in millions of GBP) of outstanding consumer credit excluding student loans (not seasonally adjusted) for each month of 2016, and broke out how much of that total outstanding amount was on credit cards. The author averaged the monthly totals for all twelve months of 2016 and arrived at an average of £65,213 million for the amount of outstanding consumer credit excluding student loans attributed to credit cards over the course of 2016, and an average of £186,668 million for the total amount of outstanding consumer credit excluding student loans over the course of 2016. Thus, credit cards accounted for 34.9 percent of the market for consumer credit excluding student loans over the course of 2016. When the 34.9 percent credit card market share was added to that of the £236.6 billion consumer loan market described previously, the total market share of consumer loans was reduced to approximately 65 percent of the consumer credit market under consideration. Individual banks' shares of the consumer credit market were therefore reduced accordingly. For example, Barclays Bank's market share was reduced from 23.9 to 15.6 percent when the market under consideration was broadened to include credit cards. Although the data for consumer loans and credit cards come from different sources, may include loans to consumers outside of the United Kingdom, and measure different time frames and therefore cannot be reconciled with each other, combining these two data sets provides the best approximation of individual banks' share of the consumer credit market combined with credit cards' share of the consumer credit market.

The consumer loan data for each bank was obtained from a Capital IQ Company Screening Report, "Consumer Loans [FY 2016] (£GBPmm, Historical rate)," Capital IQ Inc., a division of Standard & Poor's, accessed July 19, 2017. The credit card market share data was calculated from Bank of England, Bankstats, A Money & Lending, A5.6, "Consumer Credit Excluding Student Loans," Excel workbook, "NSA Amts Outstanding" worksheet, last updated June 29, 2017, http://www.bankofengland.co.uk/statistics/pages/bankstats/current/default.aspx, accessed July 2017.

35. The 22.2 percent average purchase rate (APR) for credit cards in the United Kingdom in 2016 was calculated by the author based on two

numbers published by Moneyfacts.co.uk in 2016: an average percentage rate (APR) for credit cards of 21.6 percent on February 29, and a rate of 22.8 percent on September 6. Moneyfacts.co.uk, "Credit Card Interest Rate Hits an All Time High," February 29, 2016; Moneyfacts.co.uk, "Credit Card Interest Hits New Record High," September 6, 2016.

36. Thales Teixeira, Rosalind Picard, and Rana el Kaliouby, "Why, When, and How Much to Entertain Consumers in Advertisements? A Web-Based Facial Tracking Field Study," *Marketing Science* 33, no. 6 (2014): 809–827.
37. John R. Hauser, "Consideration-Set Heuristics," *Journal of Business Research* 67, no. 8 (2014): 1688–1699.
38. "Know Your Industries: 90+ Market Maps Covering Fintech, CPG, Auto Tech, Healthcare, and More," CB Insights, August 2017.
39. "Most Popular Father's Day Gifts," MarketWatch, June 14, 2013.
40. Peter Henderson, "Some Uber and Lyft Riders Are Giving Up Their Own Cars: Reuters/Ipsos Poll," Reuters, May 25, 2017.
41. Sophie Kleeman, "Here's What Happened to All 53 of Marissa Mayer's Yahoo Acquisitions," Gizmodo, June 15, 2016.
42. Seth Fiegerman, "End of an Era: Yahoo Is No Longer an Independent Company," CNN, June 13, 2017.

Chapter 7

1. For other examples, see Thales S. Teixeira and Morgan Brown, "Airbnb, Etsy, Uber: Growing from One Thousand to One Million Customers," Harvard Business School Case 516-108, June 2016 (revised January 2018), and Thales S. Teixeira and Morgan Brown. "Airbnb, Etsy, Uber: Acquiring the First Thousand Customers," Harvard Business School Case 516-094, May 2016 (revised January 2018).
2. Austin Carr, "19_Airbnb: For Turning Spare Rooms into the World's Hottest Hotel Chain," *Fast Company*, February 7, 2012.
3. Jordan Crook and Anna Escher, "A Brief History of Airbnb," TechCrunch, June 28, 2015.
4. Michael Blanding, "How Uber, Airbnb, and Etsy Attracted Their First 1,000 Customers," *HBS Working Knowledge*, July 13, 2016; Teixeira and Brown. "Airbnb, Etsy, Uber: Acquiring the First Thousand Customers."

5. Teixeira and Brown, "Airbnb, Etsy, Uber: Growing from One Thousand to One Million Customers."
6. Teixeira and Brown, "Airbnb, Etsy, Uber: Acquiring the First Thousand Customers."
7. Teixeira and Brown, "Airbnb, Etsy, Uber: Growing from One Thousand to One Million Customers."
8. Thales S. Teixeira and Michael Blanding, "How Uber, Airbnb and Etsy Turned 1,000 Customers into 1 Million," *Forbes*, November 16, 2016.
9. Blanding, "How Uber, Airbnb, and Etsy Attracted Their First 1,000 Customers."

Chapter 8

1. Chris Zook and Jimmy Allen, "Strategies for Growth," Insights, Bain & Company, November 1, 1999.
2. Zook and Allen, "Strategies for Growth."
3. Chris Zook and James Allen, "Growth Outside the Core," *Harvard Business Review*, December 2003.
4. Tracey Lien, "Uber Conquered Taxis. Now It's Going After Everything Else," *Los Angeles Times*, May 7, 2016.
5. Alexander Valtsev, "Alibaba Group: The Most Attractive Growth Stock in 2016," Seeking Alpha, March 29, 2016.
6. Constance Gustke, "China's $500 Billion Mobile Shopping Mania," CNBC, March 14, 2016.
7. Heather Somerville, "Airbnb Offers Travel Services in Push to Diversify," Reuters, November 17, 2016.
8. Leigh Gallagher, "Q&A with Brian Chesky: Disruption, Leadership, and Airbnb's Future," *Fortune*, March 27, 2017.
9. Christopher Tkaczyk, "Kayak's Vision for the Future of Online Travel Booking," *Fortune*, August 18, 2017.
10. Walter Isaacson, *Steve Jobs* (New York: Simon & Schuster, 2011).
11. Isaacson, *Steve Jobs*.

Chapter 9

1. Victor Luckerson, "Netflix Accounts for More than a Third of All Internet Traffic," *Time*, May 29, 2015.
2. Mathew Ingram, "Here's Why Comcast Decided to Call a Truce with Netflix," *Fortune*, July 5, 2016.
3. Georg Szalai, "Comcast CEO Touts 'Closer' Netflix Relationship, Talks Integrating More Streaming Services," *Hollywood Reporter*, September 20, 2016.
4. Matthew S. Olson, Derek C. M. van Bever, and Seth Verry, "When Growth Stalls," *Harvard Business Review* 86, no. 3 (March 2008): 50–61.
5. Eddy Hagen (@insights4print), "#Innovation? Not everybody wants/needs it: Netflix still has nearly 4 million subscribers to DVD by mail . . . https://www.recode.net/2017/10/5/16431680/netflix-streaming-video-subscription-price-change-dvd-mail," Twitter, October 6, 2018, https://twitter.com/insights4print/status/916261769517158400.
6. Robbie Bach did state, "In my experience, licking the cookie is not unique to the Microsoft culture."
7. Gary Rivlin, "The Problem with Microsoft," *Fortune*, March 29, 2011.
8. In early 2017, Westfield Digital Labs was rebranded as Westfield Retail Solutions. See Adrienne Pasquarelli, "No ETA for the Mall of the Future: Westfield Rebrands Digital Labs Unit," AdAge, February 8, 2017.
9. A few months after I interviewed Kaufman, Europe's largest real estate investment trust offered to acquire the high-end mall operator.
10. Kaufman elaborated on this point, remarking: "How to get people to do what we need them to do? What's in it for them? It is not for lack of enthusiasm, but for lack of incentives. That's why most strategies fail, for me. The organizational issues get in the way of speed. Change agents are not only fighting the speed of market, but also internally pulled back by the organization's inertia. A lot of times, in my experience, they have the right ideas but the organization can't get out of its way. Organizational resistance happens because incentives are not aligned at the individual level. Think of employees like customers. How are you shaping their behavior? How are you incentivizing commitment from the traditional part of the business to invest in the new and highly uncertain initiatives? In the

[Silicon] Valley, they have [stock] options. You need to align incentives so everybody has a stake."

11. Geoff Colvin, "How Intuit Reinvents Itself," *Fortune*, October 20, 2017.
12. Colvin, "How Intuit Reinvents Itself."
13. Colvin, "How Intuit Reinvents Itself."
14. "Intuit's First 'Founders Innovation Award' Winner, Hugh Molotsi," posted by IntuitInc, August 31, 2011, YouTube, https://www.youtube.com/watch?v=GtgseZmJH4I.
15. David Kirkpatrick, "Throw It at the Wall and See If It Sticks," *Fortune*, December 12, 2005.
16. Apart from a layoff of 399 employees in 2015 that was due to "realignment," according to a company spokesperson.
17. Lara O'Reilly, "The 30 Biggest Media Companies in the World," Business Insider, May 31, 2016.
18. Robert A. Burgelman, Robert E. Siegel, and Jason Luther, "Axel Springer in 2014: Strategic Leadership of the Digital Media Transformation," Stanford GSB, E522, 2014.
19. Burgelman, Siegel, and Luther, "Axel Springer in 2014."
20. Robert A. Burgelman, Robert Siegel, and Ryan Kissick, "Axel Springer in 2016: From Transformation to Acceleration?," Stanford GSB, E610, 2016.
21. Burgelman, Siegel, and Luther. "Axel Springer in 2014."

Chapter 10

1. Jeffrey Ball, "Inside Oil Giant Shell's Race to Remake Itself for a Low-Price World," *Fortune*, January 24, 2018.
2. Ball, "Inside Oil Giant Shell's Race to Remake Itself for a Low-Price World."
3. This is one of those sayings that has been attributed to just about everyone, according to the website Quote Investigator (https://quoteinvestigator.com/2013/10/20/no-predict/#return-note-7474-2), but this version is a translation from Karl Kristian Steincke, *Farvel Og Tak: Minder Og Meninger* (Copenhagen: Fremad, 1948), 227.
4. "Expanding the Innovation Horizon: The Global CEO Study 2006," IBM Global Business Services, 22.

5. "Marketplace Without Boundaries? Responding to Disruption," 18th Global CEO Survey, PriceWaterhouseCoopers, 2015, 18.
6. Roger T. Ames and Max Kaltenmark, "Laozi," *Encyclopaedia Britannica*, https://www.britannica.com/biography/Laozi.
7. Amos Tversky and Daniel Kahneman, "The Framing of Decisions and the Psychology of Choice," *Science* 211 (January 30, 1981): 453–458.
8. Richard Thaler and Cass Sunstein, *Nudge: Improving Decisions About Health, Wealth and Happiness* (New Haven, CT: Yale University Press, 2008), 81–102.
9. John Kemp, "Spontaneous Change, Unpredictability and Consumption Externalities," *Journal of Artificial Societies and Social Simulation* 2, no. 3 (1999).
10. Website of MSCI, one of the owners of GICS classification standard, https://www.msci.com/gics, retrieved November 2017.
11. Data for 2016 for the U.S. households based on Consumer Expenditure Survey, Bureau of Labor Statistics, U.S. Department of Labor, available at https://www.bls.gov/cex/tables.htm.
12. Aaron Smith, "Shared, Collaborative and On Demand: The New Digital Economy," Pew Research Center, May 19, 2016.
13. Heather Saul, "Why Mark Zuckerberg Wears the Same Clothes to Work Every Day," *Independent*, January 26, 2016.
14. Brian Moylan, "How to Perfect the Art of a Work Uniform," *New York Times*, June 5, 2017.
15. Bryan Pearson, "Kroger's Meal Kits Could Make a Meal of the Industry," *Forbes*, May 17, 2017; Shannon Liao, "Walmart Now Sells Meal Kits, Just like Amazon and Blue Apron," The Verge, December 7, 2017.
16. Michael Ruhlman, *Grocery: The Buying and Selling of Food in America* (New York: Abrams, 2017).
17. "Having Rescued Recorded Music, Spotify May Upend the Industry Again," *Economist*, January 11, 2018.
18. Emily Dreyfuss, "The Pharmacy of the Future Is Ready for Your Bathroom Counter," *Wired*, June 15, 2017.
19. The Bureau of Labor Statistics (BLS) compiled price data on new cars, toys, TVs, software, household energy, public transportation, education, college tuition fees, childcare, food and beverages, housing, and medical care. The BLS reports on the monthly Consumer Price Index (CPI)

of individual goods and services for urban consumers at national, state, and city levels. Data used in this sequence are based on the U.S. national average of urban consumers, relative to December 1997 (which has been given the value of zero). CPI is presented on an annual basis, which we have derived as the average of the monthly CPIs in a given year. The data are available at https://beta.bls.gov/dataQuery/search, accessed December 2017.

20. For example, the average tuition and fees at public four-year colleges in the United States increased from $4,740 in 2017 dollars in 1997–98 to $9,970 in 2017–18 (an increase of 110 percent), and average tuition at private nonprofit colleges increased in 20 years from $21,160 to $34,740 (an increase of 65 percent). Source: "Trends in College Pricing 2017," College Board, 2017.
21. "Not What It Used to Be: American Universities Represent Declining Value for Money to Their Students," *Economist*, December 1, 2012.
22. For example, the average health insurance premium for family coverage grew in the United States from $9,249 in 2003 to $18,764 in 2017, according to data reported by the Kaiser Employer Survey to the National Conference of State Legislators. Sources: "Data Brief: Paying the Price," Commonwealth Fund, August 2009, and "Health Insurance: Premiums and Increases," National Conference of State Legislators, http://www.ncsl.org/research/health/health-insurance-premiums.aspx, accessed April 2018.
23. For example, the median home value in the United States has risen from $119,600 in 2000 to $199,200 in 2017, according to the U.S. Census and the real estate analytics company Zillow. Source: Emmie Martin, "Here's How Much Housing Prices Have Skyrocketed over the Last 50 Years," CNBC, June 23, 2017.
24. The major drivers for the rise in food prices in the United States over the past two decades were high oil prices (raising shipping costs), climate changes (creating more drought), subsidies to corn production for biofuels (taking the product out of the food chain), limits to stockpiling food by the World Trade Organization (leading to price volatility), and people switching to meat in their diets. K. Amadeo, "Why Food Prices Are Rising, the Trends and 2018 Forecast," The Balance, March 19, 2018.

25. For example, according to analysts at Schroders, an asset management company, while the affordability of a new car in the United States has significantly improved since the 1990s, the total cost of ownership has risen 40 to 50 percent between the 1990s and the 2010s as a result of higher fuel prices, road tax, congestion charging, parking charges, etc. See K. Davidson, "The End of the Road: Has the Developed World Reached 'Peak Car'?," Schroders, January 2015.
26. Average transaction price for light vehicles in the United States was $36,113 in December 2017, according to Kelley Blue Book, a vehicle market information company. The national average domestic itinerary fare for the fourth quarter of 2017 was $347, according to the Bureau of Transportation Statistics.
27. Prices of clothing dropped as production shifted to cheaper labor markets, low-cost retailers grabbed market share, and social changes such as fewer people needing a separate office wardrobe. See L. Rupp, C. Whiteaker, M. Townsend, and K. Bhasin, "The Death of Clothing," *Bloomberg Businessweek*, February 5, 2018.
28. The decrease in prices of electronic goods is driven by technology innovation leading to cheaper components, proliferation of devices, and competition between manufacturers and retailers. For example, between 1997 and 2015, prices of personal computers and peripheral equipment decreased 96 percent, television prices dropped 95 percent, audio equipment prices declined by 60 percent, and prices of photographic equipment and supplies were 57 percent lower. See "Long-Term Price Trends for Computers, TVs, and Related Items," *Economics Daily,* U.S. Bureau of Labor Statistics, October 13, 2015.
29. In a recent international survey, all twenty-two of Australia's metropolitan areas were found to be unaffordable for middle-income families, and fifteen of them were rated as severely unaffordable. Middle-income housing affordability is rated using the "median multiple," which is the median house price divided by the median household income. The indicator has been recommended by the World Bank and the United Nations. Markets are rated affordable when the median multiple is 3.0 or lower. The markets become severely unaffordable when they cross the median multiple of 5.1 or higher. The median multiple for all twenty-two

Australian metropolitan areas is 5.9. Source: "14th Annual Demographia International Housing Affordability Survey: 2018," 12. The median house price in Sydney skyrocketed fifteenfold between 1980 and 2016, from AU$64,800 to AU$999,600. See M. Thomas, "Housing Affordability in Australia," Parliament of Australia, https://www.aph.gov.au/About_Parliament/Parliamentary_Departments/Parliamentary_Library/pubs/BriefingBook45p/HousingAffordability, accessed April 2018.

30. For more analysis of the differences between American and German public transport systems, see R. Buehler and J. Pucher, "Demand for Public Transport in Germany and the USA: An Analysis of Rider Characteristics," *Transport Reviews* 32, no. 5 (2012): 541–567.
31. Quote by Toby Clark, director of research for Europe at Mintel, in A. Monaghan, "Britons Spend More on Food and Leisure, Less on Booze, Smoking and Drugs," *Guardian*, February 16, 2017.
32. The data on consumer expenditures on food, alcoholic beverages, and tobacco consumed at home in 2016 were collected by Euromonitor International and calculated by the U.S. Department of Agriculture's Economic Research Service: https://www.ers.usda.gov/data-products/food-expenditures.aspx.
33. International data for 2016 from OECD's Global Health Expenditure Database at http://stats.oecd.org/Index.aspx?DataSetCode=SHA, accessed April 2018.
34. The American Time Use Survey methodology is described in "Technical Note," in "American Time Use Survey—2016 Results," Bureau of Labor Statistics, U.S. Department of Labor, June 27, 2017, 5–9.

Epilogue

1. A long strand of psychological research has shown that when people exhibit heightened aggression, they behave differently, losing track of others around them and forgetting about their needs.
2. Eugene F. Soltes, *Why They Do It: Inside the Mind of the White-Collar Criminal* (New York: PublicAffairs, 2016).
3. A. H. Buss and M. Perry, "The Aggression Questionnaire," *Journal of Personality and Social Psychology* 63, no. 3 (1992): 452–459.

Note on Terminology

1. J. L. Bower and C. M. Christensen, "Disruptive Technologies: Catching the Wave," *Harvard Business Review* 73, no. 1 (1995).
2. Clayton M. Christensen, *The Innovator's Dilemma: When New Technologies Cause Great Firms to Fail* (Boston: Harvard Business School Press, 1997).
3. "Disrupt," Merriam-Webster.com, accessed July 2018.
4. See, for example, Clayton M. Christensen and Michael E. Raynor, *The Innovator's Solution: Creating and Sustaining Successful Growth* (Boston: Harvard Business School Press, 2003). In more recent articles, Christensen uses the term "disruption theory" to refer to his theory of disruptive innovation. I think this is misguided. It created confusion by implying that the word "disruption" should be used only when referring to his specific theory of how, in some cases, incumbents lose significant market share to new entrants using a certain class of innovations.
5. M. E. Porter, *The Competitive Advantage: Creating and Sustaining Superior Performance* (New York: Free Press, 1985).
6. David Court, Dave Elzinga, Susan Mulder, and Ole Jørgen Vetvik, "The Consumer Decision Journey," *McKinsey Quarterly*, June 2009; Thales S. Teixeira, "Marketing Communications," Harvard Business School Background Note 513-041, August 2012.

Note on Differences Between Decoupling and Disruptive Innovation

1. Joseph L. Bower and Clayton M. Christensen, "Disruptive Technologies: Catching the Wave," *Harvard Business Review* 73, no. 1 (1995): 43.
2. "Tesla's Not as Disruptive as You Might Think," *Harvard Business Review,* May 2015, 22.
3. Clayton M. Christensen, Michael E. Raynor, and Rory McDonald, "What Is Disruptive Innovation?," *Harvard Business Review,* December 2015, 44.

INDEX

D

ABOUT THE AUTHOR

THALES TEIXEIRA is the Lumry Family Associate Professor of Business Administration at the Harvard Business School. A specialist in digital marketing strategy and e-commerce, Teixeira is a pioneer in the economics of attention, an emerging field that explores how to use consumer attention effectively to acquire and engage consumers (www.economicsofattention.com). His work has been featured widely in mainstream publications such as the *Harvard Business Review*, *Forbes*, the *Economist*, and the *New York Times*. Professor Teixeira serves as a reviewer for the Food and Drug Administration and for a number of academic journals. Among his most recent clients are large companies such as BMW, Siemens, Bayer, Nike, YouTube, and Microsoft, and he advises countless startups. He speaks often at companies and large conferences, including past invited presentations at Facebook, the National Retail Federation Week, Netflix, Unilever, Google, Cannes Lions Festival, and Walt Disney Studios. Professor Teixeira holds a PhD from the University of Michigan. He is originally from Brazil.